VOICES AND VEILS
FEMINISM AND ISLAM IN FRENCH WOMEN'S WRITING AND ACTIVISM

RESEARCH MONOGRAPHS IN FRENCH STUDIES

The *Research Monographs in French Studies* (RMFS) form a separate series within the Legenda programme and are published in association with the Society for French Studies. Individual members of the Society are entitled to purchase all RMFS titles at a discount.

The series seeks to publish the best new work in all areas of the literature, thought, theory, culture, film and language of the French-speaking world. Its distinctiveness lies in the relative brevity of its publications (50,000–60,000 words). As innovation is a priority of the series, volumes should predominantly consist of new material, although, subject to appropriate modification, previously published research may form up to one third of the whole. Proposals may include critical editions as well as critical studies. They should be sent with one or two sample chapters for consideration to Professor Ann Jefferson, New College, Oxford OX1 3BN.

Editorial Committee
Ann Jefferson, New College, Oxford (General Editor)
Adrian Armstrong, University of Manchester
Janice Carruthers, Queen's University Belfast
Nicholas Harrison, King's College London
Neil Kenny, Cambridge University
Bill Marshall, University of Stirling

Advisory Committee
Wendy Ayres-Bennett, New Hall, Cambridge
Celia Britton, University College London
Sarah Kay, Princeton University
Diana Knight, University of Nottingham
Michael Moriarty, Queen Mary University of London
Keith Reader, University of Glasgow

PUBLISHED IN THIS SERIES

www.rmfs.mhra.org.uk

Voices and Veils

Feminism and Islam in French Women's Writing and Activism

❖

ANNA KEMP

LEGENDA

Research Monographs in French Studies 29
Modern Humanities Research Association and Maney Publishing
2010

Published by the
Modern Humanities Research Association and Maney Publishing
1 Carlton House Terrace
London SW1Y 5AF
United Kingdom

LEGENDA is an imprint of the
Modern Humanities Research Association and Maney Publishing

Maney Publishing is the trading name of W. S. Maney & Son Ltd,
whose registered office is at Suite 1C, Joseph's Well, Hanover Walk, Leeds LS3 1AB

ISBN 978-1-906540-26-5

First published 2010

Printed in Great Britain

Cover: 875 Design

Copy-Editor: Richard Correll

CONTENTS

FOR MY FAMILY, FOR ANNIE AND FOR FRANÇOIS

ACKNOWLEDGEMENTS

I am very grateful to the French Department at King's College London for their tremendous support in the writing of the thesis upon which this book is based. In particular, I am indebted to Siobhán McIlvanney, my supervisor, for her insight, enthusiasm, and support. I also thank Nicholas Harrison, for his expert guidance, encouragement and efficiency in the final phases, Patrick ffrench for his valuable input in the early stages, and Jim Wolfreys for his contributions and insights. I am also very grateful to Simon Gaunt for his guidance and generosity, to my examiners, Alec Hargreaves and Azzedine Haddour for their many helpful comments and subsequent support, to Ann Jefferson at Legenda for her invaluable suggestions and encouragement, and to the anonymous readers for their constructive criticism and advice. Furthermore, I am indebted to the Queen's College Oxford and to the trustees of the Hamilton Junior Research Fellowship in French whose generous support has allowed me to complete this research and prepare it for publication.

Part of Chapter 2 appeared in different form in my article 'Marianne d'aujourd'hui?: The Figure of the beurette in Contemporary French Feminist Discourses', *Modern & Contemporary France*, Vol.17, No.1, February 2009, 19-33, and I thank the editors for their advice in the writing of that paper. I also thank Houria Bouteldja, Christine Delphy, Sonia Kichah, Anne Souyris, Dounia Bouzar, Ismahane Chouder and Samia Said for the interviews they kindly gave me in April 2006, and for the interest they showed in my work. Finally, I thank my editor at Legenda, Graham Nelson, for his patience, good-humour and expertise and my copy-editor Richard Correll for his eagle-eyed accuracy and helpful suggestions.

Furthermore, I am indebted to the Queen's College Oxford, in particular to Roger Pearson, and to the trustees of the Hamilton Junior Research Fellowship in French whose generous support has allowed me to complete this research and prepare it for publication.

A.K., Oxford, June 2010

INTRODUCTION

In February 2004, I was browsing the aisles of a large Parisian bookseller. The French headscarf affair was at its height, and the national media was filling vast stretches of airtime and spilling great quantities of ink over the question of whether or not Muslim schoolgirls should be allowed to wear their headscarves to class. Judging by the books on display, the French publishing industry had quickly followed suit. In the windows and on the show tables were dozens of essays and pamphlets offering analyses of the controversy, alongside an assortment of titles on the more general subjects of Islam, immigration, integration, insecurity and terrorism. As this variety of topics suggested, the public interest in the *affaire du foulard* stretched far beyond the question of headscarves, to cover a wide range of issues all loosely connected, in the public imagination, to the presence of Islam in France. But despite the large selection of titles, there was one particular set of images that appeared on book covers with striking frequency: those representing Muslim women. Scanning the display tables, I was struck that these images fell, broadly, into two categories. On the one hand there was the generic image of the veiled Muslim woman, her face either entirely concealed by an Afghan burkha or reduced to a pair of kohl-rimmed eyes, while on the other, there were images of young unveiled women of North African origin, smiling and dressed in Western style clothes. Whereas the former tended to appear on the covers of books dealing with the issue of the veil, Islamic extremism or Islam in general,[1] the latter most often appeared on the covers of testimonies by French women of Muslim origin that described the author's struggle for emancipation from the religious and cultural traditions of their parents or communities.[2] Two images: the Muslim woman as Westernized and emancipated, and the Muslim woman as veiled and oppressed. The message was implicit but clear: France and the Western world were in harmony with humanist and feminist principles, while Islam was defined by its perceived oppression of women.

These two contrasting representations of Muslim women dominated not only Parisian bookshelves but the debate as a whole. In fact, the public appetite for tales of women's emancipation from religious and cultural tradition seemed insatiable. There was a proliferation of television documentaries and articles on the appalling treatment of Muslim women in the so-called *terres de l'islam*, and women who had escaped the veil or who were seen to have resisted sexism within their communities were invited onto chat shows to talk about their ordeals. But despite the scale and range of the debates, there was one glaring absence. Where were the *voilées*, the veiled girls, themselves? Where were the women whose lives would be directly affected by the outcome of the affair and why were they not invited to participate in the discussions? With very few exceptions, French Muslim women who, like the schoolgirls, claimed that they wore the headscarf of their own accord, were nowhere to be seen. Between the image of the emancipated Westernized woman and the iconic Afghan burkha, there was little room for women who claimed to be fully French, Muslim *and* feminist.

This study has emerged from a desire to identify and investigate the writings and discourses of French Muslim women whose voices were actively excluded from the affair and continue to be marginalized in public debate.[3] Since February 2004, I have sought out literary, sociological and journalistic writing by French women of Muslim origin, or by Muslim women writing in French, that offers alternative perspectives on the experiences of Muslim women in France and beyond, and complicates dominant analyses that imagine the West defending women's rights against an Islamic menace. Though marginalized, boycotted or excluded from mainstream publishing and debate, these voices are formulating compelling critiques of mainstream discourses and suggesting new possibilities for feminist collaborations in both a French and a global context.

There has already been significant academic interest in the phenomenon of *beur* women's writing, that is, novels and autobiographies written by young French women of North African immigrant origin.[4] Most of this criticism deals with texts written in the 1980s and 1990s and, as the *beur* tag suggests, the work is often considered in relation to the politics of the time, in particular to the *beur* movement. The *beur* movement, as I shall explain more fully in the second chapter, invested hope in the French model of integration and the egalitarian values it is supposed to embody and was mobilized by a desire, on the part of the children of Maghrebi immigrants, to be accepted as *des Français comme les autres* — as French as everyone else. However, the political climate has changed in recent years and continues to develop rapidly. Since the attacks on the United States on 11 September 2001, France, like many other Western countries, has witnessed an accelerating hostility towards people identified as Muslim and has further integrated 'Islam' as a core reference in debates on immigration, integration and national identity. As I shall later argue, this 'Islamization' of debates has been paralleled by a 'gendering' of debates whereby the perceived status of women is taken as definitive proof of the supposed stagnation of Islamic culture and the superiority of the French cultural model, injecting new life into colonial constructions of the Muslim woman as symbolic of the West's relationship to Islam.

This altered climate is reflected in the work considered in this study, most of which has been published in recent years. Broadly speaking, much *beur* women's writing of the 1980s and 1990s, though often critical of French society, invests faith in the process of integration that, it is hoped, will emancipate young Muslim women from the oppressive cultural traditions of their families, and allow them to enjoy the same freedoms and privileges as their white, middle-class French counterparts. Many books produced today continue to conform to this model, and (as the frequency of reprints indicates) they satisfy a significant public demand. However, there are also a number of writers who distance themselves from this formula and some of the presumptions around which it is structured. These writers tend to be disillusioned with the promise of integration and more overtly critical of it. They show greater awareness of the ways in which their words may be framed and exploited in support of an agenda that they have not chosen and they develop compelling counter-narratives of their own. They also pay more explicit attention to their identity, not only as the descendants of immigrants, but as Muslims, and take into account the ways in which the global political context affects how others perceive them and how they perceive themselves.

The writings of these authors and activists will be the focus of the latter half of this study but, in order to appreciate the nature of their resistance, it is necessary to begin with a consideration of what they are up against. Part I of this book will consider French feminist representations of Muslim women, tracing a genealogy of ideas from the nineteenth century onwards, with a view to dissecting its disavowed ethnocentrism and the role this plays in perpetuating neocolonial structures of power. The first chapter goes back to the early days of French feminism to examine representations of Muslim women in writing by French women of the colonial era. A good deal of popular and critical attention has been paid to British women's travel writing, such as the letters of the eighteenth-century aristocrat Lady Mary Wortley Montagu,[5] but rather less attention has been paid to the writings of French colonial women. However, as I shall argue, French colonial women's writing testifies to the crucial role women played in France's colonial project. French women did not merely visit the colonies as tourists or to shop for fashionable Oriental goods; many invested tremendous energy in France's 'civilizing' mission, in particular with a view to 'liberating' their Muslim sisters. The complicity between feminist and colonial discourses that emerges from these texts produces what I shall call a 'colonial feminism' that imagines an idealized French womanhood in opposition to a vision of Muslim-Arab women as the embodiment of female oppression and that ultimately betrays its feminist agenda to work in the service of French imperialism. In the second chapter, I shall analyse dominant representations of Muslim women produced during the recent *affaire du foulard*, arguing that it is possible to identify an enduring colonial legacy that constructs Muslim womanhood as the antithesis of French feminist values, while consecrating a certain notion of French femininity as an ideal to be emulated. 'Colonial feminism', as I shall demonstrate, was closely intertwined with colonial ideology and strategy. In a similar way, contemporary feminist discourses are entangled in a gendered model of integration that does not safeguard women's emancipation, so much as reassert dominant gender norms in the service of a nativist notion of French identity.

A historical perspective on present-day events seems appropriate, even necessary, given the republican establishment's tendency to gloss over more painful aspects of French colonial history, in particular the memory of the Algerian War of Independence and its aftermath. Paradoxically, France's oft-cited denial of its colonial history has, in recent years, generated substantial public interest around this very subject. In February 2005, for example, there was controversy surrounding the introduction of a law (later repealed) obliging schools to present the country's colonial exploits in a favourable light,[6] and in September 2006 the dictionary definition of 'colonialism' came under scrutiny as, in the eyes of its critics, it laid too great an emphasis on the supposed benefits of colonialism for colonized peoples.[7]

Furthermore, France's disavowed colonial past has become a key reference for a number of dissident movements who demand not only that France acknowledge certain aspects of its history but that the republican establishment recognize an enduring colonial legacy that continues to determine its relationship to its ethnic and religious minorities.[8] In a similar vein, the first part of this study will argue that contemporary feminists in France have, in several important ways, inherited directly from their colonial predecessors. This is not simply a French problem however. Though Part I will focus on the specificities of the French case, it will situate these issues in relation to more widely circulating discourses that construct Muslim women as victims and Western women as their models and saviours. Indeed, the notion that Muslim women need to be rescued by their white sisters has become an established part of Western neocolonial discourse One need only think of the ways in which Afghan women's rights (championed by Laura Bush) became a crucial means of rallying public pinion behind the invasion of Afghanistan in 2001.

However, the concerns expressed in this book about representations of Muslim women as victims and the ends to which these representations may be deployed, in no way constitutes a denial of the appalling violence inflicted on many Muslim women by Muslim men both in colonial times and our own. The hideous crimes of the Taliban are well documented and, beyond the institutionalised misogyny of fundamentalist regimes, patriarchal interpretations of Islam have restricted women's freedoms to varying degrees around the world. It is not my intention to condone, out of a misguided respect for cultural difference, any form of gender oppression carried out (to the horror of many Muslims) in the name of Islam. Nor is it to suggest that non-Muslim feminists should simply leave their Muslim sisters to their own devices for fear of being accused of cultural imperialism (as my discusion of collaborations between non-Muslim and Muslim French feminists should make clear). Rather, this book will consider what happens when (often legitimate) feminist concerns for the welfare of Muslim women are recuperated to a politically conservative agenda that ultimately works in the interest of existing structures of power and against the feminist values it purports to defend.

Having considered the ways in which contemporary French feminist constructions of Muslim womanhood are informed by a colonial legacy, the second chapter will lead into a discussion of contemporary literary texts by considering how representations of Muslim women as victims or veiled threats shape the production and reception of writing by French women of Muslim or North African origin. Particular attention will be paid to autobiographical writing produced through a collaboration between a Muslim woman writer and a majority-ethnic French woman editor. Taking Samira Bellil's *Dans l'enfer des tournantes* [*Inside the Hell of Gang Rape*] as a case in point,[9] I shall argue that, although such collaborations potentially provide valuable opportunities for marginalized women to tell their stories, more often than not they see the writer's story pressed into the service of dominant interests, denying her a voice at the very moment she is presumed to speak. In particular, I will look at how these collaborations construct the figure of the young, emancipated Maghrebi woman, or *beurette*, as the poster girl for a French model of integration that demands a high degree of conformity to French (and more broadly, Western) cultural norms — norms that are, in many ways, far from emancipatory.

Part II of this book will then turn to the ways in which French Muslim women writers and activists are questioning the *beurette* stereotype and moving beyond the reductive parameters of mainstream feminist discourses. Chapters 3 and 4 will consider literary texts, specifically: *Ce pays dont je meurs* [*This Country that Kills Me*] by Fawzia Zouari,[10] and *Moze* and *'Musulman' Roman* [*'Muslim': A Novel*] by Zahia Rahmani.[11] These texts are very diverse in content and style, but they all communicate a distinct mistrust of discourses that force Muslim women into stereotypes and speaking positions that are not of their choosing, and reveal a powerful desire to carve out a space of agency in which they might negotiate their own sense of belonging. Indeed, 'belonging' is an important notion for these writers. Far from figuring their positions on the margin of society as sites of potential subversion (as some other examples of postcolonial writing tend to do), these writers are attuned to the pain of exclusion and emphasise the importance of finding a place from which to speak, however limited and unstable. As a result, the work of these writers does not easily lend itself to readings that privilege marginality and see emancipatory potential in the dismantling of categories of identity. Rather than reject notions of a secure and stable identity as necessarily falsifying and reductive, these writers emphasise the importance of fantasizing a sense of identity and being seen to belong, especially for those whose sense of self is under constant assault.

In a similar vein, French Muslim women activists do not reject, but seek to rehabilitate feminist and republican ideals. The discourses of these activists will be the subject of the final chapter. For this chapter, I travelled to Paris and Lyons where I interviewed Muslim and non-Muslim feminists and activists seeking to articulate alternatives to dominant narratives of emancipation. In their view, mainstream feminisms in France are both failing to represent the diverse experiences of French women, and failing to address the sexism that endures at the heart of French society, by constructing conservative notions of womanhood as an ideal for all to aspire to. Although Muslim women's voices remain on the margins of mainstream debate and feminist activism, they are starting to forge a critique of the ways in which Western feminists' obsession with the Muslim woman is ultimately self-defeating, while articulating models of feminist collaboration that have implications beyond the French context. In particular, these activists harness their feminist agenda to a practical ideal of citizenship as participation that resists both the false universalism of dominant French discourses of emancipation, and the isolating relativism of multicultural approaches to women's rights. Between the images of the burkha-clad victim and the smiling *beurette*, new representations of Muslim women as actively engaged citizens and feminists are beginning to emerge, offering feminist and humanist ideals a real chance to renew themselves.

Notes to the Introduction

1. See for example, Chadorrt Djavann, *Bas les voiles!* (Paris: Gallimard, 2003); Régis Debray, *Ce que nous voile le voile* (Paris: Gallimard, 2004); Michèle Vianes, *Les Islamistes en manœuvre* (Paris: Hors Commerce, 2004).

2. See for example, Loubna Méliane, *Vivre libre* (Paris: Oh! éditions, 2003), Aïcha Benaïssa and Sophie Ponchelet, *Née en France: Histoire d'une jeune beur* (Paris: Presse Pocket, 1991).

3. The treatment of Faiza Silmi is a case in point. Silmi is a Moroccan woman who, despite having lived in France for eight years, speaking fluent French and having three French children by her French husband, was refused citizenship in August 2008 on the basis that her choice to wear the niqab was irreconcilable with 'French' values, in particular that of gender equality. Silmi's and her family's explanations to the contrary were drowned out by a massive media consensus in favour of the decision. See Laura Agustín, 'What not to wear — if you want to be French', *The Guardian*, 6 August 2008 <http://www.guardian.co.uk/commentisfree/2008/aug/06/france.islam> [accessed 28 February 2009].

4. For an excellent introduction to the key dynamics of *beur* women's writing see Siobhán McIlvanney, 'The articulation of *beur* female identity in the works of Farida Belghoul, Ferrudja Kessas and Soraya Nini', in *Women's Writing in Contemporary France: New Writers, New Literatures in the 1990s*, ed. by Gill Rye and Michael Worton (Manchester: Manchester University Press, 2002), pp. 130–41.

5. See for example Jane Robinson's popular anthology, *Unsuitable for Ladies: An Anthology of Women Travellers* (Oxford: Oxford University Press, 1994).

6. The law of 23 February 2005 was originally intended to oblige schoolteachers to recognize the role of the *harkis* (Algerians who fought on the side of the French during the Algerian War of Independence). However, a clause was added insisting that schools had a duty to recognize the positive role of the French presence overseas, particularly in North Africa. Opponents of the law signed a petition stating that the law imposed an official lie. See Jon Henley, 'French angry at law to teach glory of colonialism', *The Guardian*, 15 April 2005, section Higher Education. <http://www.guardian.co.uk/world/2005/apr/15/highereducation.artsandhumanities> [accessed 30 November 2005]

7. The 2007 edition of *Le Petit Robert* stirred up controversy when it defined colonialism in terms of a 'mise en valeur' [beneficial exploitation] of colonized countries. See, 'Polémique autour de la définition de "colonisation" et "coloniser" par le Petit Robert' [Controversy over the dictionary definitions of "colonization" and "colonize"], *Le Monde*, 6 September 2006.

8. The dissident movement *Les Indigènes de la République* [The Natives of the Republic] lays particular emphasis on what it sees as enduring structures of colonial power. Indeed, rather than refer to themselves as an 'anti-racist' organization, the *Indigènes* regard themselves as 'anti-colonial'.

9. Samira Bellil, *Dans l'enfer des tournantes*, 2nd edn (Paris: Editions Denoël, 2003). First published in 2002.

10. Fawzia Zouari, *Ce pays dont je meurs*, 2nd edn (Tunisie: L'Or du temps, 2000). First published in France (Paris: Editions Ramsay, 1999).

11. Zahia Rahmani, *'Musulman' Roman* (Abbeville: Sabine Wespieser Editeur, 2005); *Moze* (Abbeville: Sabine Wespieser Editeur, 2003).

PART I

Looking into the Veil

CHAPTER 1

Colonial Daughters, Feminist Sisters: 'Colonial Feminism' and the Muslim Woman

Well over a century before girls in headscarves were excluded from schools in the name of the Republic, humanist principles were being cited in support of French imperialism. Despite the fact that France's seizure and domination of its colonies often entailed the brutal repression of indigenous peoples, the French colonial project was animated, in part, by a zealous republican ideology informed by the emancipatory ideals of the Enlightenment. The colonial administration of the Third Republic professed its commitment to improving the lives of France's colonial subjects by reshaping them in line with a French vision of modernity. Indeed, far from imagining themselves as oppressors, many members of the French colonial administration saw themselves as liberators whose mission it was to bring the benefits of Western civilization to the backward peoples of Africa and Asia. France's 'civilizing' imperative came to be known as the *mission civilisatrice* and, by the end of the nineteenth century, it had become one of the prime arguments in favour of French expansionism.[1]

French women became an increasingly important asset to the colonial *mission civilisatrice* as their participation in education and healthcare, framed by their role as mothers, gave them exceptional access to indigenous homes and, above all, to indigenous women who, it was believed, were more sympathetic to French culture than their male counterparts. In particular, indigenous women's presumed desire to liberate themselves from oppressive cultural traditions became the fulcrum around which French hopes of successfully dominating the colonies and assimilating their peoples would turn, bringing colonial and feminist imperatives into ever closer contact with one another. This chapter will lay the groundwork for my analysis of contemporary feminist discourses by examining three examples of what I shall call 'colonial-feminist' writing: writing by French women of the colonial era that articulates a feminist agenda within a colonial frame.

The three colonial women writers considered in the chapter all participated, in different ways, in the colonial enterprise, and they all identified with the occidental feminist discourses of their time. Their texts were written during France's imperial presence in North Africa, from the colonization of Algeria in the 1830s to the end of the Algerian War of Independence in 1962, and they all describe the writers' travels in Africa and their responses to the Muslim women they encountered. Although French colonial ambitions and the beginnings of modern French feminism both predate this period, colonial and feminist discourses and strategies nonetheless become increasingly interconnected during this time as the colonial authorities co-opted feminist discourses to fit their agenda, while French feminists exploited colonial discourses to suit theirs. Colonial women's writing on Muslim women is so diverse that it is impossible to claim that the works considered here are representative in all respects. However, I have selected these texts for two reasons: firstly, when viewed chronologically they reveal feminism's progressive entanglement in colonial strategy; and secondly they plot the emergence of a distinctive French feminist identity constructed in relation to the figure of the Muslim–Arab woman.

The first of these three texts is Suzanne Voilquin's *Souvenirs d'une fille du peuple ou la Saint-simonienne en Egypte, 1834 à 1836* [*Memoirs of a Daughter of the People or the Saint-Simonist Woman in Egypt*].[2] Voilquin's text, the writing of which coincides with the first stirrings of an organized, autonomous women's movement in France, points to an emerging awareness of French women's potential involvement in the colonial enterprise. Sixty-four years after Voilquin's stay in Egypt and following the mass settlement of French women and families in Algeria, Hubertine Auclert's *Les Femmes arabes en Algérie* [*Arab Women in Algeria*][3] seeks to turn this potential into reality by pushing for the inclusion of French women in the colonial administration and sets the stage for a spate of studies on the welfare of Algerian women. Finally, by the time Marie Bugéja published her treatise on the necessity to 'civilize' Algerian women for the good of French Algeria, *Nos sœurs musulmanes* [*Our Muslim Sisters*],[4] in 1921, French women's involvement in the colonial project had become part of mainstream policy, with women playing a strategically important role in the *mission civilisatrice*. By studying these three writers in turn, this chapter aims to demonstrate the gradual merging of colonial and feminist discourses, and the developing interest in the figure of the Muslim woman.

However, I do not wish to argue that these writers were simply 'racists', any more than I would wish to depict them as heroines merely seeking to improve the lot of Muslim women in the face of male colonial indifference. Just as it would be unfair to suggest that colonial women writers did nothing more than cynically exploit their position of cultural 'superiority' to further their own agenda, it would also be naïve to assume that their discourses necessarily challenged the hegemonic male colonial perspective. It is perhaps more revealing to consider how French women, being of the 'inferior' sex yet of the 'superior' race, occupied an intermediary position in colonial society that allowed them to function as cultural mediators, and to explore the contradictions this gave rise to as they hovered (often uncomfortably) between complicity with and criticism of colonial discourse and policy. At the centre of these contradictions is the figure of the Muslim woman as she is variously represented in terms both of sameness and difference, the opposite of the ideal French woman yet symbolic of all women's struggles, a colonial daughter and a feminist sister.

Suzanne Voilquin: Imagining the Emancipated Woman

Suzanne Voilquin was a writer and activist who became involved in the utopian socialist movement of Saint-Simonism. Saint-Simonism combined a socialist agenda with aspirations to sexual equality and Voilquin, herself from a modest background, was quickly converted to its cause when, as a young woman, she attended a public lecture organized by the Saint-Simonists in Paris. Two years later, in 1832, she founded and edited the first proletarian women's newspaper, *La Tribune des Femmes* [*The Women's Forum*], with a number of fellow *saint-simoniennes* before travelling to Cairo to work at a Saint-Simonist colony where she spent two years caring for plague victims. *Souvenirs d'une fille du peuple ou la Saint-simonienne en Egypte, 1834 à 1836* (henceforth *Souvenirs*) is an autobiographical work that narrates Voilquin's life story from early childhood to her departure from Africa. The first part of the text lays particular emphasis on Voilquin's participation in the Saint-Simonist movement in Paris and her involvement with *La Tribune des Femmes*, while the second half is dedicated to her time in Egypt. Most critical writing on Suzanne Voilquin's feminism tends to focus on her involvement with *La Tribune* and her feminist insights as found in the first half of *Souvenirs*.[5] Less attention, however, is paid to the ways in which Voilquin's thinking develops during her time in Cairo. Indeed, Voilquin's feminist vision undergoes significant changes when she encounters Egyptian Muslim women and it is perhaps in relation to the figure of the 'oppressed' Muslim woman that Voilquin's notion of an ideal French womanhood takes shape.

In order to explain the dynamics of her feminism, it is first necessary to outline Voilquin's relationship to Saint-Simonism. The number of pages devoted to her time with the Saint-Simonists is testimony to the tremendous impact that her involvement with the movement had on her life and thought. Saint-Simonism was a utopian socialist movement that preached the sharing of wealth, the abolition of inheritance and, crucially, the enfranchisement of women. As historians Claire Goldberg Moses and Leslie Wahl Rabine have explained, the feminism of the Saint-Simonist movement emphasized the 'natural' differences between the sexes in deliberate opposition to the 'equality' arguments fashioned by Revolutionary feminists. Feminists of the French Revolution, such as Olympe de Gouges, were Enlightenment rationalists who tended to ascribe differences between men and women to culture as opposed to nature.[6] However, by the 1830s, socialist reformers were arguing that the Revolution's espousal of universal rights masked entrenched inequalities and that it was necessary to acknowledge distinctions between social classes and the 'natural' differences between men and women in order to address these problems. The Saint-Simonists, in tune with a Romantic sensibility, idealized 'feminine' virtues and imagined Woman to be symbolic of the peace, compassion and harmony of a new social order that would replace what they saw as a 'masculine' politics of force and conflict.

However the feminism that Voilquin encountered when she joined the movement was very much a masculine invention conceived by the group's male leaders, Prosper Enfantin and Saint-Amand Bazard. Despite their celebration of 'feminine' virtues, Enfantin and Bazard did not seek to guarantee women's equality within the Saint-Simonist hierarchy itself. This inequality was reflected in Enfantin's decision to create a couple-pope supposed to reflect the duality of God as both male and female. But while Enfantin cast himself in the male role, the female throne was left empty in expectation of a promised Woman Messiah who would, at an unspecified time in the future, announce a new morality for humankind. The privileging of 'feminine' virtues, in other words, did not mean that women themselves were accorded a privileged position within the Saint-Simonist movement. Instead, the idealized Woman Messiah displaced the needs, desires and energies of real women, prompting Voilquin to complain of 'le fossé qui sépare pour les hommes l'énoncé d'un principe et sa traduction pratique' [The gap that, for men, separates the articulation of a principle and its application] (*Souvenirs*, 6).

In November 1831, Enfantin definitively excluded women from positions of influence within the Saint-Simonist hierarchy, prompting Voilquin and fellow Saint-Simonist women to found *La Tribune*. The editors received no moral or financial support from the male Saint-Simonists who ridiculed the perceived lack of organization amongst the female journalists.[7] However, this apparent lack of organization was in fact a conscious decision to form a non-hierarchical collective in opposition to the doctrinal hierarchy of the men. Several of the paper's contributors point to the need for an independent woman-centred philosophy, distinct from the male vision of female emancipation. Joséphine Félicité writes: 'Les femmes seules diront quelle liberté elles veulent' [Only women can say what kind of freedom women want], while Adrienne Bassac insists: 'il faut un nouveau monde où les femmes puissent se conduire d'après leurs inspirations' [a new world is needed in which women can pursue their own dreams].[8] This 'nouveau monde' was imagined to be one in which women of all classes and backgrounds would work as equals to emancipate themselves and each other. From this perspective, the notion of a top-down chain of command was nonsensical. Voilquin writes: 'Aux hommes [...] de former hiérarchie, mais nous, Mesdames, ayons la prétention de représenter dès aujourd'hui la face de liberté qui doit régner sur le monde' [Let the men [...] form hierarchies. From now on, we women can claim to represent the face of liberty that must reign over the world].[9]

The founders of *La Tribune* not only envisaged equality of the sexes but equality amongst women. Voilquin had been outraged by attempts on the part of bourgeois Saint-Simonist women to establish authority over their working-class counterparts. Recalling this episode in *Souvenirs* she remarks:

> Selon moi, penser à hiérarchiser les femmes avant qu'elles n'eussent fait acte de volonté libre, avant qu'elles ne se connussent elles-mêmes, c'était un non-sens, c'était dire à la femme: 'Nous vous déclarons libre mais marchez dans nos pas, répétez nos discours et grandissez, si vous pouvez, sous notre souffle et notre inspiration' (*Souvenirs*, 113).

> [In my view, to think of organizing women into hierarchies before they knew their own will, indeed before they even knew themselves, was nonsense. It was a way of saying to women: 'We declare you to be free but follow in our footsteps, repeat what we say and develop, if you are able, under our influence.']

In opposition to the condescending maternalism of their middle-class peers, Voilquin and her fellow editors developed a vision of equality, partnership and dialogue between women that was the driving force behind *La Tribune*.

According to Goldberg Moses, *La Tribune* represents the first manifestation of an autonomous French women's movement as it is likely to have been the first female collective venture whose purpose was specifically and exclusively feminist.[10] It only printed articles by women and sought to replace Enfantin's notion of the elusive Woman Messiah with the diverse voices of French women themselves. Women from all walks of life were encouraged to contribute to the paper which pledged to represent all women, whatever their status, religion or views, in order to forge a collective female consciousness.[11] According to Voilquin, the ideal Woman was to be found in *all* women and the new social order that she aspired to would be created, not by a single Woman Messiah, but by the collective efforts of many. In *Souvenirs* she writes:

> Selon moi, toute femme devra d'abord se manifester, en dehors de l'influence masculine, par des sentiments ou des actes de sa libre volonté [...] [C]es femmes se rechercheront par la force des choses, afin de former entre elles un concile où chacune apportera sa pierre à l'édifice moral de l'avenir. C'est ce sentiment, *tout féminin,* qui créera ce que les saint-simoniens appellent la Mère! [Original emphasis] (*Souvenirs*, 190)

> [In my view, all women must first of all assert their free will and feelings beyond the sphere of masculine influence [...] [T]hese women will come together of necessity and form an alliance in which each individual woman will place a stone from which the moral edifice of the future will be built. It is this *wholly feminine* sentiment that will create what the Saint-Simonists call the Mother!]

The *saint-simoniennes'* faith in a feminine principle and their desire to create a new 'feminine' social order has led Goldberg Moses and Wahl Rabine, amongst others, to see them as predecessors of French 'difference' theorists, such as Hélène Cixous and Luce Irigaray, who also seek alternatives to 'masculine' subjectivity by identifying a 'feminine' principle that would replace hierarchical relationships with multiple, reciprocal ones.[12] Indeed, in Voilquin's text, the 'sentiment, *tout féminin*' described above, is embodied in a notion of an ideal woman or what the editors of the *Tribune* call *la femme nouvelle*; the feminist subject of the future who would belong to a utopia governed by 'feminine' principles.

However, Voilquin's projection towards a non-hierarchical, non-exclusive 'feminine' community in the Parisian section of *Souvenirs* is undermined by her representations of Egyptian women in the latter half of the book. Although Egypt never became part of the French Empire, the Saint-Simonist movement in Cairo was nonetheless engaged in a civilizing, colonizing venture, the purpose of which was to 'improve' Egyptian society. Saint-Simonism was driven by a strong missionary zeal and, after the movement was suppressed in France in the early 1830s, many Saint-Simonists emigrated to establish colonies in America, the Orient and the Pacific. Voilquin's journey to Cairo and the work she undertook there was very unusual for a French woman of the 1830s. In general, North Africa and the colonies were considered to be no place for a white woman, and (with the exception of prostitutes employed to serve the French military) women were not yet officially part of the colonial project.[13] At the time of Voilquin's stay in Egypt, the French army was still battling for control of Algeria which would remain under military dominion until 1871 when the country came under civil rule following the suppression of native insurrections. It was only then, once the focus switched from military to cultural domination of the colony, that the status of Muslim women became a concern for colonial policy, ultimately leading to the enrolment of European women in the *mission civilisatrice*.

At the time Voilquin was writing, the potential roles of both Muslim and French women within the colonial context were yet to be fully imagined. However, Voilquin's representations of Muslim women point forward to these later developments. Although Voilquin's writing at times suggests an alternative 'feminine' sensibility that subverts 'masculine' structures of power, when faced with the Muslim woman, Voilquin falls back on a conventional hierarchical model that figures the Muslim woman as the excluded Other against which *la femme nouvelle* defines herself. Despite Voilquin's claim in *La Tribune des Femmes* that Saint-Simonist feminism is open to all women regardless of their views, religion or background, she hesitates to extend this invitation to Muslim-Arab women who, more often than not, are figured as irretrievably Other. Occasionally however, Voilquin implicitly identifies with Muslim women on the basis of a shared female oppression. This hesitation between exclusion and identification, I shall argue, is at the heart of colonial-feminist thinking and comes to form the basis of colonial policy with regard to Muslim women.

Back in Paris, Voilquin had been appalled by the creation of a hierarchy amongst Saint-Simonist women, which saw the leaders' bourgeois wives acting as tutors to their working-class 'inferiors'. Yet in *Souvenirs*, Voilquin does not hesitate to establish a racial and cultural hierarchy of women, whereby white European women occupy the top rung of the ladder and black female slaves languish at the bottom. This kind of hierarchy is consistent with the popular nineteenth-century notion of a 'ladder of civilization' that ranked 'advanced' or 'civilized' societies over 'primitive' or 'backward' ones.[14] But although this concept of a 'ladder of civilization' was common currency at the time, Voilquin's decision to rank ethnic groups according to their women points forward to much later colonial strategy which would transform the perceived status of women into *the* barometer of progress.

Voilquin imagines the level of 'civilization' of each ethnic or racial group to be visible on the bodies of its women who are ranked according to their physical proximity to an idealized European physiognomy. The women of the more 'civilized' Armenians are among the most attractive, their beauty described in terms of their resemblance to European women. Voilquin writes: 'Leurs femmes sont généralement belles; dans l'ovale de leur visage, dans la régularité des traits de l'Arménienne, on retrouve le type si vanté des Géorgiennes dont elles sont les dignes descendantes' [Their women are generally beautiful; in the oval shape of their faces and the symmetry of their features Armenian women resemble the much admired Georgians of whom they are the noble descendants] (*Souvenirs*, 321). Conversely, Voilquin considers Arab women to be ugly in their divergence from the European ideal:

> Généralement les femmes arabes ne sont pas jolies; les lignes si pures de l'ovale européen ne se retrouvent chez aucune d'elles; leurs dents sont très blanches ; mais leur bouche, leur nez, leur front étroit, un peu déprimé, tous ces traits sont sans grâce, sans finesse et surtout sans expression. Leurs yeux seuls sont beaux, noirs et brillants, quand toutefois leur enfance a pu échapper aux effets de l'ophtalmie (*Souvenirs*, 321).

> [In general Arab women are not pretty. None of them share the pure lines of the oval European face. Their teeth are very white, but their mouths, their noses, their low, slightly depressed, brows, all of these features are without grace, without subtlety and above all without expression. Only their eyes are beautiful, black and brilliant — if they have been spared childhood blindness that is.]

It is significant that the only attractive feature Voilquin attributes to Arab women is their eyes for, as she later goes on to explain, 'elles n'ont libre que le regard' [only their eyes are free] (*Souvenirs*, 242), the rest of the face and body being hidden beneath a veil. In Voilquin's analysis, women's beauty is in direct proportion to the degree of *liberté* they are imagined to possess, *liberté* being a key ingredient of civilization and progress. Consequently, the perceived ugliness of Arab women is seen as a product of Arab cultural practices that suppress women's natural *liberté*, while French women appear as the radiant embodiment of civilized French culture.

Voilquin's construction of women's emancipation as a desirable marker of civilization is clearly a feminist move. But her feminist aims are compromised by her focus on female beauty. In Paris, Voilquin sought to establish a female-only space that would allow women to form relationships beyond the dynamics of male power. In Egypt, however, the relationship between French women and their Muslim-Arab sisters seems to be regulated by an eroticizing male colonial gaze that transforms women into rivals. Indeed, Voilquin is keen to deflate Orientalist notions of Arab women as sexually alluring. On the effects of the *hammam* (a privileged site of Orientalist fantasy) she writes:

> L'abus des bains très chauds déforme en général le sein des femmes. Ce n'est que chez les jeunes filles de dix à seize ans que cet important détail de la beauté de notre sexe pourrait soutenir la comparaison avec les femmes d'Occident. (*Souvenirs*, 264)

> [The overuse of very hot baths generally deforms women's breasts. Only young girls between ten to sixteen years old could rival Western women in terms of this most important aspect of feminine beauty.]

This is not to say that Arab women are not sexualized in Voilquin's work. Voilquin frequently eroticizes Arab women describing them variously as nymphs, caged birds and sexual slaves, but their sexuality is represented as deviant and impure in contrast to European women's modest virtue. On watching a crowd of Egyptian women caress a holy man to wake him from his meditations, Voilquin remarks: 'Oh pudeur! Me disais-je, en voyant l'air placide de ces femmes [...] ton charme si poétique est-il bien inhérent à nos âmes, ou bien subsiste-t-il dans l'opinion que nos mères chrétiennes ont imposée à nos esprits dans notre enfance?' [Oh modesty! I would cry on observing the nonchalance of these women [...] is your poetic charm innate, or does it arise from those virtues that our Christian mothers instilled in us as children?] (*Souvenirs*, 317). The colonial context in which Voilquin writes does not bring women together in a recognition of their shared oppression, but subordinates them to an eroticizing male gaze that forces them apart. While Voilquin constructs the French woman as the embodiment of civilization, beautiful, radiant and pure, the body of the Oriental woman appears abject and depraved, symbolic of the perceived backwardness and degeneration of Muslim-Arab culture.

Voilquin's idealization of French femininity aims to valorize French women in the eyes of French men and turn them into a prized asset, but such a move produces deep contradictions. Despite her former criticism of the subordinate status of French women in *La Tribune des Femmes*, in Egypt Voilquin confuses her ideals of emancipation with the rather less impressive reality of women's situation in order to imagine French women as the embodiment of women's natural *liberté*. When a group of Arab women questions Voilquin on the lives of her French counterparts, she enthusiastically sings the praises of French womanhood:

> Je me transformai en agent provocateur et me mis à critiquer leurs voiles épais et incommodes, leur réclusion; puis je cherchai à leur faire comprendre nos usages polis et sociables. En France, leur dis-je, les raguel (hommes) font constamment partie de nos assemblées; ils nous accompagnent dans nos promenades; partout nous sommes placées au premier rang, le visage découvert et la tête ornée de fleurs!
>
> Que de soupirs et d'exclamations s'échappèrent de leur poitrine en écoutant ces féeries d'Occident! (*Souvenirs*, 322–23)

> [I decided to stir things up a bit and set about criticizing their heavy, uncomfortable veils and their seclusion. Then I tried to help them understand our own manners and customs. In France, I told them, the raguel (men) are always beside us; they accompany us when we take a stroll and it is 'ladies first' wherever we go. Our faces are uncovered and our hair is decorated with flowers!
>
> What sighs and exclamations escaped their lips when they heard these fairytales of the West!]

The delight with which Voilquin narrates her Western fairytales suggests that her encounters with Arab women do not so much facilitate her critique of women's situation, as produce an assertion of Western gender norms as an ideal of emancipation.

However the Muslim-Arab woman does not only appear as the extreme opposite of the ideal French woman. Reading between the lines, there is also an unacknowledged tendency towards identification. The Muslim-Arab woman represents everything that Voilquin feels is wrong with the treatment of women in French society. Voilquin's perception of harem wives as 'pauvres recluses' subjugated to the will of their 'maître' echoes her earlier criticisms in *La Tribune des Femmes* of the Napoleonic civil code which in her opinion reduced French wives to little more than slaves.[15] 'La misère, le délaissement, le peu de garanties qui entourent l'existence [des femmes arabes]' [The poverty, the neglect, the few guarantees that circumscribe the lives [of Arab women]] (*Souvenirs*, 358) that is described in *Souvenirs*, is elsewhere seen as the lot of the married French woman. Furthermore, there are similarities between Voilquin's perception of Egyptian women as 'bad mothers' whose lack of education prevents them from raising their daughters successfully, and her own relationship with her devoutly Catholic mother. Egyptian mothers are described as uneducated, superstitious and therefore incapable of emancipating their daughters: 'En vieillissant, ces femmes s'approprient une foule de superstitions; elles aident à leur tour à parfaire l'éducation de la génération suivante' [As they get older, these women accumulate a host of superstitions and, in their turn, they help to scupper the education of their daughters] (*Souvenirs*, 316). Similarly, Voilquin's mother is described as silent and submissive, having been brought up in 'la plus complète ignorance' [total ignorance] (*Souvenirs*, 63). Self-emancipation for Voilquin necessitates a rejection of her 'bad' mother in order to embrace the 'good' mother, figured as the ideal woman of the future, *la femme nouvelle*. In a similar way, Voilquin represses the 'bad' Oriental mother in order to bring 'ce que les saint-simoniens appellent la Mère' into existence. Voilquin does not, however, explicitly acknowledge these similarities. Instead, she projects her anxieties concerning the oppression of women in France onto the figure of the Muslim woman in order to clear the way for a purified and idealized image of the emancipated French woman.

The discourse of identification implicit in Voilquin's work is more apparent in her desire to educate Muslim-Arab women. Though Voilquin most often represents Arab womanhood as the negative opposite of French femininity, she also sees potential for the enlightenment and eventual emancipation of Arab women. Her desire to convert Arab women to French values is most concretely expressed in her (unrealized) project to create a girls' school in Cairo with fellow *saint-simonienne*, Clorinde Rogé. She writes: 'Toutes deux, nous nous proposons d'attaquer par des moyens divers, l'ignorance abrutissante des femmes de ce pays, qui en fait des automates et non des êtres vivants' [We both decided to attack, in different ways, the mind-numbing ignorance of the women of this country — an ignorance that makes them into automatons rather than human beings] (*Souvenirs*, 329), and explains that it is through the education of women that the country will be transformed: 'Si ce moyen réussit, elles seront alors à même de s'assimiler notre littérature, nos pensées et notre moralité française [... il faut] régénérer ce pays par l'esprit, c'est à dire par l'éducation' [If this method succeeds, the women will be ready to assimilate French literature, thought and morality [...we must] regenerate this country through the mind, that is to say, through education] (*Souvenirs*, 327). The only path to emancipation, in Voilquin's mind, is via the civilizing influence of French culture. Despite her resistance to the maternalism of her bourgeois peers in Paris, in the colonial context Voilquin does not hesitate to assume the role of tutor and emancipator, reconstructing the relationships of authority and privilege that *La Tribune* had sought to undermine. Whereas, in the Parisian section of the book, Voilquin distinguishes between the contemporary status of French women and the ideal woman of the future towards whom all women should aspire, in her account of Egypt the notion of the ideal woman and that of the French woman are conflated to produce French femininity as the luminous opposite of Muslim-Arab womanhood. This problematic construction of the French woman as the embodiment of emancipation is taken up, in different ways, by Auclert and Bugéja and, as we shall see in the next chapter, may be seen to endure into contemporary feminist discourses on Muslim women.

Voilquin's desire to educate colonized peoples and assimilate them to French culture was in keeping with colonial policy of the 1830s and 1840s which oversaw the establishment of a number of schools in French territories, the most famous of which was Mme Allix's school for girls in Algeria.[16] This early initiative was, however, abandoned in 1861 on the grounds that the education of Arab girls was premature and alienated indigenous peoples, and it was not until the 1920s that the education of Arab women was back on the colonial agenda. Publishing at the turn of the century, our next writer, Hubertine Auclert was, in her insistence on the necessity to educate and assimilate Arab women both for their own good and the good of the colony, speaking against the current of public opinion. But many of her insights, building on those of earlier colonial-feminists, would eventually form the basis of French colonial policy with regard to Muslim women.

Hubertine Auclert: The Feminization of Colonialism

Hubertine Auclert, founder of the French women's suffrage movement and editor of the feminist newspaper *La Citoyenne* [*The Woman Citizen*], travelled to Algeria in 1888 where she studied the condition of Arab women. Twelve years later, her findings were published in *Les Femmes arabes en Algérie*, a two-hundred-and-fifty-page work that considers various aspects of indigenous Algerian women's lives, including marriage, divorce, inheritance rights, prostitution and polygamy. However, *Les Femmes arabes en Algérie* (henceforth *Femmes arabes*), is not only an anthropological study but also a political treatise that condemns what Auclert perceives to be French men's mismanagement of the colony, and makes the case for a greater involvement of women in the colonial enterprise. Like Voilquin, Auclert deplores the suffering of Muslim-Arab women and makes a case for their emancipation but, expressed over fifty years later, her 'colonial feminism' is articulated quite differently from that of her predecessor. In order to better appreciate these differences, it is first necessary to understand the changes in the political and social climate between the 1830s and the turn of the century — changes that would allow Auclert to knit feminist and colonial discourses ever more closely together.

In the mid-nineteenth century, a series of repressive laws stifled feminist activity but, by the dawn of the Third Republic, the transformation of the political scene by a number of liberal laws encouraged the re-emergence of feminist activism. In particular, the press law of 1868 ended administrative censorship and extended freedom of assembly, allowing for the emergence of a number of new women's rights groups such as the Société pour l'Amélioration du Sort de la Femme [Society for the Betterment of Women's Situation] and La Ligue Française pour le Droit des Femmes [The French League for Women's Rights]. These new feminists were predominantly republicans who revived the feminism of the Revolution with its emphasis on rights and equality. Unlike the Saint-Simonists, their aspirations were not tied to socialist ideals. Ties between feminism and socialism had been weakened following the enforced exile of feminist-socialist activists in 1871 for taking part in the Paris commune uprising, and feminism's class-base shifted to become largely bourgeois and liberal in orientation.[17] Hubertine Auclert, however, remained a committed socialist and had an ambivalent relationship to the dominant feminism of the time, her radical views eventually resulting in her marginalization. Nonetheless, in spite of these tensions, Auclert was profoundly republican in her emphasis on equality and the goal of her organization *Suffrage des femmes* [Women's Suffrage] was the equal treatment of the sexes in public, private and political life.[18]

The energetic republicanism of the late nineteenth century not only informed feminist activism but also fuelled the 'civilizing' aims of French colonialism. Before the establishment of a civilian regime in Algeria in 1871, there were not sufficient numbers of French women in the colony to make any significant contribution to the *mission civilisatrice*. However, the large-scale settlement of European families in Algeria during the final decades of the nineteenth century levelled up the gender imbalance, and changes at home began to lay the foundations for women's involvement in colonial affairs. As the historian Eugen Weber explains,[19] what the colonial administration was trying to achieve in Algeria was similar to that which the French republican establishment was trying to accomplish in rural France and amongst the French working classes. The republican mission to modernize and eradicate ignorance and superstition began at home, and bourgeois women were allocated a key role in these domestic reforms. As Janet Horne explains, this role was shaped, in part, by the work of sociologist Frédéric Le Play who, drawing on notions of women as guardians of society's traditions and values, argued that women, in their role as mothers, were responsible for preserving the values of society by passing them on to their children.[20] This gave women exceptional political and social responsibility and, in Le Play's analysis, made them the primary agents of progress. Taking inspiration from Le Play's studies, republican reformers such as Emile Cheysson argued that bourgeois women held the key to social cohesion in the Republic, and women were subsequently enlisted to visit the homes of working-class families in order to exert their supposedly beneficial influence on working-class mothers. If working-class families could adopt or aspire to 'superior' middle-class values, Cheysson argued, class conflict could be quelled. Bourgeois women appeared as the perfect agents of this change, as they could most easily gain access to working-class homes, firstly because women, unlike bourgeois men, were perceived to be inherently apolitical and more altruistic, and secondly because women from all social backgrounds were expected to bond in their shared role as mothers.[21]

Meanwhile in Algeria, the French colonial gaze was beginning to fix upon the figure of the Muslim-Arab woman. General Eugène Daumas appears to have been the earliest official to express the notion that women-centred policies might also enable the successful colonization and pacification of Algeria. Daumas's study of indigenous Algerian women, *La Femme arabe*, argues that knowledge of and influence over Arab women might lead to the better understanding and domination of Arab society.[22] It was vital, he claimed, to gain access to the women in order to be able to transmit the culture and values of the colonizing society into the heart of Algerian homes, and thus destroy indigenous culture. Daumas's work would ultimately become fundamental to the colonial ethnographic perception that constructed the Muslim woman as both the gateway and obstacle to colonial domination but, written during the early decades of colonial rule, it was well ahead of its time. However, by the end of the nineteenth century, once the role of women in domestic social policy was firmly established in the imagination of republican reformers, the stage was set for the elaboration of women's role in the colonies. Hubertine Auclert's *Les Femmes arabes en Algérie*, published in 1900, borrows from both the sociological discourses advanced by Le Play and looks back to Daumas's views on Algerian women as the key to colonial domination, to produce an argument in favour of the full assimilation of the indigenous Algerian population, for the benefit of both Arab women and the French colonial project. In championing assimilation, Auclert was swimming against the tide of official opinion, policy-makers having for the most part renounced that objective for French Algeria. However, as we shall see in the next section, her arguments laid the groundwork for later colonial practice.

Auclert's key contention in *Les Femmes arabes* is that the education and assimilation of Muslim-Arab women is not only moral, but critical to the success of French Algeria and, crucially, can only be brought about by the inclusion of French women in the colonial administration and the political sphere more broadly. In her study of colonial women writers, *Femmes arabes et sœurs musulmanes*, Denise Brahimi argues that Auclert's arguments in favour of assimilation combat racism and sexism in mutually re-enforcing ways. According to Brahimi, sexism and racism are, for Auclert, two manifestations of the same oppression making colonized women doubly oppressed and therefore doubly in need of protection.[23] However, as Brahimi acknowledges, Auclert's outspoken and courageous denunciation of the colonial administration is not a criticism of the colonial enterprise itself. My reading of Auclert's work will suggest that Auclert's balancing of racist and sexist concerns is perhaps not as fortuitous as Brahimi suggests. Auclert not only embraces the colonial project but strategically exploits colonial discourses and nurtures colonial fantasies in order to make her case for the emancipation of Arab women and the inclusion of French women in the colonial administration. Ultimately, this complicity with colonial power does not facilitate the realization of her feminist aims, but severely compromises them.

Throughout *Les Femmes arabes*, Auclert expresses her disgust at French men's mishandling of the colonial enterprise and their mistreatment of the indigenous population. Although she fervently believes in the necessity to 'civilize' Algeria and never questions the premises of the colonial mission itself, Auclert is appalled by the viciously repressive ways in which her fellow citizens have subjugated the colony and its people. In the opening pages, she remarks: 'En Algérie, il n'y a qu'une toute petite élite de Français qui classe dans l'humanité la race arabe' [In Algeria, there is only a small elite of French people who would consider the Arab race to be part of humanity] (*Femmes arabes*, 3) and criticizes the colonial administration's ritual humiliation of indigenous Algerians. Auclert explains this behaviour as resulting from a lack of female influence in the centres of colonial power. She writes: 'Loin de la mère patrie, les hommes qui vivent entre eux, privés de l'élément féminin, retournent à l'état sauvage; on ne peut s'expliquer autrement, la cruauté des fonctionnaires envers les indigènes' [Far from the mother country, the men who live among themselves, with no female influence, regress to a state of savagery. There is no other way of explaining the cruelty with which these officials treat the indigenous population] (*Femmes arabes*, 31). In Auclert's analysis, the violent subjugation of indigenous Algerians by the male colonial authorities needs to be replaced by a female-led colonial strategy that would promote the full assimilation of the Algerian population to French nationhood by granting them the same rights and political representation as their European counterparts.

In particular, Auclert attacks what she sees as the complicity between the male French colonial administration and a small patriarchal Arab elite that disempowers the great majority of indigenous Algerians, especially Algerian women. In her analysis, the colonial administration supports the Arab elite in order to keep the Arab people ignorant of their rights, subjugated by feudalism and consequently easier to dominate. The assimilation of the indigenous population, she argues, would upset this order: 'Le peuple arabe a en effet tout à gagner à devenir français; ses maîtres, eux, ont à perdre en même temps que leurs privilèges, leur meilleure source de revenus' [The Arab people have everything to gain in becoming French; their masters however would lose both their privileges and their best source of income] (*Femmes arabes*, 22). Consequently, the colonial authorities, in Auclert's analysis, are reluctant to involve themselves in what they considered to be 'Arab' affairs, leaving it to the Arab elite to ensure the subjugation of the people. This means that a double legislation applies, whereby French settlers and indigenous Algerians form two separate groups that are not always subject to the same rule of law. In Auclert's view, this double system is especially detrimental to Arab women who, despite living under French rule, continue to be subject to patriarchal Arab traditions. In a letter to the President of the Chamber of Deputies, in which she petitions for a ban on polygamous marriages, Auclert urges: 'On a déjà laissé trop longtemps les Arabes garder leurs lois, leurs mœurs, leur langue. Ne croyez-vous pas qu'il est urgent d'en faire des enfants de la République, de les instruire, de les assimiler aux Français?' [For too long, we have let the Arabs keep their laws, morality and language. Don't you think that it is urgent to make them children of the Republic, to educate and assimilate them?] (*Femmes arabes*, 69). Furthermore, in Auclert's view, the French administration's complicity with the enforcement of Arab patriarchal tradition reaps material rewards. Referring to inheritance laws, she explains: 'Quand la musulmane, qui ne touche qu'un tiers de la succession paternelle, n'a pas de coheritiers mâles, l'Etat français s'empare des deux autres tiers' [When the Muslim woman, who in any case only receives a third of the inheritance, does not have any male co-inheritors, the French state takes the other two thirds]. She goes on to describe this arrangement as 'une convention tacite de brigands, où les Français semblent dire aux musulmans: "Nous vous laissons détrousser les femmes, à condition que quand vous ne serez pas là, ce sera nous qui les détrousserons!"' [a pact between thieves by which the French seem to be telling Muslim men: 'We'll let you steal from your women as long as we can steal from them if you are not around!'] (*Femmes arabes*, 140–41). Auclert detects the workings of an aggressive patriarchy behind both French colonial rule and Arab traditions, and promotes the empowerment of French women and the assimilation of indigenous women as a means of undermining it.

However, the emancipation of women was hardly a popular agenda in late nineteenth century France and so, in *Femmes arabes*, Auclert attempts to make her demands more palatable by couching them in terms of the celebrated colonial project. For Auclert, the colonies presented an opportunity for French women to prove themselves worthy of inclusion in public and political life. Indeed, her insistence on the usefulness of French women in the colonial context was part of a broader feminist agenda to advance French women's political and civil status. If the reader could be persuaded that the participation of women in colonial affairs would work in favour of the greater glory of the French nation then, Auclert imagined, they might be more easily persuaded of women's usefulness in other areas of public life. With this in mind, Auclert stresses that assimilation would not only benefit the indigenous population and empower French women but would (most importantly) be in the long-term interests of French imperialism. Whereas elements of the male colonial administration thought the Arab population could be better dominated and exploited if they remained entrenched in their 'backward' traditions, Auclert argues that, on the contrary, French Algeria would be stronger and more prosperous if the Algerian population were 'civilized' through education and political integration. She writes: 'Le meilleur moyen de les empêcher de se rebeller c'est de les charger de concourir à faire prospère et libre leur pays' [The best way to prevent them from rebelling is to involve them in the process of making their country free and prosperous] (*Femmes arabes*, 249). In Auclert's view, the success of the colony depends on assimilation, and this begins with the conversion of Muslim-Arab women to French values by means of public education. In her words: 'Les indigènes très subtils savent bien que la cloche de l'école commune [...] sonnerait le glas de leur résistance à la francisation. Aussi sont-ils [...] rebelles à tout développement intellectuel féminin: "Si nos femmes étaient instruites, disent les musulmans, elles seraient les alliées des roumis"' [More intuitive natives are well aware that the sound of the school bell will signal the end of their resistance to gallicization. By the same token they are opposed to their women's intellectual development: 'If our women were educated,' they say, 'they would be the allies of the French'] (*Femmes arabes*, 144).[24] By considering women's emancipation in terms of French imperial power, Auclert is able to push for the participation of French women in the colonial project.

The following passage is particularly telling in this respect and it is worth examining more closely to reveal the ways in which Auclert draws on both republican representations of women as agents of social reform and familiar orientalist tropes in order to foster a complicity between feminism and the French colonial mission. Auclert's argument (like Cheysson's interpretation of Le Play) revolves around the question of access, and in the following passage she argues that French women's relatively easy access to Muslim homes and Muslim women makes them the perfect agents of French power:

> Ces femmes quelque peu initiées à la langue arabe, n'exciteraient pas plus la méfiance qu'elles ne blesseraient la susceptibilité musulmane. Sous un prétexte

quelconque, en vue par exemple d'établir l'état civil des femmes indigènes, elles
porteraient la francisation à domicile.

En pénétrant sous les tentes et dans les maisons aux portes verrouillées elles
familiariseraient les musulmanes avec notre manière de vivre et de penser. Les
Arabes déja très admirateurs des qualités utilitaires de la Française seraient en la
voyant communiquer son savoir-faire à leurs compagnes, moralement conquis
à notre pays. (*Femmes arabes*, 27)

[These women, who have so little command of Arabic, will not raise suspicions
nor offend Muslim sensibilities. Under some pretext, for example that of
establishing the civil status of native women, they will bring France into the
heart of the home.

By penetrating the tents and the locked doors of the houses they will
familiarize Muslim women with our ways of living and thinking. The Arabs,
who are already great admirers of the resourcefulness of Frenchwomen, will be
morally converted to France on seeing them share their savoir-faire with their
wives.]

Auclert transfers Cheysson's notion of the bourgeois French woman as guarantor
of social harmony in France into the colonial context in order to suggest that
women have a key role to play in the assimilation of the Algerian population. Only
women, she argues, can get past the 'portes verrouillées' to penetrate to the heart of
the Muslim home, to the allegorical essence of Algeria itself: the Muslim woman.
Despite Auclert's fervent feminist agenda, in this instance she strategically employs
the notion of women as uneducated and apolitical in order to make her point. Just
as Cheysson imagines that working-class women will be less suspicious of bourgeois
women than men, Auclert exploits the conventional notion of women as apolitical
to argue for their inclusion in colonial policy. In Auclert's analysis, the French
woman is the Trojan horse that will breach the native population's stronghold of
resistance; the 'impenetrable' Muslim home and the 'inaccessible', veiled Muslim
woman.

Moreover, Auclert plays on colonial anxieties with regard to the notion of the
Muslim woman as veiled and deceptive. The veiled Muslim woman's power to see
without being seen has frequently been described as a source of anxiety for the
male colonizer as it robs him of the panoptic vision which reduces the colonized to
objects under his surveillance and control.[25] Auclert's strategy soothes this anxiety
as, in this case, it is the French woman who appears as 'veiled' and deceptive,
restoring the colonial play of gazes. The French woman is able to infiltrate the
Muslim home on the pretence that she is naïvely apolitical; her real agenda *cannot
be seen*. At the same time, the Muslim interior is opened up to her scrutiny and she
may see the Muslim woman unveiled. The intimacy she fosters on the grounds
of gender identification allows her to familiarize the Muslim woman with 'notre
manière de vivre et de penser' and win her over to the colonial cause. In this way,
Auclert puts the French woman in a position of power vis-à-vis her Muslim sisters.
By penetrating into the private space of the Muslim family, she turns the Muslim
woman into an object of inquiry while denying her the possibility of returning the
gaze; the French woman's true motives remaining opaque.

Although Hubertine Auclert was sincerely committed to Muslim women's welfare, in this passage her concern for Muslim women simply serves as a pretext on which to gain access to the Muslim home and thus secure the cultural conquest of Algeria. Elsewhere she writes: 'Pour nous Français, notre intérêt en Algérie doit primer tout' [For us French, our interest in Algeria must be a priority], and explains that France has '*un intérêt réel, un intérêt politique, à instruire les musulmanes*' [*a real interest, a political interest in educating Muslim women*] [original emphasis] (*Femmes arabes*, 145). The well-being of Muslim women is, for Auclert, a good in its own right, but her tendency to frame her arguments in terms of a greater colonial agenda subordinates the interests of Muslim women to the glory of France. Furthermore, Auclert's strategic privileging of French colonial interests means that Muslim women's emancipation appears secondary to the political emancipation of French women. Indeed the former is imagined to depend on the latter. Referring to the colonial administration's tolerance of polygamy she writes: 'Si les Françaises votaient et légiféraient, il y a longtemps que leurs sœurs africaines seraient délivrées de l'outrageante polygamie et de l'intolérable promiscuité avec leurs co-épouses' [If Frenchwomen voted and legislated, their African sisters would have been released from the outrageous practice of polygamy and the degrading cohabitation with other wives a long time ago] (*Femmes arabes*, 63). Auclert's sincere defence of indigenous women is compromised by her endorsement of a colonial regime that constructs French culture as the guiding light of civilization and, in Auclert's analysis, French women as its torch-bearers. As a result, the voices of Algerian women themselves are barely audible.

This is in spite of Auclert's professed intentions. Auclert complains of the male colonial authorities' failure to consult the indigenous population. French women, she argues, would by contrast ensure that even the most marginalized voices would be heard: 'Des femmes enquêteuses songeraient à prendre l'avis du peuple arabe avant de consulter les présidents de douars. Elles interrogeraient les êtres qui chez les conquis sont les plus opprimés, les plus privés de liberté: les femmes arabes' [If women conducted surveys they would take care to hear the views of the Arab people before consulting their leaders. They would ask the opinions of those who are the most oppressed amongst the colonized, the most deprived of freedom: Arab women] (*Femmes arabes*, 23). However, there is little evidence of this in Auclert's book. Despite colonial women travellers' relatively privileged access to Muslim women, barriers of language, culture and class severely restricted communication and, like male writers, they too relied on the citation of familiar oriental tropes and types.[26] Auclert's representations of Arab women are usually generalized and the text as a whole is dominated by the monolithic figure of the 'Arab Woman'.

Like Voilquin, Auclert constructs the Arab Woman as a cipher for French women's fears and desires. The Arab Woman as projection of French women's fears is perhaps most apparent in Auclert's violent condemnation of polygamy. Polygamy, in Auclert's analysis, entails the brutal exploitation of women who are reduced to little more than sexual and domestic slaves. But, as Brahimi has suggested, Auclert's hostility to Arab marriage may also be understood in terms of French women's anxieties about their own marital status. Indeed, polygamous marriage and repudiation facilitated and legitimized what married middle-class Frenchwomen most dreaded — adultery and abandonment.[27] The French institution of marriage made women socially, emotionally and financially vulnerable, so the 'proper' regulation of sexuality (that is to say its containment within monogamous marriage and reproduction) was of vital importance. Auclert refracts these anxieties through a colonial lens to argue that the proper regulation of sexuality is not only a concern for women, but for colonial power. According to Auclert, the colonial authorities allow Arab men to remain polygamous as it renders them easier to dominate. She writes: 'Pendant que le polygame s'abrutit [...] dans le "chenil conjugal", avec les multiples ouvrières-épouses qui lui permettent d'être si majestueusement fainéant, il ne songe en effet, à defendre ni sa liberté ni son bien' [As long as the polygamist remains in the mind-numbing confines of his 'conjugal kennel', surrounded by his numerous worker-wives who allow him to be gloriously lazy, he does not dream of defending his freedom nor his interests] (*Femmes arabes*, 78). In Auclert's view, however, French tolerance of such practices not only compromises France's humanist principles but saps the potential strength of French Algeria, which would benefit from the full assimilation of indigenous Algerians to French culture.

The Muslim-Arab woman is not only a repository for French women's fears, but a projection of their desires. Auclert constructs the indigenous Algerian woman as symbolic of all women's potential for emancipation. However, like Voilquin, her tendency to subordinate her feminist agenda to colonial concerns produces profound contradictions. Despite her denunciation of French society's mistreatment of women, Auclert imagines that the Arab woman's most ardent desire is to loosen the shackles of Arab tradition and Islamic orthodoxy in order to become like French women. She writes:

> Le rêve des musulmanes dont la vie s'écoule dans les cours intérieurs et dans des maisons sans fenêtres, est d'être assimilées aux Françaises affranchies de la réclusion. Les mahometanes envient autant le sort des Européennes, que les oiseaux en cage envient le sort de ceux qui volent dans l'éspace. (*Femmes arabes*, 24)

> [The dream of those Muslim women whose lives ebb away in closed courtyards and windowless houses, is to be released from their prisons and to become like Frenchwomen. Muslim women envy the situation of European women just as caged birds envy those that are free to fly.]

The notion that Arab women wish to become like their French sisters flatters the colonizers' sense of cultural superiority and inscribes Auclert's feminism firmly within the colonial frame but, as for Voilquin, her need to appeal to male colonial powers also compromises her position. This compromise is perhaps most explicit in her assertion that if Arab women were familiarized with French values they would abandon their husbands, preferring to prostitute themselves to French men than remain in a polygamous marriage. She writes: 'dès qu'elle peut se soustraire à la claustration, elle jette le Coran par dessus la Casbah et préfère se donner à vingt Français, plutôt que de se laisser achêter par un seul mari mahometan' [as soon as she is able to escape her confinement, she throws the Koran out of the Casbah and would rather give herself to twenty Frenchmen than be bought by a single Muslim husband] (*Femmes arabes*, 93). Despite Auclert's condemnation of French men's eroticization of Arab women elsewhere in her text, in this instance she does not shy away from appealing to the voyeurism of her male readers, equating Muslim women's emancipation with their sexual availability. Comments such as these are clearly a strategy to persuade the (male) reader of the benefits of 'emancipating' Arab women, rather than a genuine reflection of Muslim–Arab women's own desires and demands, but this strategy undermines Auclert's feminist agenda with regard to both French and Algerian women. By implicitly constructing the French woman as the embodiment of emancipation and the envy of her Arab sisters she weakens her otherwise vigorous critique of French women's situation, and by projecting French women's fears and desires onto the figure of the Arab woman she erases Algerian women's specificity in a colonizing gesture of appropriation. As we shall see in the next chapter, these are also features of contemporary feminist discourses on the Muslim woman.

Although Auclert did not live to see her strategies for a 'feminized' colonialism put into practice, by the time our next writer, Marie Bugéja, was putting pen to paper, many of Auclert's ideas were becoming part of mainstream colonial discourse.

Marie Bugéja: Maternal Imperialist

In *L'An V de la révolution algérienne* [*A Dying Colonialism*],[28] written at the height of the Algerian war, Frantz Fanon describes the explicit adoption of a gendered strategy whereby the colonial authorities perceived Algerian women to have power and influence in their role as mothers and sought to weaken the colony's capacity for resistance by striking at the matriarchal heart of the Algerian family home. He writes:

> Derrière le patriarcat visible, manifeste, on affirme l'existence, plus capitale, d'un matriarcat de base. Le rôle de la mère algérienne, ceux de la grand-mère, de la tante, de la 'vieille' sont inventoriés et précisés.
>
> L'administration coloniale peut alors définir une doctrine politique précise: 'Si nous voulons frapper la société algérienne dans sa contexture, dans ses facultés de résistance, il nous faut d'abord conquérir les femmes; il faut que nous allions les chercher derrière le voile où elles se dissimulent et dans les maisons où l'homme les cache'.[29]

> [Behind the manifest, visible patriarchy it is possible to discern the workings of a more fundamental matriarchy. The role of the Algerian mother along with that of the grandmother, the aunt, the elderly woman are inventoried and explained.
>
> The colonial administration can then define a precise political doctrine: 'If we want to strike the core structure of Algerian society, right at the heart of its resistance, we must first conquer the women; we must seek them out behind the veils that hide them and in the houses where men cloister them'.]

By the time Fanon was writing in the 1950s, this thinking had become part of mainstream colonial strategy, but the notion that Algerian women's role as mothers could provide the key to colonial rule was most fully and vigorously developed some years earlier by the novelist and essayist Marie Bugéja. In her 1921 treatise on the necessity to educate Muslim women, *Nos sœurs musulmanes*, Bugéja argues that Algerian Muslim women must be taught the French way of life not only for their own sakes, but above all for the good of the colony. Like Auclert, Bugéja saw French women as the Trojan horses that would penetrate the Algerian home and instil French values in the women who would then pass them on to their children. However, whereas Auclert is primarily motivated by feminist concerns, Bugéja's desire to educate Muslim women works principally in the interests of the colonial project. She argues that the education of Muslim women is 'une double question d'humanité et de patriotisme' [a matter of both humanity and patriotism] (*Nos sœurs*, 13), as it is in France's interests to ensure that Algerian women become allied to the colonial mission. She writes: 'Croyez-moi; l'influence de la femme est grande; cette Musulmane peut devenir notre auxiliaire le plus précieux ou notre adversaire le plus tenace dans l'évolution des masses indigènes' [Believe me; the women wield tremendous influence. The Muslim woman may become either our most precious ally or our most unyielding obstacle to the development of native peoples].[30] Convinced of the vital role of women in the pacification and domination of the colony, she describes the purpose of her book as 'l'œuvre de rénovation de la musulmane algérienne pour le plus grand bien du foyer musulman, et pour la gloire toujours plus éclatante de notre France' [the renewal of the Algerian Muslim woman for the benefit of the Muslim home and for the ever more radiant glory of France] (*Nos sœurs*, 133). But whereas Auclert (despite the aforementioned contradictions) envisages the *rénovation* of Muslim women in terms of their integration into the public and political sphere, Bugéja, in keeping with the feminism of her time, seeks to rehabilitate the Muslim woman by assimilating her to a conservative ideal of bourgeois femininity as mothers serving the nation.

Marie Bugéja was of Breton origin but was born in Algeria and identified herself as *une Algéroise*. However, at the time she wrote *Nos sœurs musulmanes* her politics were much more in keeping with metropolitan attitudes than with those of the settler community in which she lived. Whereas most settlers in Algeria strongly opposed the assimilation of Algerians into the French nation and were intent on maintaining rigid boundaries between colonizer and colonized, metropolitan attitudes were increasingly sympathetic to the view that Algerians could and should be transformed into model Frenchmen.[31] In particular, the Great War of 1914–18 had a significant impact on metropolitan attitudes towards the colonies and their peoples. During the war, the French colonies supplied over 500,000 soldiers to fight in the trenches and over 200,000 workers to keep war industries running. By supplying troops, workers and raw materials in defence of the mother country, the colonies had proved themselves to be useful, renewing enthusiasm for the *mission civilisatrice* and silencing many of the critics who believed the colonies to be a waste of resources.

The First World War also had a significant impact on debates surrounding French women's social and political status. During the war, bourgeois feminists took care to shape their demands for reform within the broader frame of national interests. In particular, motherhood was figured as a social and national duty, an expression of devotion to France and the cement that would bind the nation together.[32] Indeed, as Brahimi has noted, wartime had no place for the divisive and adversarial feminism of firebrands like Auclert.[33] The national mood favoured patriotic unity and feminists fashioned their arguments accordingly. By the time Bugéja was writing at the end of the war, the emphasis on motherhood as service to the nation and civic duty was especially strong, as women were encouraged to repopulate a devastated and grieving France.

Aligning herself with the dominant concerns of her day, Bugéja uses familial metaphors to frame her arguments in favour of assimilation and the education of Muslim women. Indeed, the title of her work, *Nos sœurs musulmanes*, constructs France's colonial others as part of an extended family, suggesting a reassuring cohesion and stability. However, as Horne argues, the invocation of the family as a metaphor of social relations (a basic idiom in the language of both domestic and colonial republican reform) disguised profound differences of wealth and power.[34] As my reading of *Nos sœurs musulmanes* will suggest, Bugéja's professed identification with her Muslim 'sisters' — an identification founded on a supposedly shared female experience — naturalizes a conservative notion of French womanhood while concealing the entrenched inequalities between women in the colonial context. Indeed, the unequal balance of power is already implicit in Bugéja's use of the possessive adjective '*Nos*'.

Whereas Hubertine Auclert assumes the seemingly objective distance of the social scientist, Marie Bugéja represents herself as having an intimate relationship with Muslim women, posing as their confidante and narrating her conversations with them. Eschewing social or political analysis in favour of establishing affective bonds, she writes: 'J'ai causé bien des fois avec mes sœurs musulmanes et je les ai aimées; elles m'ont fait des confidences. Mon livre est un livre vécu; il a au moins le mérite de la sincérité' [I have often conversed with my Muslim sisters and have taken them to my heart. They have trusted and confided in me. My book is based on lived experience and has, at least, the virtue of sincerity] (*Nos sœurs*, 23). Bugéja's emphasis on the intimacy of these relationships lends her book an aura of authenticity grounded in received notions of a shared feminine sensibility. As a woman, indeed as an *Algéroise*, Bugéja considers herself to have privileged access to the secrets of Algerian womanhood remarking: 'comment les hommes auraient-ils pu approcher les musulmanes, les fréquenter, recevoir leur confidences [...] il faut une femme et — oserai-je le dire — une Algérienne' [how could men hope to become close to Muslim women, to visit them, to hear their private thoughts [...] only a woman and — dare I say it — an Algerian woman, is capable of doing so] (*Nos sœurs*, 82–83). In reality, Bugéja, like Auclert, had limited access to Algerian women as she spoke only a few words of Berber and no Arabic. This meant that her contact with Algerian Muslim women was generally restricted to meeting elite women from wealthy households who could speak a little French. However, as Brahimi has noted, this suited Bugéja as it allowed her to draw attention to similarities between Algerian women and middle-class French women, thus rehabilitating the Algerian woman by assimilating her to a model of bourgeois French femininity.[35] Indeed, focusing on the upper echelons of colonial society was a way for Bugéja to remind her readers that not all Algerian women were 'pouilleuses' [dirty low-life] or 'danseuses' [erotic dancers] (*Nos sœurs*, 87) — some were already respectable *bourgeoises* and others were capable of evolving towards this model.

In Bugéja's account, there is a natural understanding and complicity between women that transcends differences of culture and class. Unlike Auclert, Bugéja's identification with Algerian women is not grounded in a common struggle against a universal patriarchy, but is based, first and foremost, on women's supposed common experience as mothers. Sweeping cultural, class and linguistic barriers to one side she writes: 'Mauresques aux haïks splendides, pauvresses aux haillons déchirés, Françaises à la civilisation très haute ou aux mains rudes et laborieuses, nous ne sommes toutes que des mères' [Moorish women in splendid veils, poor women in rags, Frenchwomen at the pinnacle of civilization or with work-roughened hands, we are all mothers] (*Nos sœurs*, 19). Indeed, the first chapter of her book is entitled 'Aux mères musulmanes' [To Muslim mothers] and addresses them directly, emphasizing their common experience as mothers of young men who fought in the trenches for the glory of France. In another of her publications, *Visions d'Algérie* [*Visions of Algeria*],[36] Bugéja reports the words of an Algerian mother whose son was wounded on the battlefields:

> [I]l m'a dit que les Françaises ont été bonnes pour lui et pour tous les nôtres. Tu est française, à ta figure je vois que tu es bonne [...].
> Je répondis à cette mère inquiète: 'Ton fils est sous le ciel de la France et il combat sous son drapeau, c'est un brave qui fait tout son devoir, tu dois être fière d'avoir un tel enfant'. Elle me baisa les mains avec effusion, puis brusquement se redressa sans souci de la chute de son fagot, et me dit: 'Merci, ô Française; mon fils, c'est vrai, aime ton pays et moi, sa mère, j'aime ce qu'il aime'. (Visions, 147)

> [He told me that Frenchwomen were good to him and to all our men. You are French and I can tell from your face that you are good too [...].
> I replied to this anxious mother: 'Your son is under a French sky and fighting under the French flag. He is a brave fellow who is doing his duty. You must be proud to have such a child.' She kissed my hands effusively, then suddenly stood up straight without a care for her firewood that tumbled to the ground. And she said to me: 'Thank you, O Frenchwoman; it is true that my son loves your country and as his mother I love what he loves'.]

Bugéja's choice of the First World War as the point of contact between herself and the Algerian woman is significant because it frames the common concerns of French and Algerian women within the context of French patriotism. The relationship between French and Muslim women is mediated, first and foremost, by their common role as mothers serving the French nation. The Algerian woman's son is 'sous le ciel de la France' and Bugéja invites her to join in the pride of French mothers for their fallen sons.

Yet despite Bugéja's emphasis on a natural sisterhood between women as mothers, the relationship between French women and their Algerian counterparts is clearly more maternal than sisterly. For Bugéja, it is Frenchwomen's moral and patriotic duty to educate Muslim women and convert them to a French way of life and this is best achieved through the cultivation of a maternal bond. Muslim women, she insists, have a daughterly admiration for French women. In *Visions d'Algérie*, Bugéja claims to have inspired love and respect in Muslim women of all social classes and after dinner in the company of Muslim women, she feels certain that they secretly long to resemble her: 'je sors avec la certitude que les femmes musulmanes, ces cloîtrées qui vivent en dehors de la société moderne, sentent s'ébaucher dans leurs âmes un rêve encore obscur mais séduisant; elles se plaisent à nous imiter et sont prêtes à nous aimer' [I leave certain that Muslim women, these cloistered beings that live beyond modern society, feel an as yet elusive but seductive dream taking shape in their souls. They enjoy imitating us and are ready to love us] (*Nos sœurs*, 74). Furthermore, according to Bugéja, French women have a responsibility and duty to ensure the development of their protégées. She writes: 'Avec notre liberté d'action et de mouvement, nous devons toutes, femmes françaises, ne pas refuser notre concours à celles dont la voix est assourdie au fond du gynécée' [With our liberty of action and movement, we Frenchwomen, must all come to the aid of those whose voices are stifled in the gynaeceum] (*Nos sœurs*, 133). Algerian women are not active in their own emancipation. Rather, they are waiting to be rescued by French women. Lastly, Bugéja's maternalism is tied to her notion of France as the mother country. It is France's responsibility to nourish, nurture and educate the colonies and, within this frame, it is the duty of French women to 'mother' their underdeveloped Muslim contemporaries. As Horne has remarked, this kind of familial discourse naturalizes, and was used to legitimize, colonial rule.[37]

Bugéja's discourse of identification with Muslim women serves colonial culture by concealing the real differences that separate French colonial women from their colonized Others. Convinced of the justness of the colonizing mission, Bugéja does not acknowledge the oppression of Algerian women as colonized subjects and instead focuses exclusively on their oppression at the hands of Algerian men. Her failure to acknowledge the ways in which Algerian women's opportunities were severely limited by the colonial situation reduces the 'rights' she defends to mere abstractions. For example, although Bugéja condemns women's enforced domestic drudgery and argues for the education of Muslim women, she sees no contradiction in the fact that, in colonial society, one of the only jobs available to Algerian women who broke away from tradition to earn their own living was as poorly paid servants in European homes. Furthermore, schools for Algerians did not teach the same subjects as those for their French counterparts but instead produced workers for low-status jobs that would serve the interests of the colonial project: manual labour for boys and domestic labour for girls. Bugéja describes the school programme as follows: 'On leur inculque des principes de propreté et d'hygiène; on les prépare à être d'excellentes ménagères; balayages, raccommodage, blanchissage, repassage simple et à l'amidon, cuisine, elles apprennent tout' [We instil principles of cleanliness and hygiene in them. We prepare them to be excellent housekeepers; sweeping, darning, laundering, ironing with and without starch, cooking, they learn everything] (*Nos sœurs*, 89).

Bugéja's proclaimed solidarity with Algerian women glosses over the real advantages bestowed on French women as mistresses of the colonial masters, and ultimately serves to reinforce these privileges. With reference to works by a variety of French colonial women writers, Sakinna Messaadi remarks: 'Ce zèle humaniste et protecteur à l'égard de la femme colonisée n'était pas désintéressé. Il servait plutôt à déguiser le statut subalterne de la femme colonisée, à l'intérieur d'un système

colonial, rehaussant ainsi le prestige des écrivains en tant que "leaders féministes"'
[This humanist zeal to protect the colonized woman was not disinterested. Rather,
it served to disguise the subaltern status of the colonized woman within the colonial
system while adding to the prestige of the writers as 'feminist leaders'].[38] Although
Bugéja's agenda may not have been as overtly cynical as Messaadi suggests (she did
after all campaign for Muslim women's welfare in spite of resistance from the settler
community), by substituting a feminist discourse that denigrates Algerian culture
on grounds of sexism for an analysis of the oppressive power relations of colonialism,
she asserts French women's superiority over their Muslim 'sisters'. Furthermore,
Bugéja's writing naturalizes French women's oppression by constructing middle-
class French femininity as the jewel in the crown of civilization. French women,
in her account are already emancipated and as such are fully qualified to be the
saviours, educators, confidantes and spokeswomen for their Algerian others.

What emerges from a study of these three colonial-feminist texts is the tendency
to represent the Muslim woman in one of two ways. Either she is represented
as the negative opposite of an idealized vision of French womanhood, or as
fundamentally the same: a woman who despite her cultural origins, aspires to
be just like her French 'sisters'. Voilquin, Auclert and Bugéja, in their different
ways, oscillate between these two poles in order to imagine an idealized vision
of French womanhood, advance the prospects of French women in the colonies
and justify and strengthen the colonial mission. Whether they choose to represent
Muslim women as the enemies or as the allies of women's freedom, only one path
to emancipation is thought to be possible and it is embodied in an idealized image
of the white, republican Frenchwoman. Muslim women's difference, according to
this logic, is simply reduced to the reverse image of French femininity as they are
translated into the colonial-feminist subject's own terms.

   The following chapter will reveal how a similar logic persists in contemporary
feminist discourses surrounding French Muslim women, in particular those
produced in response to the *affaire du foulard*. But first, as a way of providing the
historical backdrop to the *affaire*, it is useful to consider colonial-feminist responses
to the Muslim veil.

Colonial Feminism and the Veil

The desire to penetrate the mysteries of the Orient by lifting the Muslim woman's
veil is a frequent and much-discussed trope of orientalist discourse.[39] In this
fantasy, the Oriental woman is figured as the truth and essence of the Orient itself.
However, the all-encompassing veil places her (along with the pleasures and threats
she embodies) beyond the visual control of the colonizer, thus limiting his power.
As Meyda Yegenoglu argues, this refusal to yield to the Western gaze gives rise to
the suspicion that the Oriental woman is hiding something, that she is concealing
her (the Orient's) real nature behind the folds of her veil, and as such her allure
is lined with menace. The ambivalence and frustration produced by this refusal
are expressed in male travellers' accounts. The Italian writer Edmondo de Amicis

remarks, with a mixture of enchantment and irritation: 'it is impossible to say what they contrive to do with those two veils [...] making them serve at once to display, to conceal, to promise, to propose a problem, or to betray some little marvel unexpectedly',[40] while the French Romantic Théophile Gautier sulks that men should not bother going to Turkey as only women are able to enter the harems and glimpse the legendary odalisques.[41] Locked out of the harem and teased by the veil, the male colonizer responds with aggressive and elaborate fantasies of unveiling and possessing the Oriental woman and by analogy, the Orient itself. The erotic postcards that form the object of Malek Alloula's famous study are manifestations of this fantasy, as are the countless depictions of unveiled Oriental women by painters such as Delacroix, Ingres and, in the twentieth century, Matisse.[42]

But as we have seen, and as Gautier's peevish envy confirms, the veil did not pose such an obstacle to colonial women travellers. The Orient was coded 'feminine' and therefore, as Bugéja is keen to stress, it was by means of a feminine sensibility that its secrets could be disclosed. Indeed, colonial women frequently boasted of their privileged access to life behind the veil and variously sought either to disenchant their male counterparts with the banal 'truth' of life in the harem or to titillate them with salacious anecdotes.[43] Yet colonial feminists are just as invested in discourses of unveiling as colonial men. Their concern was not only to penetrate behind the veil, but to free the indigenous woman from it in order to transform her into a Frenchwoman. This desire to unveil and liberate the Muslim woman is also a colonizing gesture, but one that differs in important ways from that of colonial men.

The masculine fantasy of unveiling is perhaps most powerfully expressed by Fanon in his essay 'L'Algérie se dévoile' ['Algeria unveils'] in which he draws a clear comparison between the desire to possess the Algerian woman's body and the ravishment of Algeria. Fanon observes that, '[c]haque fois que l'Européen, dans des rêves à contenu érotique rencontre la femme algérienne, se manifestent les particularités de ses relations avec la société colonisée' [every time the European encounters the Algerian woman in erotic fantasy, the particularities of his relationship to the colonized society as a whole are revealed],[44] and he goes on to describe a dream pattern that inevitably culminates in the violent rape of a helpless Algerian body. Although Fanon characterizes the desire for domination and penetration as a masculine fantasy, this phallic violence also haunts colonial women's writing. As we have seen, colonial feminists occupy a 'masculine' position in relation to Algerian women by constructing them as their repressed Other, the ground upon which they build their subjectivity, and this position of phallic power is manifest in colonial feminists' repetition of a 'masculine' fantasy of domination. The clearest example of this eroticizing female gaze is provided by Mme Jean Pommerol whose description of an encounter with a veiled Mozabite woman has all the characteristics of male sexual intimidation. In *Une femme chez les Sahariennes*, she describes waiting in an alley for a woman to pass:

> J'essayai de suivre et d'aborder, entre les parois d'une ruelle blanche, l'une de ces couvertures ambulantes dont j'ai parlé. Elle glissait, fuyait devant moi, éperdue, s'appuyant aux murailles comme pour leur demander de l'engloutir et de la protéger. Mais j'avais sur elle l'avantage de ma liberté de mouvements.

Je l'atteins, cette Faffa ou cette Mamma. Je la touche du doigt. Elle pousse un cri. Je lui dis ce mot de politesse locale: 'Tu es jolie!' Elle se débat. J'essaie gentiment d'entr'ouvrir son voile et je reçois une bourrade qui m'ôte toute envie de persévérer![45]

[Between the walls of a whitewashed alley, I tried to follow and sidle up to one of those walking tents I mentioned earlier. She was slipping, fleeing in front of me, distraught, pressing close to the walls as if asking them to swallow her up and protect her. But I had the advantage of my freedom of movement. I catch up with this Faffa or Mamma. I touch her with my finger. She cries out. I try a local nicety: 'You are pretty!' I say. She struggles. I gently try to open her veil and receive an almighty slap that quoshes all desire to persevere!]

Pommerol's loitering followed by a pursuit in which she exploits her superior strength (in terms of increased mobility and speed), her near enjoyment of the woman's terror and her use of physical flattery are all characteristic of male sexual harassment. Although Fanon's description of the male rape fantasy is far more violent, it is similar to Pommerol's anecdote in terms of the power struggle that takes place. In both cases, the eroticization and intimidation of the veiled woman suggests the greater power of the colonizer — male or female.

But while the masculine fantasy privileges discourses of difference, constructing the Orient and the Oriental woman as a seductive and dangerous Other that must be dominated and exploited, colonial feminism doubles this phallic aggression with discourses of identification. In her reading of Lady Mary Wortley Montagu's Letters, Lisa Lowe argues that colonial feminist texts like Montagu's subvert masculine Orientalist discourses through a rhetoric of similitude that likens the situation of indigenous women to their Western counterparts, establishing a relationship of equality and solidarity rather than one of domination.[46] However, I would agree with Yegenoglu that this rhetoric of identification does little to undermine dominant Orientalist discourses as it is part and parcel of the imperialist act of subject constitution.[47] As we have seen in the writings of Voilquin, Auclert and Bugéja, such discourses of similitude deny the alterity of the Other woman by reducing her to the colonial-feminist subject's own terms, and this is nowhere more apparent than in colonial feminist discourses on unveiling. Indeed, if colonial feminists reveal a phallic aggression in their desire to unveil Muslim women this is because it is not only the emancipation of the Muslim woman imagined to be at stake, but that of French women themselves.

The unveiling of the Muslim woman is critical to colonial-feminist thinking as it symbolizes the transformation of the 'oppressed' Muslim woman into an 'emancipated' French woman. Colonial feminists were convinced that, once the layers of cultural difference had been peeled back, Muslim women would be seen to have the same desires, the same ambitions, and the same capacity to be 'civilized' as their French counterparts. If only the veil could be lifted, if only she could escape the clutches of her menfolk — or so the logic ran — the Muslim woman would become just like her European 'sisters'. This logic is underwritten by the assumption that Algerian patriarchy, symbolized by the veil, is unnatural and artificial, whereas French society enables the spontaneous blossoming of natural womanhood. In other words, unveiling the Algerian woman did not so much entail the transformation of a Muslim essence, as a stripping back of layers of Muslim cultural artifice to discover the kernel of a natural femininity (synonymous with French womanhood) that could then flourish under the protection of French society.

This logic is visible in Voilquin's representations of Egyptian women. In Voilquin's analysis, the Egyptian woman appears as the triumph of artifice over nature. She is all floating veils and jangling bracelets; deprived of an enlightened education, she has no internal life. Voilquin writes: 'La femme [...] n'a nulle consistance dans ce pays' [Women have no substance in this country] (*Souvenirs*, 315). Indeed, enslaved by an unnatural and oppressive patriarchy, Egyptian women appear unable to develop their 'natural' and individual identities and are instead reduced to identical, empty shells. Voilquin comments: 'L'existence de ces femmes n'a pas de variété, de mouvement; aussi chez toutes l'expression du visage est la même; le type par conséquent reste uniforme' [These women's lives have no variety, no movement. Furthermore they all have the same facial expressions. Thus they form a uniform type]. This depiction of Muslim women is in keeping with masculinist discourses of woman as pure appearance, a fascinating, seductive spectacle that masks her lack of substance.[48] But in typically contradictory fashion, Voilquin is subsequently keen to establish that Muslim women do in fact have an essence and that this essence is shared with French women. Voilquin appeals to the luminaries of the Enlightenment to liberate her Muslim sisters from such unnatural oppression and discover their 'natural' selves. She writes: 'O philosophes [...] affranchissez notre sexe, afin de voir toutes ces femmes s'épanouir au soleil de la liberté dans la diversité de leur nature' [O philosophers [...] free our sex so that all these women may blossom under the sun of liberty in the full diversity of their natures] (*Souvenirs*, 242). French culture, embodied here by Enlightenment thinkers, is imagined to be synonymous with nature. If only Egyptian women were to strip off their veils and stand beneath the natural sun of enlightened French culture, they would achieve their liberty.

This investment in the notion of a 'natural body' does not account for the ways in which ideas of what is 'natural' are shaped by cultural contexts.[49] Colonial-feminist discourses like that of Voilquin, pass off the culturally specific dimensions of an idealized French body as natural with the result that any divergence from this norm appears as an aberration. But if veiling can be read as a means of disciplining the body in line with Algerian configurations of power, then unveiling or not veiling can be seen as a product of European power matrices. As Fanon's description of a newly unveiled woman illustrates, unveiling involves the inscription of the Algerian woman's body into French cultural codes. He writes:

> Impression de corps déchiqueté, lancé à la dérive; les membres semblent s'allonger indéfiniment. Quand l'Algérienne doit traverser une rue, pendant longtemps il y a l'erreur de jugement sur la distance exacte à parcourir. Le corps dévoilé paraît s'échapper, s'en aller en morceaux [...]. L'absence du voile altère le schéma corporel de l'Algérienne. Il lui faut inventer rapidement de nouvelles dimensions à son corps, de nouveaux moyens de contrôle musculaire. Il lui faut se créer une démarche de femme-dévoilée-dehors.[50]

[An impression that her body is fragmented, drifting, her limbs seeming to stretch to infinity. When the Algerian woman crosses the street she will, for a long time, misjudge the exact distance she must travel. The unveiled body seems to escape her, to go to pieces [...]. The absence of the veil alters the Algerian woman's sense of her bodily contours. She must quickly invent new dimensions of her body and new means of muscular control. She needs to learn a new step, as an unveiled-woman-outside.]

The newly unveiled woman does not simply walk free, but must relearn her body. Whereas feminist discourses imagine the veil to be external to the Muslim woman's body, Fanon's description shows it to be a constitutive part of it. There is no 'inside' and 'outside', no 'with' or 'without' the veil as the Muslim woman's body is both disciplined and produced by the veil itself. For the Algerian woman that Fanon describes, removing the veil does not mean rediscovering her 'natural' body, denied to her by Algerian patriarchy, but instead involves a violent separation from her adult female body as she knows it, and its reinscription into a set of specifically European norms. Colonial feminist discourse, however, by naturalizing an idealized notion of French womanhood was able to sustain the fantasy that beneath every Muslim veil there was a potential European woman waiting to be freed.

Through the rhetoric of unveiling, colonial feminists were able to project their own dreams of emancipation onto the body of the Muslim woman. But this was a profoundly contradictory manoeuvre. By constructing the French woman as the ideal vision of women's emancipation, colonial feminists disavowed their own oppression displacing their anxieties, frustrations and disappointments onto the bodies of their colonial others. At the same time the fantasy of the unveiled and liberated Muslim woman allowed them to dream of their own, as yet unrealized, freedom. While French women were struggling to advance their situation at home, the colonial situation allowed them to imagine that they could force 'emancipation' on others and by doing so fantasize their own liberation. Colonial feminist texts might not subvert the dynamics of power implicit in masculine orientalist narratives, but they do differ from masculine orientalism in the way these power relations are articulated. For colonial feminists, the veil not only signifies resistance to colonial power, it denies them the fantasy of their own future empowerment. Indeed, the two are inextricably linked as it is the French woman's power over her colonial others that permits this fantasy in the first place.

This aggressive desire to 'free' the Muslim woman perhaps found its ultimate expression in the events of 13 May 1958 when domestic servants threatened with losing their jobs, poor women tempted with bribes and prostitutes with nothing to lose, were brought to the square in Algiers and publicly unveiled beneath a banner that read 'Soyons comme la femme française' [Let's be like the French Woman]. This notorious event was organized to coincide with a coup by right-wing elements of the military led by General Jacques Massu, culminating in the overthrow of the Fourth Republic and the return of Charles de Gaulle as president. Perceiving the Fourth Republic to be weak and indecisive in the face of swelling Algerian nationalism, Massu sought to seize back control of French Algeria and this involved pushing Algerian women, once again, to the foreground of colonial strategy.[51] During the war of Algerian independence the Muslim woman's veil became a prime symbol in France's struggle to maintain control of the colony.[52] As the frontier around which colonial fantasies of penetration were structured, the 'battle of the veil' was of tremendous symbolic and strategic importance transforming the veil from a traditional and religious garment into the symbol of Algerian resistance to French rule. In Fanon's words 'A l'offensive colonialiste autour du voile, le colonisé oppose le culte du voile' [In response to the colonizer's attack on the veil, the colonized make a cult of the veil].[53]

In her survey of masculine representations of the Algerian woman Rachida Titah argues that the war of independence provided an unprecedented opportunity for Algerian women to escape the confines of masculine fantasy and, for a time at least, to define themselves on their own terms.[54] However, one might also argue that the terms by which Algerian women defined themselves in their efforts to oust the French were borrowed from colonial feminist discourses. During the war, Algerian women appropriated colonial feminist stereotypes and used them against the French to devastating effect. Far from imagining their emancipation as dependent upon their gallicization, many Algerian women perceived their liberty to go hand in hand with a free Algeria and rallied to the side of their brothers and fathers to play an active role in the resistance. Most notoriously, women used their voluminous veils to set bombs and to transport bomb-making equipment through the streets of Algiers. Just as French women gained access to Muslim households by exploiting the stereotype of women as apolitical, Algerian women resistants relied on the image of Algerian women as 'harmless Fatmas' to dodge security. In Fanon's words: 'Il ne s'agit plus seulement de se voiler. Il faut se faire une telle "tête de Fatma" que le soldat soit rassuré: celle-ci est bien incapable de faire quoi que ce soit' [It was no longer a matter of simply veiling. It was necessary to pass oneself off as a 'Fatma' so that the soldier would be reassured that this woman was incapable of posing a threat].[55] Once the French authorities had wised up to the technique of transporting bombs under veils, female Algerian militants instead earned their trust by dressing as French women and transporting grenades in their handbags, this time exploiting the notion of the unveiled woman as ally.[56] This mimicking of colonial-feminist stereotypes of the Westernized and emancipated algérienne, saw France's dream of securing colonial domination through the 'emancipation' of indigenous women, turn rapidly into a nightmare.

Indeed, the French received news of Algerian women's participation in bombing campaigns as a devastating betrayal, and the female bombers themselves inspired a mix of fascination, outrage and stunned confusion. As Titah recalls, an enraged French press published photos of these ' "tricheuses" déguisées en Parisiennes' [treacherous women disguised as Parisian ladies] and called for them to be punished for 'la déception qu'elles avaient provoquée' [the disappointment they had caused].[57] The depth of disappointment experienced by the French was in proportion to the degree of hope they had invested in Algerian women. Taking the example of the FLN militant, Zohra Drif, Donald Reid explains that what made women like Drif so appalling to the French was that they had been exposed to French culture and had benefited from a French education. Indeed, Drif was a prize-winning student who had attended law-school and, according to the French officer who interrogated her, dressed like a European and was perfectly versed in French culture.[58] She was precisely the kind of woman that, according to colonial feminist logic, should have been underpinning not undermining French rule. But, as we have seen, colonial feminists' defence of and professed solidarity with Algerian women as women annihilated their identity as Algerians and as victims of colonization, and it was this identity that was violently reclaimed during the war years. As Reid points out, exposure to French cultural institutions did not impede the nationalism of women like Drif but instead served as a catalyst for engagement.[59]

For Fanon, women's liberation would be born of the struggle for national liberation and he describes how some young women defied the authority of their fathers and brothers to mix freely with men outside their family, sharing their camps, and frequently choosing their own husbands from among their comrades. Other accounts, however, suggest that this was something of an overstatement if not a romanticization of events, pointing to the initial reluctance of FLN leaders to recruit women and their subsequent failure to safeguard women's freedoms after liberation.[60] As Titah explains, the freedoms tasted during the revolution were short-lived. After an initial period of unveiling as a response to decolonization, the veil was reinstituted as a symbol of national unity and resistance to Western power and this went hand in hand with the institutionalization of a defensive patriarchy that saw women who played a significant part in the War of Independence excluded from the political sphere and relegated to traditional roles.[61] Feminist activity in Algeria since independence owes little however to the missionary efforts of French feminists who, by seeking identification with Algerian women along gender lines alone, failed to acknowledge their status as colonized subjects within an oppressive colonial system. Instead Algerian feminists have tended to look back to the heroines of the war as models of female emancipation.[62] Since the terrorization of women during the civil war of the 1990s, feminist activity in Algeria has made some gains, advancing and retreating in fits and starts, but women in Algeria remain relegated to a subordinate position that compares unfavourably with the position of women in neighbouring countries such as Tunisia and Morocco.

Tracing the development of colonial feminism through the writing of Voilquin, Auclert and Bugéja reveals not only the gradual entanglement of colonial and feminist discourses, but the progressive undermining of these writers' feminist concerns as they become ever more tightly harnessed to colonial power. Tensions between colonial and feminist agendas produce clear contradictions in Voilquin's and Auclert's work as they oscillate between criticizing the status of French women at home and constructing the French woman as the embodiment of emancipation in the colonies. These contradictions are spuriously resolved by Bugéja's substitution of a dissident feminist agenda for the promotion of bourgeois French motherhood and, by the time Algerian women were being forcibly and publicly unveiled, colonial women's feminist concerns had been entirely engulfed by the colonial project. Feminism's alliance with colonialism, though it produced some material benefits (mostly for French women), was ultimately self-destructive, annihilating the voices of Muslim women and naturalizing French women's oppression.

The next chapter will seek to show how these discourses endure into contemporary French feminist representations of Muslim women that, as I shall argue, continue to be grounded in a 'colonial' logic that serves the interests of the French republican establishment over and above those of French Muslim women, or indeed French women in general.

Notes to Chapter 1

1. Jules Ferry (1832–1893), architect of French republican education, along with many other influential men of his day, fervently supported the *mission civilisatrice*, arguing that it was France's moral duty to civilize the 'inferior' races. See Jean-Michel Gaillard, *Jules Ferry* (Paris: Fayard, 1989), p. 540.
2. Suzanne Voilquin, *Souvenirs d'une fille du peuple ou la Saint-simonienne en Egypte, 1834 à 1836*, Introduction de Lydia Elhadad (Paris: François Maspéro, 1978). First published in 1866 (Paris: E. Sauzet).
3. Hubertine Auclert, *Les Femmes arabes en Algérie* (Paris: Société d'Editions Littéraires, 1900).
4. Marie Bugéja, *Nos sœurs musulmanes: Nouvelle édition*, 2nd edn (Paris: Editions France Afrique, 1931). First published in Algiers, in 1921 (E. Pfister).
5. See for example Claire Goldberg Moses, *French Feminism in the Nineteenth Century* (Albany: State University of New York Press, 1984) and Claire Goldberg Moses and Leslie Wahl Rabine, *Feminism, Socialism and French Romanticism* (Bloomington: Indiana University Press, 1993).
6. Olympe de Gouges, 'Les Droits de la femme', in *Ecrits politiques, 1788–1791, préface d'Olivier Blanc* (Paris: Côté-femmes, 1993), pp. 204–15.
7. See Lydia Elhadad's introduction to *Souvenirs*, pp. 5–48 (p. 29).
8. Quoted in Elhadad, p. 31.
9. Ibid, p. 46.
10. See Goldberg Moses, p. 63.
11. See Goldberg Moses and Wahl Rabine, p. 68.
12. Ibid, pp. 85–144.
13. Julia Clancy-Smith claims that the official silence regarding the presence of European women during the conquest can be explained by the fact that the majority worked as prostitutes. See Julia Clancy-Smith, 'Islam, Gender and Identities: French Algeria', in *Domesticating the Empire: Race Gender and Family Life in French and Dutch Colonialism*, ed. by Julia Clancy-Smith and Frances Gouda (Charlottesville and London: University Press of Virginia, 1998), pp. 154–74 (p. 159).
14. For a discussion of this notion in British and French contexts, in particular in relation to the political thought of John Stuart Mill, see Anthony Bogues, 'John Stuart Mill and "The Negro Question": Race, Colonialism and the Ladder of Civilization', in *Race and Racism in Modern Philosophy*, ed. by Andrew Valls (Ithaca, NY: Cornell University Press, 2005), pp. 217–34.
15. See Goldberg Moses and Wahl Rabine, p. 366.
16. See Rebecca Rogers, 'Telling Stories about the Colonies: British and French Women in Algeria in the Nineteenth Century', *Gender and History*, 21 (2009), 39–59.
17. For a more detailed account see Goldberg Moses.
18. Hubertine Auclert, *Les Femmes au gouvernail* (Paris: Marcel Giard, 1923), p. 6.
19. Eugen Weber, *Peasants into Frenchmen: The Modernisation of Rural France, 1880–1914* (London: Chatto and Windus, 1977).
20. See Janet R. Horne, 'In Pursuit of Greater France', in Clancy-Smith and Gouda, eds, *Domesticating the Empire*, pp. 21–42.
21. Horne, p. 32.
22. Eugène Daumas, *La Femme arabe*, 2nd edn (Algiers: A. Jourdan, 1912). Though written during the early decades of colonization *La Femme arabe* was not published until 1912. It nonetheless anticipated and provided inspiration for the work of a number of colonial scholars at the turn of the century, in particular Adrien Leclerc and Louis Milliot.
23. Denise Brahimi, *Femmes arabes et sœurs musulmanes* (Paris: Editions Tierce, 1984), p. 15.
24. Auclert condemned the closing of girls' schools in the 1860s arguing that, by factoring women out of the colonial project, France had weakened its dominion over the Algerian people. See Rogers, p. 53.

25. For a detailed analysis on the play of colonial gazes, see Meyda Yegenoglu, *Colonial Fantasies: Towards a Feminist Reading of Orientalism* (Cambridge: Cambridge University Press, 1998).

26. Brahimi, p. 10.

27. Ibid, p. 11.

28. Frantz Fanon, *L'An V de la révolution algérienne* (Paris: François Maspéro, 1960); published in English as *A Dying Colonialism*, trans. by Haakon Chevalier (New York: Grove Press, 1965).

29. Ibid, p. 16.

30. Ibid, p. 96.

31. Jeanne M. Bowlan, 'Civilizing Gender Relations in Algeria: The Paradoxical Case of Marie Bugéja', in Clancy-Smith and Gouda, eds, *Domesticating the Empire*, pp. 175–92 (p. 179).

32. Horne, pp. 35–36.

33. Brahimi, p. 312.

34. Horne, pp. 25–26.

35. Brahimi, p. 220.

36. Marie Bugéja, *Visions d'Algérie* (Algiers: Baconnier frères, 1929).

37. Horne, p. 22.

38. Sakinna Messaadi, 'Nos sœurs musulmanes': *Ou le mythe féministe, civilisateur, évangélisateur du messianisme colonialiste dans l'Algérie colonisée* (Algiers: Editions Distribution HOUMA, 2001), p. 35.

39. See for example Alain Buisine, *L'Orient voilé* (Paris: Zulma, 1993) and Malek Alloula, *Le Harem colonial: Images d'un sous-érotisme* (Paris: Garance, 1981).

40. Yegenoglu, p. 44.

41. Ibid, p. 75.

42. Famous examples are Eugène Delacroix's *Femmes d'Alger dans leur appartement*, Jean-Dominique Ingres's *Le Bain turc* and Henri Matisse's various *Odalisques*.

43. In her letters, Lady Mary Wortley Montagu challenges the accuracy of French men's descriptions of Turkey and Turkish women, yet she also plays to masculine fantasies in a bid to seduce her readers. For a discussion of Montagu's letters see Yegenoglu, pp. 79–90.

44. Fanon, p. 28.

45. Mme Jean Pommerol, *Une femme chez les Sahariennes: Entre Laghouat et In-Salah* (Paris: Editions Flammarion, 1900; repr. 1990), p. 169.

46. Lisa Lowe, *Critical Terrains: French and British Orientalisms* (Ithaca, NY: Cornell University Press, 1994).

47. Yegenoglu, p. 82.

48. One clear examples of this particular kind of misogyny is provided by Baudelaire, see 'Eloge du maquillage' in *Baudelaire: Œuvres completes* (Paris: Gallimard, 1961), pp. 1182–85.

49. As Elizabeth Grosz argues, drawing on a Foulcaultian understanding of power as creative, bodies are not ahistorical, precultural or presocial but always-already inscribed by social pressures. See Elizabeth Grosz, *Volatile Bodies: Toward a Corporeal Feminism* (Bloomington: Indiana University Press, 1994).

50. Fanon, p. 41.

51. Indeed, the unveiling ceremony was presided over by Massu's wife, Suzanne. See Donald Reid, 'The World of Frantz Fanon's *L'Algérie se dévoile*', *French Studies*, 61 (2007), 460–75.

52. Fanon, p. 23.

53. Ibid, p. 28.

54. Rachida Titah, *La Galerie des absentes: La Femme algérienne dans l'imaginaire masculine* (La Tour-d'Aigues: Editions de l'Aube, 1996), pp. 156–59.

55. Fanon, p. 45.

56. This technique is famously represented in Gillo Pontecorvo's film, *La Bataille d'Alger*. Casbah Film. 1957.

57. Titah, p. 108.

58. Reid, p. 467.

59. Ibid, p. 475.

60. Reid criticizes Fanon for making women's emancipation conditional on national liberation 'with no evidence that achievement of one liberation brings another'. Reid, p. 475.

61. Titah, p. 112.

62. In 1985, for example, women protesting the regressive Family Code rallied at the site of female militant Hassiba Ben Bouali's death, and in 1992 women marching against Islamist attacks on women held banners declaring 'Hassiba Ben Bouali, Nous ne te trahirons pas' [Hassiba Ben Bouali, we won't betray you]. See Susan Slyomovics, '"Hassiba Ben Bouali, If You Could See Our Algeria": Women and Public Space in Algeria', in *Political Islam: Essays from Middle East Report*, ed. by Joel Beinin and Joe Sork (Berkeley: University of California Press, 1997), pp. 211–19.

CHAPTER 2

Voices and Ventriloquisms: 'Nativist Feminism' and the Muslim Woman

On 28 May 2005, the streets of Marseilles filled with marchers participating in the *Marche Mondiale des Femmes.* According to the organizers, the purpose of the march was to bring together women from all walks of life in a spirit of equality, freedom, solidarity, justice and peace.[1] However, the feminist organization *Le Collectif féministe pour l'égalité* [The Feminist Collective for Equality] (CFPE) reported that the presence of veiled Muslim women in their group provoked anger and disgust amongst a number of other women on the march. In a press release published on the Muslim women's internet forum *Saphirnet,*[2] CFPE reported that they had to deal with 'bousculades et invectives' [shoving and insults] that sought to marginalize them as if they were 'une présence honteuse dont il faudrait se défaire' [a shameful presence that should be got rid of].[3] Similar scenes had been reported the previous year at the International Women's Day celebrations in Paris, where a number of veiled and non-veiled women and men protested against the imminent exclusion of veiled Muslim girls from public schools.[4] Although the primary focus of both marches was solidarity in the face of sexism, the animosity shown towards veiled women suggested that, in the eyes of many of the marchers, the *voilées* were not entitled to make the same demands as non-veiled women. Both reports mention the occasional welcome show of solidarity from fellow demonstrators, but the reaction of the majority of marchers was overwhelmingly hostile: 'Une à une, les organisations plus ou moins féministes passent devant nous, clamant des slogans antisexistes et nous regardant avec gêne, mépris ou haine' [One by one, the feminist organizations pass by us shouting anti-sexist slogans while looking at us with embarrassment, scorn or hatred].[5] Why was it that demonstrations supposedly representing the interests of *all* women should stigmatize a number of their participants? What was it about the Muslim veil that provoked such hostility from many French feminist associations, and what room did this leave for French Muslim women to identify themselves both as feminists and as French citizens?

This chapter will seek answers to these questions by looking at the dominant feminist discourses that emerged during the notorious *affaire du foulard* and which became a powerful mobilizing force behind the 2004 ban on Islamic headscarves in state schools. The *affaire du foulard* first erupted in 1989, against the backdrop of the Rushdie affair, when three schoolgirls were suspended from a school in Creil for refusing to remove their Islamic headscarves in class. Their headmaster claimed to be acting in accordance both with the Ferry laws of the 1880s, which first mandated the secular school system in France, and with legislation dating from the beginning of the twentieth century that prohibited the wearing of proselytizing religious or political symbols. What started as a local scuffle soon assumed the proportions of a national debate in which those who opposed the wearing of the headscarf claimed that it transgressed the republican principle supposed to ensure the separation of Church and State, otherwise known as *laïcité*. The 1989 controversy subsided when Lionel Jospin, then Minister for Education, insisted that, although the French school system should discourage the wearing of the Islamic headscarf, it had no right to exclude the girls on that basis, as existing laws protected the girls' right to publicly express their religious convictions provided that this did not interfere with the school curriculum or assume proselytizing dimensions. But tensions continued to mount with a resurgence of the debate in 1994 and, most recently, in 2003–04. This time, the debate swept widely over a range of issues including immigration and integration, youth culture and violence in the *banlieues*, the presence of Islam in France, international terrorism and, significantly, sexual equality. Although the matter of sexual equality had not been absent from previous *affaires*, discussion had tended to be dominated by the *laïc* argument. However in 2003–04, against a background of international anxiety surrounding Islam and the status of Muslim women, the debate took on a strong feminist dimension that condemned the wearing of the veil on the grounds that it contravened women's rights and represented the infiltration of French society by a fundamentalist and patriarchal Islam. This prohibitionist feminist position, sustained by France's political and media classes, monopolized the debate to the near total exclusion of dissenting voices from many grassroots women's organizations, trade unions, the education sector and the Muslim population, and exerted significant influence over public opinion which eventually swung in favour of legislation. In July 2003 President Chirac commissioned a group of academics, philosophers and public intellectuals headed by Bernard Stasi to investigate the matter and, in December 2003, they submitted a report in favour of legislation resulting in an official ban on all religious symbols deemed 'ostensible' [showy] in public schools.[6] This ban also covered Jewish yarmulkes and large Christian crosses, but the chief target of the law was widely understood to be Muslim headscarves.

We have already seen how colonial feminism served colonial ideology and strategy, often to the detriment of its feminist agenda. This chapter will consider the ways in which certain contemporary French feminisms, in a similar fashion, may be recuperated by conservative agendas in ways that ultimately work against their feminist imperatives. The 'feminism' that gained momentum during the *affaire* has a good deal in common with colonial-feminism in its construction of a glorified French femininity in opposition to a vilified vision of the Muslim woman and, by extension, an idealized vision of the Republic in conflict with a perceived Islamic menace. Part of the purpose of this chapter is to reveal these similarities, but there are also shades of difference. While the colonial-feminism of Voilquin and Auclert was fundamentally contradictory in its tendency to condemn the situation of women in France while simultaneously holding up French womanhood as an ideal to be emulated, the 'feminism' of the veil controversy more closely resembles that of Bugéja who, as we have seen, resolves this contradiction by imagining sexual equality to be already a defining feature of French culture. In other words, the feminism of the affair confuses republican ideals of sexual equality with a much grimmer reality ultimately remaining uncritical of an enduring sexism at the core of French society. So, while Voilquin and Auclert sought to justify French and Muslim women's emancipation in the name of the colonies, the feminism of the affair, as this chapter shall argue, constructed gender equality as a republican achievement under threat, legitimizing neocolonial attitudes and transforming feminism, as a forward-looking political position, into a defence of a reified (and regressive) notion of 'femininity'.

So what should we call this kind of feminism? Although such discourses dominated the debate, they did not represent the feminist community as a whole. Indeed, these discourses were not just articulated by feminists but were repeated by a whole range of public voices, from intellectuals and politicians, to writers and celebrities. Furthermore, I do not wish to suggest that the feminism of the affair is a complete philosophy in itself, nor that those feminists who participated in such discourses have not done valuable feminist work at other times and in other contexts. Bearing these qualifications in mind, however, it is possible to identify a clear strand of 'feminist' thinking in relation to Muslim women that surfaced during the controversy and this will be the object of my study. In order to distinguish this strand from the many dissenting feminist voices and to highlight the ways in which it invests in a nostalgic notion of French identity (and French femininity) perceived to be under siege, I shall refer to it as 'nativist feminism' and to its proponents as 'nativist feminists'. But before we look more closely at 'nativist feminism' and its construction of the Muslim woman, it is first necessary to say more about the specificity of the relationship between contemporary France and its Muslim population.

Muslims in France: Disillusionment and Disaffection

Today, Islam is the second largest religion in France and, although precise figures do not exist, different commentators estimate that there are between 3.5 and 6 million Muslims living in the country. This imprecision is due to the fact that official population statistics do not account for ethnic or religious origin, meaning that estimates tend to be vague and can vary according to the statistician's agenda. The large number of Muslims in France is above all due to immigration from France's ex-colonies in West and North Africa that began in the late nineteenth century, but peaked between 1945 and 1974 when France encouraged migrants to fill its post-war labour deficit. However, it is important to note that not all Muslims in France are of immigrant origin, and that not all immigrants are Muslims. Furthermore, some self-identify as Muslim as a form of cultural allegiance even if they are non-practising, and the diversity of Islamic schools and traditions means that even those who practise do not make up one homogeneous group.[7] Bearing this in mind, it is nonetheless safe to say that a great number of French Muslims are of North African immigrant origin and occupy the lowest rungs of French society, filling the worst paid jobs and living in the most run-down districts. Although a handful of this population have broken through class and ethnic barriers to escape poverty, French Muslims continue to make up a significant proportion of France's poorest social strata which suffer most from job insecurity, unemployment, crime and bad housing, all of which are aggravated by institutionalized and ambient racism.[8] For this reason, discussion of the French Muslim community is frequently tied into broader debates concerning poverty and insecurity in the neglected suburbs of French cities known more commonly as *les banlieues*.

Of course, France is not the only European country with a sizeable Muslim population, nor is it the only one to have experienced veil controversies. In Britain in 2006 the *niqab*, a Muslim veil that covers part of the face, came under fire on the grounds that it inhibited interpersonal identification and signified a rejection of British values.[9] But whereas the UK debate was framed by security issues and by a broad questioning of multiculturalism in the wake of the 2005 London bombings, the French controversy, as we shall see, drew its energy from elsewhere and attained much greater proportions. In the eyes of many other Western nations, the French response to the headscarf was a colossal overreaction. As Alain Badiou puts it in his satirical essay *Foulard*, 'La France étonna le monde' [France stunned the world].[10] Viewing the affair from a multiculturalist perspective, British commentators were quick to read the French debate as proof of France's intolerance of difference and its failure to recognize the legitimacy of basic religious rights but, as Cécile Laborde argues, although these were both important themes, they were not the whole story.[11] In order to understand the violence of French reactions to the headscarf in schools, it is necessary to appreciate the specificity of the French model of citizenship and France's commitment to *laïcité*.

While multicultural models envisage different cultures existing alongside each other within the overarching frame of national law, French republicanism does not officially recognize racial, ethnic or cultural difference and lays greater emphasis on the unifying potential of citizenship. In theory this 'colour-blind' approach combats racism by recognizing people, not as representatives of various ethnic groups, but as equal citizens. As I shall argue in the final chapter, the primacy of citizenship is a valuable republican ideal worth defending. However, problems arise from the ways in which these ideals are (mis-)translated into practice. In practice, this official non-recognition of difference often fails to properly recognize and deal with existing problems of racism and, as far as integration is concerned, typically translates into the demand that minorities assimilate to the dominant cultural model. French colonial discourses emphasized the cultural assimilation of colonial peoples in order to secure domination of the colony and, in a not dissimilar way, contemporary French discourses on immigration tend to insist on the full cultural integration of minority groups in order to ensure national unity. As Rogers Brubaker comments, French conceptions of nationhood and citizenship demand a high level of cultural uniformity as part of the project of integration. He writes: 'While French nationhood is constituted by political unity, it is centrally expressed in the striving for cultural unity. Political inclusion has entailed cultural assimilation, for regional cultural minorities and immigrants alike.'[12] The burden of compliance, therefore, rests squarely on the shoulders of cultural minorities.

It is the republican principle of *laïcité*, or more specifically the *laïc* education system, that is intended to facilitate this desired integration and, in the playgrounds and classrooms of French state schools, cultural and religious differences are supposed to be subordinated to the notion of an all-embracing French citizenship. As Soheib Bencheikh argues in his careful discussion of the term, the definition of *laïcité* has been contested since its inception but, broadly speaking, *laïcité* can be said to refer to a particular kind of secularism that goes beyond the official separation of Church and State to constitute a broad moral and social philosophy with the aim of promoting religious freedom within the frame of citizenship.[13] However, more recent interpretations (prominent during the *affaire du foulard*) have transformed *laïcité* into an uncritical secular ideology that is actively hostile to the expression of religious or cultural difference. Consequently, the presence of Islamic headscarves in French schools was seen by a large part of the French political and media classes as a direct assault on the principle of *laïcité* and, by extension, the integrity of the French Republic. President Chirac himself protested: 'Les Français étant ce qu'ils sont, le port du voile, qu'on le veuille ou non, est une sorte d'aggression' [Like it or not, the French, being what they are, see the wearing of the veil as a kind of affront].[14]

Chirac's words assume the existence of an inflexible and exclusive French identity that is fundamentally incompatible with the veil. The French, according to Chirac, are what they are and cannot be expected to tolerate alien cultural practices. But where does this leave those who identify themselves as both Muslim and French? In recent years the descendants of France's immigrant population have experienced a sharpening sense of exclusion that has given rise to disaffection with mainstream politics. This sense of disempowerment follows on from the dissipation of the *beur* movement of the 1980s and 1990s which, for a time, had seemed to promise integration and acceptance. The term *beur*, an inversion of the word *Arabe*, expressed a new aspect of French identity; that of the children of Maghrebi immigrants to France who wished to be accepted as French citizens with the same rights and opportunities as their majority-ethnic counterparts. Unlike their parents, who had never considered themselves to be *chez eux* in France and who often harboured hopes of returning to their countries of origin, the *beurs* were raised and educated in France and demanded the same rights and privileges as other young French people. Rather than being united by a sense of religious or ethnic community, this generation was galvanized by a shared sense of exclusion and discrimination, and from this mobilization against injustice emerged what came to be known as the *beur* movement.[15]

However, this movement was quickly co-opted by the political Left who offered massive financial and media support to the anti-racist organization *SOS Racisme*, drowning out the grassroots radicalism of some previous *beur* mobilizations. The

Left's endorsement of the organization was seen by many *beur* activists as a political move by the *Parti Socialiste* to widen Mitterrand's basis of support ahead of the 1988 election, and consequently many of them refused to unite under the SOS banner. Their fears appeared to be justified when the Socialists (once Mitterrand's election was secured) withdrew their support and reneged on their promises. Mitterrand's infamous statement in December that the number of immigrants had exceeded the *seuil de tolérance* [threshold of tolerance] was not only experienced by the organization as a profound betrayal, but also served to confirm the sense that the mainstream political Left had come to represent the French middle classes and was failing to respond to the demands of young ethnic-minority French citizens.[16] This sense of isolation was further aggravated by a sharpening sense of persecution as a result of a series of laws in the 1990s restricting the rights of immigrants, and the introduction of measures enabling police to stop and detain people suspected of being in France illegally.[17] As Carrie Tarr has noted, many young people of ethnic minorities 'suffer from the invidious *délit du faciès*, the crime of simply looking different, which makes them vulnerable to police harassment'.[18]

In recent years, this stigmatization of France's Muslim community has provoked a defensive identitarian response amongst some young Muslims. Editor of *Le Monde Diplomatique*, Alain Gresh, argues that the aggressive targeting of France's Muslim population during the *affaire du foulard* paradoxically pushed some young Muslims towards a stronger identification with their religion as a form of political resistance. He writes:

> Les débats, parfois violents, qui ont sécoué la France en 2003–2004 ont renvoyé nombre de citoyens prénommés Mohammed ou Fatima à cette identité 'réligieuse' qu'ils avaient en parti oubliée; ils se sont ainsi vus sommés de répondre de tout ce qui se passait dans le monde musulman, du 11 septembre 2001 à chaque nouvel attentat terroriste. Ils ont éprouvé dans leur travail, dans la rue, la stigmatisation dont sont victimes les 'musulmans'. Du coup, en manière de défi, certains ont décidé de reprendre à leur compte cette identité.[19]

> [The, at times violent, debates that shook France in 2003–2004 sent a number of citizens by the name of Mohammed or Fatima straight back to a religious 'identity' that they had in part forgotten. They felt that they were being implicated in everything that happened in the Muslim world, from 11 September 2001, to the latest terrorist attack. At work and in the street they felt stigmatized as Muslims. As a result, and as a defensive response, some decided to assume this identity].

In an echo of the Algerian war, Islam offers some young Muslims not only a religious identity but also a social and political one. In some cases this can lead to an identification with conservative interpretations of Islam and hypermacho behaviour amongst some young Muslim men who, feeling emasculated by the French state, retreat into a defensive assertion of patriarchal norms within their families and communities.[20] Such hypermacho behaviour was, as we shall see, a recurring theme during the *affair du foulard*.

However, according to Dounia Bouzar many young people who feel that they have been overlooked by the Republic's professed commitment to *égalité* and *fraternité* do not simply find a defensive, readymade identity in the teachings of Islam, but a restored sense of community and social justice. She writes: 'Face à cette société qu'ils vivent comme extrêmement inégalitaire et discriminatoire, les valeurs d'égalité et de solidarité prônées par les prédicateurs sont fondamentales et redonnent espoir à ces jeunes qui ont perdu confiance dans le système social et ses représentants' [In the face of social inequality and discrimination, the values of equality and solidarity that are offered by the preachers make a deep impression and give hope to young people who have lost faith in the social system and its representatives].[21] Bouzar's analysis of the Islamic teachings that appeal to young French Muslims suggests an emphasis on solidarity, community and equality. In particular, she observes that young Muslims and Muslim associations have been influenced by the work of the Swiss Muslim academic and activist Tariq Ramadan, whose work will be discussed more fully in the last chapter. According to Bouzar, Ramadan's work has been so influential because it emphasizes the social message of Islam, in particular its commitment to social justice. In *L'Islam, la foi et la politique* [*Islam, Faith and Politics*], for example, Ramadan stresses the egalitarian aspect of the journey to Mecca: 'riches et pauvres sur la même ligne, riche et pauvres unis' [rich and poor together, rich and poor united] while in *Islam, modernité et modernisme* [*Islam, Modernity and Modernism*] he emphasizes Islam's message of social justice: 'Être musulman, c'est développer le principe de justice sociale: développement d'une conscience sociale fondée sur la justice et engagée dans son application' [To be a Muslim is to develop the principle of social justice: it is the development of a social conscience founded on justice and committed to its application].[22] By marking out solidarity as an important feature of Islam, Bouzar claims, Muslim associations, Muslim scholars and imams have been able to step in where the French State has failed, offering an inclusive understanding of Liberty, Equality and Fraternity.

What Farhad Khosrokhavar calls *l'islam des jeunes*,[23] and Bouzar *l'islam des banlieues*, differs from the Islam practised by previous generations in that it is firmly anchored in life in contemporary France. While earlier generations saw their religion as belonging to their country of origin, today's young Muslims shape their relationship to Islam through their experience as French citizens. This may, on the one hand, be produced as a defensive reaction to stigmatization, but it may also exist as a positive attempt to restore a sense of community and to introduce Islam as a legitimate reference in the construction of French identity. With this in mind, the schoolgirls' insistence on their right to wear an Islamic headscarf may, in some cases, be seen not only as an expression of religious belief or gender identity, but also as a positive political statement — a way of rethinking the boundaries of French identity by insisting on their rights as both French citizens and as Muslims. I will return to the matter of Muslim women's activism in the final chapter. For now, I shall focus on the ways in which dominant feminist discourses constructed Muslim women during the *affaire*.

'The Woman Question': From *SOS Racisme* to *Ni putes ni soumises*

Just as colonial feminists imagined the status of women to be the barometer of civilization and progress, the nativist feminist discourse that dominated the *affaire du foulard* imagined the perceived differences between French and Muslim women to be the primary marker of cultural difference and proof of the superiority of the French cultural model. This logic is clearly expressed by Jeanne-Hélène Kaltenbach, member of the *Haut Conseil à l'Intégration*, and the demographer Michèle Tribalat:

> L'identité française, c'est d'abord l'esprit des lois qui la régissent. Or l'essentiel des différences entre le droit français et les codes de statut personnel inspirés par l'islam porte sur le droit de la famille et sur le droit des femmes. La femme n'est pas une question mais LA question.[24]

> [French identity is above all embedded in the spirit of French law. The essential differences between French law and Islamic notions of the status of the individual are to be found in family law and women's rights. The status of women is not an issue, it is THE issue].

'The woman question' is not simply one of many cultural differences but '*l'essentiel des différences*' that distinguishes and separates a certain notion of French identity from Islam. During the 2003–04 *affaire*, this view of Islam as incompatible with (or diametrically opposed to) French identity on the grounds of the perceived status of women saw the rallying together of feminist and *laïc* discourses in defence of a notion of authentic Frenchness perceived to be under threat. The alignment of these arguments is best expressed by Michèle Vianes, founder and president of the feminist association *Regards de Femmes*:

> Interdire le voile, c'est organiser la fusion entre combats laïques et féministes. Fusion évidente. Être laïque, c'est se battre pour l'égalité des droits entre les citoyens, c'est notamment le but des féministes. Celles-ci ont toujours dû lutter contre le poids des traditions religieuses sur la société; la séparation des Eglises et de l'Etat est préalable pour que les femmes accèdent aux droits fondamentaux de la personne humaine. Tous deux se définissent également par leur caractère universel. À même combat, mêmes ennemis.[25]

> [To ban the veil is to bring together the secular and feminist struggles. This is an obvious collaboration. Secularism means fighting for the equal rights of citizens and this is also the goal of feminism. Feminists have always resisted the weight of religious tradition on society. The separation of Church and State is indispensable if women are to be guaranteed their basic human rights. Both struggles are defined by their universal character. Same struggle, same enemies.]

Vianes's automatic association of *laïcité* and feminism was repeated by various commentators throughout the debate, but the history of female emancipation in France does not entirely bear this out. Although the inclusion of girls in Ferry's public education reforms was intended to emancipate them from the grip of the Catholic Church and facilitate their enlightenment, this did not translate into political rights and, while male suffrage was secured in 1848, French women had to wait until 1945 before they could vote. Furthermore, it was only in the 1960s that conventions of the patriarchal family were challenged in law, at last allowing women to manage their finances or gain employment without their husbands' permission.[26] Nonetheless, during the headscarf controversy, the association of feminism and *laïcité* was a powerful rhetorical tool as it marked religion in general, and Islam in particular, as the enemies of both feminism and the French State, thus excluding the possibility of being both Muslim and feminist.

Indeed, the nativist feminism that emerged during the *affaire du foulard* refuses to acknowledge Islam as a legitimate reference in the construction of French identity and instead, in an echo of colonial feminism, sustains an assimilationist discourse by which successful integration is measured in terms of conformity to a 'French' cultural model. Furthermore, nativist feminists, like their colonial predecessors, imagine successful integration to hinge on the figure of the Muslim woman. Where colonial-feminist discourse saw the Muslim–Arab woman as the means of breaking down resistance to colonial rule and assimilating indigenous peoples, nativist feminism represents young Muslim women as the key to the successful assimilation of the French Muslim population. In particular, nativist feminists invest great hope in the stereotype of the young aspirational Muslim woman, or *la beurette*, whose supposed identification with feminist ideals leads her to abandon her cultural, ethnic and religious heritage in order to align herself with a 'French' model of womanhood and citizenship.[27] Like colonial-feminist stereotypes of Muslim–Arab women, the *beurette* is not only supposed to ensure her own emancipation by *choosing* 'French' values over the supposedly oppressive weight of her cultural origins, but she is also supposed to transmit these values to future generations. Jane Freedman remarks: 'it is seen to be their duty [...] to see to it that their children integrate or assimilate and become "French".' As the previous chapter has shown, this stereotype of Muslim women as mothers or future mothers who must be won over to French values in order to ensure the assimilation of their children, has its roots in colonial discourses that are over a century old, but as Freedman observes, 'little has been done to moderate [this stereotype] by analysts of immigration, or indeed by French feminist researchers'.[28] Bearing in mind the gendered nature of the republican model of integration, it is easy to see why the sight of Islamic headscarves in schools was considered so provocative. In particular, the insistence of some Muslim girls that they wore the headscarf out of *choice* precipitated a confused and anxious response from the public and media alike.

During the 2004 *affaire*, this anxiety was somewhat soothed by the emergence of the organization *Ni putes ni soumises* (NPNS) who claimed to represent *les filles des quartiers* [the girls from the estates] and reinforced the *beurette* stereotype through their professed identification with mainstream feminist values.[29] The organization was formed in February 2003 in response to the death of Sohane Benziane, a young woman who was brutally murdered in Vitry-sur-Seine by boys from a neighbouring estate after refusing to submit to their sexual demands. Sohane's death quickly became emblematic of the pressure and abuse inflicted on women of North African Muslim origin by some of their male peers and NPNS was formed with the prime motive of putting an end to such violence against women. However, Fadela Amara (the organization's founder, and an ex-campaigner for *SOS Racisme*) has strong links to the *Parti Socialiste* and, from the outset, the organization has been closely tied to the mainstream political Left. This has aroused criticism from grassroots activists who believe that NPNS's agenda is manipulated to serve mainstream party political interests and that the organization has abandoned the women they purport to defend. NPNS's co-option by the republican establishment was especially visible during the *affaire du foulard* when the organization was seen by many grassroots activists to have succumbed to pressure from the *Parti Socialiste* to support the official party line. NPNS initially declared itself to be against the ban on the grounds that it was important for veiled girls to gain access to education.[30] However, a few weeks later, Amara signed a petition in the women's magazine *Elle*, in favour of a law banning visible religious symbols at school and in the public services and subsequently campaigned vigorously for legislation. This volte-face was never officially explained, but many anti-prohibitionist campaigners suspected that the change was influenced by the *Parti Socialiste's* decision on 12 November 2003 to unanimously support the ban.

Interestingly, NPNS's U-turn mimics that of *SOS Racisme* several years earlier. When the *affaire* first flared up in 1989, *SOS Racisme* alienated many of its supporters by defending the schoolgirls' right to wear headscarves. As a result, when it erupted for the second time in 1994, the organization was quick to change sides explaining its decision in terms of a perceived Islamization of France's immigrant population that had to be suppressed for the sake of French secularism. For NPNS, as for *SOS Racisme*, the decision to support the official party line guaranteed financial support and media exposure. However, like *SOS Racisme*, NPNS's rapid integration into the political establishment led to a disintegration of their grassroots support. In an article entitled 'Ni putes ni soumises, ou la parole confisquée' [Ni putes ni soumises, or the stolen voices], the collective and internet forum *Les Mots sont importants* points to the distance separating the movement's key supporters, described as predominantly white, middle-aged and middle-class, from the *beurettes* they claim to represent. The make-up of NPNS's supporters, they argue, '*n'a en soi rien d'infamant* mais pose problème lorsqu'un groupe politique a la prétention de représenter les "sans-voix" et de parler du "terrain", et que son principal ressort argumentatif est le "jeunisme" et le "basisme"' [*is not outrageous in itself*, but does pose a problem when a political group claims to represent the "voiceless", to speak from the "source", and when their key arguments rely on their supposed connection with "young people" and "grassroots activism"] [original emphasis].[31] Nonetheless, despite its reputation amongst grassroots activists as a ventriloquist's dummy,[32] NPNS was given virtually unlimited access to public platforms, and its endorsement of the *beurette* stereotype served a nativist feminist agenda in favour of the full assimilation of France's Muslim community to a 'French' cultural model.

The displacement of *SOS Racisme* by NPNS as media-darling of the republican establishment is significant in that it marks the decisive gendering of the immigration/integration debate in France. The *laïc* arguments that dominated earlier rows were, in 2003–04, overshadowed by 'feminist' arguments that opposed an oppressive Islam to a supposedly emancipatory Republic. However, the high profile of the figure of the Muslim woman in public debates has not guaranteed a public voice for Muslim women themselves.

L'Affaire 2003–04: A False Debate?

In their collection of Muslim women's testimonies, *L'Une voilée, l'autre pas* [*One veiled, one not*] Saïda Kada and Dounia Bouzar debate the decision of one of their interviewees to remove her headscarf in class in order to be able to discuss subjects such as religion, secularism and colonialism with her teachers. Nassera, the interviewee, explains her decision as follows:

> J'ai décidé de ne plus couvrir mes cheveux parce que je voulais garder ma liberté de ton avec les enseignants. Je voulais continuer notre affrontement librement, sans qu'il y ait de 'parasites' entre nous. Malgré la souffrance que cela entraînait, j'ai ôté mon foulard et je l'ai assumé car cette confrontation qui me permettait de me construire était essentielle pour mon équilibre.[33]

> [I decided to stop covering my hair because I wanted to speak freely to my teachers. I wanted to continue our discussions in an open manner, without any 'obstacles' coming between us. Despite the suffering that this caused, I stuck to my decision to remove my headscarf as it allowed me to continue a dialogue that was essential to my personal development and well-being].

Whereas Bouzar sees Nassera's decision as a necessary compromise, allowing 'une libre confrontation' between student and teacher, Kada insists that a free and authentic dialogue is not possible when the terms of the debate are set by one party. She writes: 'Pour qu'il y ait authenticité, il faut que chacun puisse lui-même se définir. Sinon, on ne laisse pas place à un vrai débat [...] À partir du moment où l'on impose à l'autre une façon d'être, on ne lui demande pas d'être lui-même, on lui demande d'être présentable' [In order for authentic dialogue to be possible, each participant must be able to define her own speaking position. Otherwise there is no real debate [...] As soon as one party imposes a certain way of being on the other, they are not asking them to be themselves, rather they are asking them to be presentable].[34] Bouzar and Kada's disagreement may be seen to crystallize the dilemma facing under-represented minorities in postmodern, multi-ethnic societies. Whereas colonial-feminist writers simply spoke in Muslim women's stead, the postmodern notions of plurality and diversity favoured by Western democratic cultures promise to allow cultural others to speak for themselves. However, Nassera's story raises the questions: on what conditions may the voices of cultural others be heard, and who manages the terms of the debate? Do postmodern claims to multi-vocality represent a true break with colonialism's marginalization of its subalterns, or are they just a means of extending neocolonial forms of power?

In his analysis of the headscarf controversy, *Le Voile médiatique* [*The Media's Veil*], sociologist and activist Pierre Tévanian argues that public anxiety about the presence of veils in schools was above all the result of a top-down media campaign that drew on existing but unformulated fears concerning a threat to national identity, and transformed them into a distinct and precise Islamophobic discourse. In his analysis, strongly supported by sociological data, Tévanian seeks to show that, although the media often claimed to be responding to grassroots public concern about the veil, the evidence suggests that it was only after the media campaign that the public (or at least certain contingents of it) began to express alarm.[35] This media attention was partly the result of political manoeuvring by France's main parties, but it was also a result of the commercial pressures on media production simultaneously feeding off and shaping public opinion in order to generate stories.

Indeed, the sheer newsworthiness of the *affaire du foulard* was quite remarkable. According to the statistics gathered by Tévanian, in 2003 the weeklies *Paris Match*, *Le Figaro Magazine*, *Le Nouvel Observateur*, *L'Express*, *Le Point*, *Valeurs actuelles* and *Marianne* devoted twenty-six covers to the theme of *la laïcité* and *le voile*, while daily newspapers *Le Monde*, *Aujourd'hui en France*, *Le Figaro* and *Libération* devoted over one hundred front-page stories. In total, one thousand two hundred and eighty-four articles were published by the three main dailies (*Le Monde*, *Le Figaro*, *Libération*); on average more than one article per day, per paper.[36] However, the scale of the debate did not guarantee diversity and, as Tévanian and Gresh have shown, virtually all sections of the media rallied to the prohibitionist position. Tévanian remarks that the only notable exception was *Le Monde* which, on the whole, treated the matter with more balance and less sensationalism. As for the weeklies, Gresh is at pains to stress the imbalance of the debate. According to him, the weeklies forgot their ideological differences to pursue a prohibitionist editorial line fuelled by contributions from journalists, intellectuals and politicians, all of whom were persuaded that the Republic was in danger.[37]

As Gresh suggests, the media debate was overwhelmingly dominated by individuals and institutions that, in Stuart Hall's terms, could be described as 'primary definers' — that is to say the supposed authorities on any given news item.[38] In Hall's analysis, the media turn to primary definers with the aim of offering authoritative and impartial perspectives, but by doing so ironically and unwittingly reproduce existing structures of power as the 'primary definitions' forwarded by figures of authority frame the subsequent debate and what may or may not be said in relation to it. This appeal to 'primary definers' was manifest during the *affaire du foulard* and, for months, French airwaves and column inches were dominated by the opinions of public intellectuals, politicians, journalists and writers, who more or less unanimously assumed a prohibitionist position.[39] This over-representation on all fronts of those from the sectors of society most in favour of a ban — the professional classes and the older generations[40] — contrasted with the dramatic under-representation of French citizens most likely to be affected by the appearance of veils in schools; the teaching community, school students, working-class parents and, above all, Muslim girls and women themselves.[41] Tévanian writes: 'les élèves voilées, qui étaient pourtant les premières cibles de la loi, n'ont jamais eu la parole, mis à part quelques articles dans le quotidien *Le Monde* et quelques "micro-trottoirs" de dix secondes à la sortie des lycées dans les journaux télévisés' [the veiled students who were, after all, the prime targets of the law, never had the chance to make themselves heard, save for a few articles in *Le Monde* and some ten second televised interviews at school gates].[42] Furthermore, when, in January 2004, the main anti-prohibitionist coalition *Une école pour tou(te)s* [One school for everybody] organized demonstrations across the country, rallying ten thousand people in Paris and around fifty thousand elsewhere in France, they were, according to Tévanian, literally boycotted by televisual media and barely covered by the written press.[43] Although the supposed oppression of Muslim women was frequently cited as one of the key reasons for banning the veil in school, the voices of veiled Muslim women and girls were rarely heard.

Whereas colonial-feminist discourses gestured towards a desire to allow Muslim–Arab women to speak for themselves, then simply spoke in their place on the assumption that their superior perspective as 'civilized' French women granted them the authority to do so, the media's handling of the *affaire du foulard*, in keeping with postmodern democratic notions of diversity, sought to create at least the illusion of plurality by calling on selected representatives of France's Muslim community to have their say. But, as Tévanian argues, the media were extremely selective. The voices of young women were monopolized by the prohibitionist NPNS, who reinforced dominant discourses despite their claim to speak from the margins, while the anti-prohibitionist stance (despite wide support amongst the teaching community, young people, the working classes and Muslim women) was most often represented by conservative Muslim men who could easily be dismissed as 'fanatics'.[44] By seeking to balance primary definitions with secondary ones the media produced an illusion of multivocality. However, the ideological tone of the debate had already been set. Secondary perspectives tended either to conform to primary ones (NPNS), or to represent 'fanatical' resistance (conservative male Muslims) the extremism of which was taken to validate the mainstream position.

Furthermore, when moderate Muslim voices were occasionally invited to share their views, they were often constrained to speaking from a defensive position. This was demonstrated by Saïda Kada's appearance on Olivier Mazerolle's *100 minutes pour comprendre: Dieu, La France et la République* [*100 minutes to Understand: God, France and the Republic*] broadcast on 19 January 2004 on *France 2*. Saïda Kada was the only veiled Muslim woman to be interviewed by the Stasi commission, and it was in this capacity that she and Bernard Stasi, along with other (prohibitionist) guests, were invited onto the show. However, the way in which the debate was structured by the show's host put Kada in a defensive position that saw her fending off charges of extremism rather than expressing herself on her own terms. After a lengthy exchange amongst the show's other guests, amalgamating worldwide atrocities carried out in the name of Islam with incidents of forced marriage amongst France's Muslim population, Mazerolle expressed his shock that such things are possible in France before turning to Saïda Kada. Drawing attention to her veil he remarked: 'Quand vous entendez tout ça, vous dites: ce n'est pas vrai, ce sont des histoires, ce sont des fantasmes?' [When you hear all that, do you tell yourself that it's not true, that these are just stories, fantasies?].[45] The issue here is not to deny the existence of sexist abuses within France's Muslim population, but the way in which the accumulation of, often unspecified and unrelated, 'examples' of Islam's supposed denigration of women builds towards the interpellation of Kada as *une femme voilée* and marks her out as complicit in the oppression of women within 'her community', reducing her to the role of guilty defendant or suspect. The terms of the debate have been set and Kada is framed as an extremist whose resistance will only serve to validate the consensus.

La Beurette et La Voilée

So what are the terms in which French Muslim women might express themselves, and how exactly does nativist feminism frame their voices? An examination of texts published during the *affaire du foulard* reveals that nativist feminist discourse follows a distinctly colonial logic that represents Muslim women as either fundamentally similar or essentially other to a reified vision of 'French' womanhood. Muslim women are either figured as *beurettes* who desire to 'be like French women' and seek to liberate themselves from the oppressive weight of their presumed cultural heritage, or they are represented as *voilées*; the living embodiment of female oppression and the antithesis of everything that 'French' womanhood and culture is supposed to stand for. Between the two stereotypes of the *beurette* and the *voilée* there is little room for manoeuvre. As the novelist and critic Fawzia Zouari remarks, Muslim women are obliged to choose between 'le modèle de la femme soumise, et celui de l'occidentalisée assimilée' [the doormat, or the assimilated Westernized woman].[46] During the *affaire du foulard*, nativist feminism tended to confine French Muslim women to speaking from one of these two polarized positions.

NPNS dominated the *beurette* speaking position throughout the *affaire*. It publicly celebrated republican values and promoted a reified image of French womanhood as the yardstick of female emancipation. In an article in *Le Nouvel Observateur*, the public intellectual and feminist Elisabeth Badinter emphasizes Muslim women's desire to 'be like the French woman' in the following terms: 'Ecoutez les *Ni putes ni soumises*. Elles disent: "Libérez-nous de cette emprise familiale, religieuse, culturelle. Notre espoir, c'est de devenir des Françaises comme les autres. Et tenez bon sur les valeurs de la République. Pas de voile à l'école!"' [Listen to *Ni putes ni soumises*. They are telling us : "Free us from the grip of our families, religion and culture. Our wish is to become like other French women. And stand firm on republican values. No veils in school!"].[47] But what exactly does it mean to become 'des Françaises comme les autres'? What is this ideal image of French womanhood towards which the *beurette* is imagined to aspire? Much has been said (not least by feminists) about the assimilationism and false universalism of the republican ideal of French citizenship that, while promising *Liberté, Egalité* and *Fraternité* for all, in reality imagines the ideal French citizen as white, middle class and (as the word *Fraternité* implies) male. But there is a great deal more to be said about the ways in which this false universalism has inflected French feminism, resulting in the construction of an ideal French *woman*. Indeed, during the *affaire du foulard* it was not so much feminist values that were asserted as a certain notion of femininity and in particular an ideal of French womanhood.

In her book and manifesto *Ni putes ni soumises*, Fadela Amara describes a topology of *les filles des quartiers* that is not dissimilar to Suzanne Voilquin's hierarchization of the women of Cairo. Just as Voilquin organizes Egyptian women according to the degree of liberty she supposes them to have in comparison to an idealized vision of French womanhood, Amara measures women's divergence from or conformity to a reified image of 'French' femininity. Amara's understanding of freedom differs from that of her colonial predecessor in its emphasis on sexual emancipation but, like

Voilquin, Amara maps the degree of freedom she supposes women to have directly onto their bodies. She judges the *filles des cités* in terms of their dress and physical appearance where conformity to French dress codes is equated with sexual freedom and, by extension, freedom in general. Lipstick and jeans are associated with 'le monde extérieur [...] celui de la liberté' [the outside world [...] the free world], while the veil is equated with '[le monde] de la maison et de la cité, où les jeunes filles doivent se conformer au rôle que les hommes veulent leur faire jouer' [the world of the home and the estate, where girls must play the roles men impose on them].[48] 'Liberated' women, then, are those who resist these pressures by dressing like their white, French counterparts and assuming their 'femininity'. Amara writes: 'Elles vivent très mal l'atmosphère d'oppression dans les cités et résistent en affirmant leur féminité [...] en continuant à porter des vêtements moulants, en s'habillant à la mode, en se maquillant parfois à outrance' [The oppressive atmosphere of the estates causes them suffering and they resist by asserting their femininity [...] by continuing to wear tight clothes, by dressing fashionably, by wearing loud make-up]. Indeed, 'le maquillage est devenu une peinture de guerre, un signe de résistance' [make-up has become war-paint, a sign of resistance] and, dismissing 'les féministes des années 1970, qui jetaient leur soutien-gorge et menaient la guerre des sexes' [the feminists of the 1970s who threw away their bras and engaged in a battle of the sexes], Amara reclaims a 'femininity' that asserts: ' "Dieu m'a donné un corps que j'assume et que je mets en valeur. Si ça les gêne [les hommes], qu'ils tournent la tête" ' ['God gave me a body that I love and that I flaunt. If men are bothered by that, well they can just look away'].[49] Amara rightly insists on women's right to choose their own sexual partners, have access to contraception and take control of their sexuality, but her emphasis on sexual freedom as *the* measure of female emancipation is misleading and reductive. Firstly, this narrow focus on sexual freedom emphasizes Muslim women's mistreatment within their communities while shifting attention away from the ways in which these women suffer from social and economic exclusion, as well as sexism, within French society. Secondly, the 'sexual freedom' that is imagined is narrowly defined in terms of dominant gender norms promoting a highly eroticized and commercialized femininity that not all women can readily identify with.

Although it is conceivable (and understandable) that young women might assert their sexuality as a strategy for resisting sexism within their community, Amara's discourse conforms to what cultural critic Eric Macé describes as a typically French refusal of a supposedly American-style 'battle of the sexes', in favour of 'l'idée que les hommes et les femmes sont différents par nature et que cette différence naturelle justifie à la fois objectivement et subjectivement des rôles et des trajectoires sociales différentes, c'est-à-dire en réalité hiérarchisées' [the idea that men and women are naturally different, and that this natural difference justifies, both objectively and subjectively, different roles and social trajectories that are, in reality, hierarchized].[50] Rejecting a 'bra-burning' feminism, Amara buys into a 'feminine' feminism, represented as French in spirit, that emphasizes the complementarity rather than the equality of the sexes, thus naturalizing sexist gender norms and investing in the commercially lucrative notion that women's real power resides in their sexual allure.

Moreover, because the desirable femininity that Amara invokes is characterized as typically *French*, these interests are inflected by a certain nationalism. French culture is clearly not alone in its tendency to displace feminism with a defence of 'femininity'.[51] However, what is particular to France (as opposed to Britain or America for example) is the way in which a certain idea of the French woman is married to national interests, and indeed to national pride. As the choice of Brigitte Bardot as the model for Marianne implies, the desirable French woman is an established part of the French brand.[52] Nativist feminism, in its defence of an eroticized femininity at the service of the Republic, plays to stereotypes of the desirable Frenchwoman as a national treasure that must be defended with the same vigour as unpasteurized camembert or foie gras.

This construction of the French woman as a national commodity, along with the injunction that women who are culturally or ethnically other conform to this model, was visible in the NPNS campaign 'Mariannes d'aujourd'hui: Hommage des femmes des cités à la République' [The new face of Marianne: Women from the estates pay homage to the Republic] which saw thirteen oversized colour photographs of young women from the *cités* suspended across the façade of the *Assemblée Nationale*. Ten of the thirteen women photographed are of North African, Arab or African ethnic origin, and all of them wear variations on the *bonnet phrygien*, icon of the French Republic. The first striking feature of the exhibition is that all the women are young (in their twenties or early thirties), attractive and impeccably made-up. Many wear off-the-shoulder dresses in red white and blue and each poses for the camera, one blowing a kiss to the spectator, while another throws back her head and laughs, the overall impression reminding the viewer of an advertising campaign for a Parisian department store. This soft eroticization of the *femmes des cités* is accompanied by short texts in which each woman explains what Marianne — figurehead of the Republic and icon of French womanhood — means to her. The image of Marianne that emerges from these texts has two key dimensions. First, she is the embodiment of republican values. She is 'fière d'être Française et de vivre en République' [proud to be French and to live in the Republic] (Alice, 26), and is 'déterminée à faire respecter ses valeurs' [determined that her values be respected] (Gladys, 27). Second, she is seen to possess the distinctly 'feminine' virtues of peace, tenderness and maternity, while displaying a revulsion for power. Linda, 27, claims that 'Marianne, c'est une femme de cœur, qui regarde l'autre avec un a priori positif et chaleureux' [Marianne is a tender-hearted woman who looks upon others positively and warmly] while Gladys, 27, insists that 'Marianne c'est avant tout une femme: elle ne gère pas les relations humaines par la violence' [Marianne is above all else a woman: she doesn't deal in violence]. Furthermore, she is 'une mère protectrice tournée vers l'avenir, [qui] vit loin des histoires de pouvoir. C'est ce qui la rend sereine' [a protective mother looking to the future, far removed from power struggles. That is what makes her so serene]; appropriate, perhaps, for the façade of a seat of power that counts just a handful of women amongst its representatives. Last but not least, comes the injunction that French women can and should attempt to resemble NPNS's vision of Marianne. Clarisse, 23, insists that Marianne is 'une femme à laquelle on peut toutes ressembler. Ce n'est pas une question d'origine ou de physique mais d'engagement républicain' [a woman that we can all aspire to be. It is not a matter of origin or appearance but one of commitment to the Republic].[53] Despite the women's generalized discourse of equality and respect, the specific values attributed to Marianne are 'feminine' ones of seduction, gentleness and motherhood, all in the service of the nation. As such, the *Mariannes* project demonstrates a key tenet of the feminist discourses that dominated the *affaire*, which is the expectation that women who are ethnically or culturally Other to a reified notion of French womanhood must republicanize by feminizing. Indeed, it is through the perpetuation of a notion of femininity in line with dominant gender norms that the integrity of the Republic is assumed to be protected, replacing feminism with an unthreatening idea of the 'feminine'. And so it was that, when Diam's — a French female rapper and supporter of NPNS — appeared on the television programme *Tout le monde en parle* on the 13 March 2004, the host first invited her to talk about life in the *banlieues* where she claims to have adopted aggressive 'masculine' behaviour, before concluding with the question: 'Bon alors maintenant Diam's, vous assumez votre féminité?' [right then, Diam's, so now you've come to terms with your femininity?].[54]

In nativist feminist discourse, the stereotype of the 'feminine', integrated *beurette* is opposed to the unsettling figure of the *voilée*. However, the *voilée* of popular imagination has little in common with the real-life *voilées* whose lives were affected by the ban and who were excluded from the debate. As the ultimate symbol of Muslim 'difference', the *voilée* appears as the visible symptom of an invisible illness, the tip of a monstrous iceberg of Islamic extremism on a crash-course with the French Republic. Indeed, nativist feminist discourse places the veil at the centre of a whole network of social ills. Vianes argues:

> Refuser le foulard, c'est ôter la pièce maîtresse autour de laquelle s'est construit tout le réseau. C'est défaire l'écheveau qui a permis aux intégristes de chasser la République de certains quartiers [...] et de laisser s'installer la loi mafieuse, d'ouvrir la porte à tous les trafiquants, recel de voitures et autres marchandises, drogue, filles, armes; de semer la terreur parmi les habitants.[55]

> [To ban the veil is to remove the lynchpin that holds the whole network together. It is to destroy the web that has let extremists drive the Republic out of certain areas [...] allowing a mafia rule to develop that has opened the door to illegal traffic of all kinds, stolen cars and other goods, drugs, women, guns; spreading fear amongst the inhabitants].

According to Vianes, the 'veil' is the means by which Islamic fundamentalists seek to gain a foothold in French society with a view to infiltrating and corrupting it from within. What the veil conceals, her logic runs, is a whole network of loosely connected social and political evils that threaten to infiltrate and dominate the Republic. The chaotic accumulation of associations (Islam = veil = rape = violence = extremism = terrorism) that characterize nativist feminist representations of the veil and veiled women, build the *voilée* into a monstrous figure onto which all manner of racist fantasies may be projected. Just as colonial-feminist discourse reduced indigenous culture to the image of the inaccessible native woman who was in turn reduced to the veil, nativist feminist discourse condenses all perceived manifestations of Islam into the single iconic vision of the martyred and veiled Muslim woman thus giving tangible form to a mass of loosely connected prejudices, anxieties and fears.

Furthermore, nativist feminist discourse constructs the figure of the *voilée* as a specific threat to dominant notions of 'femininity'. In his savagely spirited analysis of the veil controversy, Badiou argues that the veil causes such offence, not because it constitutes any real threat to republican values, but because it appears to resist the commercial imperatives that underpin Western consumer culture. According to Badiou, the *voilée* appears to pose a threat to capitalism's construction of women both as consumers and as merchandise. In his words: 'On ne peut vendre, on ne sait vendre, voitures, canaris encagés, bétonneuses ou bigoudis, qu'à l'enseigne de femmes vivement dévoilées' [We can't sell, we don't know how to sell, cars, caged canaries, cement mixers or hair rollers, to anyone other than utterly unveiled women]. The presumed modesty and restraint of the *voilée* provides a disconcerting contrast to more commercially viable constructions of women as clothes horses, judicious housewives, or avid shoppers. Furthermore, in an eerie echo of colonial discourse, the *voilée* causes feelings of anger and anxiety because her modest dress hides her from view. Satirizing dominant rhetoric, Badiou remarks: 'une fille *doit* montrer ce qu'elle a à vendre. Elle doit exposer sa marchandise. Elle doit indiquer que désormais la circulation des femmes obéit au modèle généralisé, et non pas à l'échange restraint. Foin des pères et grands frères barbus! Vive le marché planétaire! Le modèle, c'est le top model' [a girl *must* show what she's got to sell. She must display her merchandise. She must confirm that the trade in women nevertheless plays by the rules of the free market model and is not an autarky. A plague on the fathers and bearded brothers! Long live the global market! The model is the supermodel].[56]

This desire to unveil the Muslim woman is also, like colonial representations of unveiling, highly sexualized. Throughout the affair the *voilée* was figured as being at the centre of a web of sexist abuse and violence, and wordplay assimilating *voile* to *viol* [rape] occurred frequently in nativist feminist discourses. In a much-quoted article in the *Nouvel Observateur* on 16 September 2003, Jacques Julliard writes: 'Inversez les deux voyelles et, dans voile, vous trouverez viol. En dissimulant ostensiblement le sexe au regard, fût-ce sous la forme symbolique de la chevelure, vous le désignez à l'attention' [Reverse the two vowels and in veil [*voile*], you will find rape [*viol*]. By hiding the female sex from the gaze, albeit symbolically in the covering of the hair, you draw attention to it].[57] Such remarks repeat the colonizer's demand that the Muslim woman's body be offered up to the Western gaze. Whereas the perceived regulation of women's sexuality by Muslim men is associated with rape, the regulation of women by dominant French society is considered no regulation at all — it is 'freedom'. However, as for Fanon's newly unveiled woman, assimilation to dominant norms does not constitute a 'liberation' but an inscription of women's bodies into new matrices of power. As Badiou remarks:

> Parce que vous imaginez qu'elle n'est pas contrôlée, de nos jours, dans nos sociétés, la sexualité féminine? Cette naïveté aurait bien faire rire Foucault. Jamais on n'as pris soin de la sexualité féminine avec autant de minutie, autant

de conseils savants, autant de discriminations assénées entre son bon et son mauvais usage [...] Le contrôle commercial est plus constant, plus sûr, plus massif que n'a jamais pu l'être le contrôle patriarcal.[58]

[Do you really think that women's sexuality isn't controlled in our day, in our societies? That kind of naivety would have made Foucault laugh till he cried. Never before have we paid such minute, careful attention to women's sexuality. Never before have we doled out such sound advice as to how it should and shouldn't be regulated [...] commercial control is more constant, more reliable, more powerful than patriarchy could ever have been.]

From this point of view the injunction on Muslim girls to uncover has nothing to do with sexual liberation and everything to do with the re-assertion of dominant norms of femininity and sexuality that construct women as consumers of beauty products, fashion and household goods as promoted by a hegemonic 'feminine' feminism diffused through women's magazines and the media.

The perceived modesty of the *voilée* is not seen to conform to the approved 'femininity' of the *beurette* and is consequently stigmatized by nativist feminists who, in a repetition of colonial feminist discourse, construct her as unattractive and possessing a perverse or grotesque sexuality. Voilquin associates the 'ugliness' of Muslim-Arab women with their perceived lack of freedom and contrasts them with a radiant and emancipated vision of French womanhood. In a similar way, Michèle Vianes imagines that the *voilées* must be unattractive and jealous of French women's right to beauty, making the provocative claim that veiled women want other women to cover up so that they do not present a source of temptation for their husbands. According to Vianes, no sexually attractive woman could possibly opt out of the pleasures of self-beautification offered by French society, leaving the veils to the 'disgracieuses, grosses ou difformes' [ungracious, fat or ungainly].[59] Whereas, in nativist feminist discourse, the *beurette* is seen to embrace a 'normal', 'natural' femininity, the *voilée* is either de-sexualized, negating her 'natural' femininity, or hyper-sexualized as a downtrodden sex slave. Chahdortt Djavann, author of *Bas les voiles!* [*Down with veils!*] — an impassioned pamphlet that combines personal testimony of life in Iran with a radical prohibitionist stance with regard to the veil — joins with Juillard in her insistence on the perversity of the veil that, by concealing women's bodies (Djavann makes no distinction between different veils or veiling practices), draws attention to them as sex objects. She writes that beneath the veil, 'le corps féminin est un objet sexuel qu'on cache, qu'on dénigre, un peu comme un accessoire sexuel qu'on aurait honte d'utiliser' [the female body is a sex object, hidden, denigrated, rather like a sex toy that one is too ashamed to use],[60] and in order to mark the divergence of the *voilées* from a 'normal' femininity, Djavann goes on to compare women who choose to veil to prostitutes who wish to draw attention to their bodies as existing for the gratification of men.[61] In this way, the deviant femininity of the *voilée* is contrasted with a naturalized image of French womanhood as compatible with *les plaisirs de la féminité* promoted in women's lifestyle magazines: beauty, fashion and seduction.

Over the course of the debate, the stereotypes of the *beurette* and the *voilée* displaced the presence of women who did not fit the bill. Sociologist and activist

Saïda Kada expresses her frustration with the false choice *beurette/voilée* imposed upon French Muslim women. She writes: 'Cela fait des années qu'on nous incite à adopter des valeurs modernes. Mais le fait qu'on passe par l'islam pour les revendiquer est insupportable! Ce qui fait violence, c'est qu'on ne prenne pas le chemin tracé pour nous: en caricaturant un peu, on a le droit de refuser l'excision à condition de renier l'islam' [For years we have been told to adopt modern values. But people can't accept that we might do this via Islam! What upsets them is the fact that we are not taking the path they have chosen for us: to caricature a little, we only have the right to refuse clitoridectomy if we renounce Islam].[62] Indeed, following nativist feminist logic, it is impossible to 'choose' Islam as a legitimate reference in the construction of a French feminist identity. The opposition *beurette/ voilée* suppresses and excludes this possibility and replaces it with the supposed 'choice' between absolute integration and absolute resistance. However, positing assimilation as the only viable alternative to fundamentalism is no real choice at all as it already assumes the 'right' answer. As Houria Bouteldja argues, it is not so much a real choice as 'le droit de faire "le bon choix"' [the right to make 'the right choice'].[63] This tendency to perceive problems via a set of false choices is characteristic of nativist feminism and Fadela Amara provides one clear example. Before supporting an outright ban on the headscarf, Amara put her faith in the secular education system and the influence of nativist feminism to show the *voilées* the error of their ways. She writes: 'Nous voulions parier sur l'école républicaine pour qu'elles arrivent à trouver les moyens d'imposer leur choix de vie et refuser ensuite le voile' [We put our faith in the republican school to empower them to make their own life-choices, and subsequently to refuse the veil].[64] By imagining that the natural choice of the educated and therefore 'liberated' woman is to reject the veil, Amara supposes that 'liberty' is the preserve of French womanhood while Muslim womanhood is associated with lack of freedom. According to nativist feminist logic, then, it is simply not possible to *choose* the veil. By representing veiled Muslim women as necessarily oppressed and voiceless, the practice of veiling does not appear as a legitimate means of self-expression, but is only conceivable as a rejection of the terms by which dialogue (as constructed by dominant discourses) is made possible.

This is not to say that nativist feminists are wrong to worry about the coercion of young girls and women into wearing headscarves. There is plenty of evidence that some Muslim girls are forced to cover their heads by their parents or community leaders.[65] Furthermore, it has always been in feminist interests to question the nature of the 'choices' women make and nativist feminists are right to ask whether all Muslim women who 'voluntarily' cover their heads are making an authentic decision. One might legitimately wonder whether Muslim women's desires and preferences are shaped and limited by an internalization of unjust patriarchal norms. One might also ask whether wearing the headscarf is, for some, simply a strategy for avoiding sexist abuse and harassment. These are important queries, but by reducing all headscarf-wearing to instances of direct or indirect coercion and refusing to listen to Muslim women on these grounds, nativist feminists oversimplify the issues facing Muslim women to the point of falsifying them, while, at the same time, offering a naïve appraisal of the situation of majority-ethnic French women.

Firstly, the singling out of the headscarf as an instance of false consciousness is highly contentious. During the affair, Elisabeth Badinter claimed that wearing ripped jeans or pink hair constituted an autonomous act while wearing the veil was an act of subservience. But, as Laborde remarks, it is striking how such discourses imagine French social pressure *not* to veil as consistent with female autonomy, while pressure to veil is constructed as coercive. Indeed, in a society in which ripped jeans and pink hair are readily tolerated it is difficult to see such fashion choices as non-conformist while choosing to veil in a hostile cultural context might, by contrast, be seen as a mark of individualism.[66] Secondly, women choose to wear the headscarf for a wide variety of reasons that cannot be reduced to nativist feminists' terms. As critics of the ban argued, and as I shall discuss in more detail in the final chapter, Muslim women should not simply be seen as passive victims but as agents in their own lives making choices within the shifting contexts in which they find themselves. Wearing the headscarf may, for example, grant the wearer a valued status and respectability functioning not only as a practical strategy for dealing with the threat of harassment, but also protecting her from the aggressive sexualization of women's bodies by commercial culture.[67] Alternatively, it may constitute an 'Islamic feminist' gesture, symbolizing a woman's embrace and reappropriation of Islam on her own terms.[68] Furthermore, some women wear the headscarf as an anti-western or anti-establishment protest, marking a sense of continuity with the anticolonial struggles of the past and expressing anger at the failure of the French state to come good on its promises.[69] As a final example, the headscarf may provide an important means for young women to reconcile the conflicting demands made of them as they find themselves caught between their affective bonds to Islam and their community, and the pressure to conform to French cultural norms. As I shall go on to argue, Muslim feminists refuse to choose between 'France' and 'Islam', 'freedom' or 'oppression', 'tradition' or 'modernity', opening up a space of agency within which they may articulate an identity that is French, feminist *and* Muslim.

The nativist feminist position that dominated the *affaire du foulard* did not, however, account for such complexity and the exclusion of veiled women on the grounds that they were alienated and manipulated resulted in an impoverished debate that traded largely in prejudice and cliché, betraying the participants' profound ignorance both of Islam and the situation of French Muslim women.[70] The result was a self-defeating law that punished the very women it was supposed to protect, excluding them from the institutions that nativist feminists imagined would safeguard their autonomy — schools. As the *voilée* was deemed voiceless, the only speaking position available to French Muslim women during the controversy was that of the *beurette*. However, as the following section will suggest, this voice was extremely vulnerable to recuperation and exploitation by a nativist feminist agenda.

'*Beur* Women's Writing': The Case of Samira Bellil

The *affaire du foulard* was not only a national controversy: it was also a publishing phenomenon. So far, my critique of nativist feminism has considered sociological, journalistic and polemical texts but nativist feminist discourse was also manifest in numerous fictions and autobiographies. The second half of this book will consider the ways in which some Muslim women writers are contesting or subverting the nativist feminist narratives that shape much of this work. This section will prepare the way for these writers by exploring the unacknowledged colonial roots of these narratives and revealing the ways in which they dispossess Muslim women of a discursive position just when they are presumed to speak.

The *affaire du foulard* saw the publication (and re-publication) of a great number of testimonies by young French women of Muslim or North African immigrant descent often written in collaboration with ethnic-majority French female writers or journalists who edited and rewrote the author's drafts. These autobiographical texts tend to repeat the themes of what has come to be known as *beur* women's writing in which the female protagonist's integration into French society is frequently imagined to ensure her self-liberation from an oppressive and violent home life.[71] *Beur* women's writing has much in common with writing by young *beur* men in its articulation of a split and strained postcolonial identity caught between the North African heritage of the family and French cultural values. However, in the case of *beur* women's writing the protagonist's desire to escape the sexism of her family environment by integrating into French society via the French education system often produces a more ambivalent representation of France. Though critical of the racism encountered there, the protagonists of these texts frequently imagine integration to ensure emancipation from the suffocating gender norms imposed at home. Undoubtedly many of the writers concerned experienced their escapes from oppressive and often violent home-lives as genuinely emancipating. However, the generally flattering image of French gender norms produced by these texts also leaves them vulnerable to recuperation by conservative discourses that hold up the figure of the *beurette* as proof of the success of an assimilationist model of integration.[72]

This recuperation of the author's testimony in the service of a nativist feminist agenda is clearly visible in the production of Samira Bellil's book *Dans l'enfer des tournantes* [Inside the Hell of Gang-rape]. *Dans l'enfer des tournantes* is an autobiographical testimony that, according to the publishers, 'dévoile la violence sexuelle qui s'est instituée et banalisée dans des cités et des banlieues où tout se réduit à un rapport de forces et de domination' [unveils the sexual violence that has become entrenched and commonplace in the estates and suburbs where all relations are reduced to a power struggle]. Bellil, victim of gang-rapes known as 'tournantes', narrates her experience of life in the *cité*, her slide into drug and alcohol abuse, and her ultimate recovery following an extended period of therapy. Although her text is presented as a straight-from-the-horse's-mouth testimony, and a rallying cry to her '"frangines", victimes, comme elle, du pire des crimes' ["sisters", victims, like her, of the worst of crimes],[73] Bellil's text is written in close collaboration with journalist Josée Stoquart who rewrote and restructured Bellil's text, as well as writing an introductory preface that frames and shapes the reader's perception of the work.[74] Indeed, in Hall's terms, Stoquart assumes the role of 'primary definer'; the voice of 'authority' that defines the vantage point from which to view the text. Although Bellil's narrative occasionally invites more complex and nuanced readings of the lives of immigrant-origin women in the *cités* and the strategies they use to protect and express themselves, Stoquart's introduction sets Bellil's narrative in terms of a simple 'emancipation' that sees the author transformed from a butch, tough-talking 'caillera'[75] to 'Samira, la petite beurette'[76] who has embraced her femininity. Indeed, after the much-hyped publication of the book, Bellil became a *marraine* [a godmother] of NPNS and figured amongst the thirteen 'Mariannes d'aujourd'hui'.

At the outset of her story, the author identifies herself as 'Sam', a streetwise *banlieuesarde* who resembles the girls Fadela Amara describes as 'les masculines'. In her typology of the *filles des quartiers*, Amara describes the behaviour of 'les masculines' as:

> celui des femmes qui veulent ressembler aux mecs, qui s'imposent pour forcer le respect. Elles adoptent les attitudes des garçons en intégrant leurs outils et leurs armes. On a ainsi vu apparaître dans les cités des phénomènes de bandes constituées uniquement de filles, habillées en jogging et baskets, tenue passe-partout pour ne pas assumer leur féminité, et qui utilisent la violence comme expression [...] sans jamais un geste tendre, qui serait perçue comme un signe de faiblesse.[77]

> [that of women who want to look like blokes, who assert themselves to force some respect. They mimic the boys' behaviour and use the same tactics and weapons. In the estates we now see girl-only gangs wearing tracksuits and trainers (a kind of uniform that hides their femininity) and expressing themselves through violence [...] they never show tenderness. That would be taken as a sign of weakness].

'Sam' assumes a 'masculine' identity in order to assert and protect herself, and as a means of adapting to the various extreme situations that she finds herself in. On more than one occasion, the narrator describes herself as having a multiple personality allowing her to play a variety of roles, and this sense of fragmentation is most frequently described as a result of her inability to 'integrate' and find her place in society: '[J]e comprends ma marginalité, mon incapacité à m'intégrer, et mon image de victime me saute aux yeux' [I see my marginality, my inability to integrate, my image as a victim stares right back at me] (*L'Enfer*, 122). However, although she expresses a strong desire to be accepted, her performance of multiple and 'masculine' identities, prevents her from identifying with the image of 'French' femininity to which she is expected to conform in order to integrate. Indeed, when she undertakes a work-experience placement as a hotel receptionist, she finds herself unable to perform the 'feminine' masquerade that is expected of her:

> Adieu baskets et jeans. Bonjour le tailleur et les talons! Ça ne dure pas bien longtemps. Je me sens déguisée, je m'ennuie et ne tiens pas plus d'un mois! J'ai vingt ans et je merde. J'essaie de donner le change, de faire comme tout

le monde. Je n'y parviens pas [...]. Je fais des petits boulots: je vends du prêt-à-porter, des sandwichs-merguez aux puces de Clignancourt. Je fournis un énorme effort pour entrer dans ce mascarade. Je joue des rôles, mais je ne suis pas moi. (*L'Enfer*, 201)

[Goodbye trainers and jeans. Hello skirt-suit and heels! It doesn't last long. I feel like an imposter. I get bored and I don't last a month! I'm twenty and I'm already screwed. I try to play the game, to be like everyone else. I can't do it [...]. I do some little jobs: I sell ready-to-wear and merguez sandwiches at Clignancourt flea-market. I make a huge effort to pull off this masquerade. I'm role-playing, but I'm not myself].

Beyond the nativist feminist logic imposed by co-author Josée Stoquart, Bellil's text at times reads as the exposition of a conflicted and ambivalent identity that does not conform to the obligatory performance of a *tailleur–talons* model of femininity which appears to Bellil as distinctly white and middle-class. However, Stoquart's paratext, along with the psychologist Fanny's intervention in the body of the narrative, invite the reader to interpret Bellil's story as a triumph of French 'feminist' values over the supposed violence and obscurantism of Muslim-Arab culture represented, in particular, by young 'immigrant' men.

Indeed, in her introduction Stoquart characterizes the young men of the *quartiers* in terms of their 'sauvagerie sexuelle' [sexual savagery] explained as a product of cultural difference loosely summarized as 'intégrisme religieux, intouchabilité de la femme, polygamie...' [religious fundamentalism, untouchability of women, polygamy...] (*L'Enfer*, 13) reducing Muslim-Arab culture to a barbaric sexism, while exonerating French culture. In order to emphasize the primitive barbarity of the *cités* and their inhabitants Stoquart's writing is shot through with animal imagery. 'La loi de la jungle' [the law of the jungle] reigns supreme, she claims, and women are obliged either to cloister themselves in the family home or risk 'dans la rue de devenir *la proie* des bandes' [becoming *the prey* of street-gangs] [my emphasis] (*L'Enfer*, 11–12). Indeed, before Stoquart's intervention and transformation of her *protégée*, Bellil herself is also described as 'un petit animal sauvage' [a little wild animal] (*L'Enfer*, 12). This eroticization and zoification of France's cultural others is perfectly in keeping with colonial depictions of indigenous cultures as sexually deviant and morally backward. Furthermore, Stoquart's description of the *cité* echoes the trepidation and voyeurism of colonial women travellers who were both intrigued and repulsed by the sexual conduct of their cultural others. Like the sleazy, violent and indomitable Casbah, Stoquart's *cité* is a place of sexual and moral lawlessness, beyond the dominion of the Republic and characterized by a perverse sexuality that is incompatible with 'normal' femininity. Stoquart perceives the sexist violence of the *cités* to be entirely alien to 'normal' French society and her pedagogical tone and choice of vocabulary are suggestive of colonial anthropology, designating Bellil and 'son monde' as distinctly Other. Terms such as '[le] *phénomène* de bande' [the gang *phenomenon*] and 'la *pratique* de la "tournante"' [the *practice* of gang-rapes] [my emphasis] represent Bellil's community as an alien culture, and turns of phrase that belong to Bellil's environment — for example '"filles à cave"'[78] (*L'Enfer*, 13) — are isolated from Stoquart's text by inverted commas. Sexism and violence against women are imagined to be the hallmarks of Muslim–Arab tradition while French culture appears synonymous with women's emancipation. As the feminist activist Christine Delphy remarks: 'Voilà comment [...] on fait d'une pierre deux coups: l'altérité des autres sexistes est confirmée, tandis que notre absence de sexisme est prouvée par l'altérité des sexistes' [That's how you kill two birds with one stone. The otherness of the sexists is confirmed, while the absence of our sexism is proven by the otherness of the sexists].[79] It is by shedding the cultural heritage of her family, and in particular by disassociating herself from her menfolk, that the author is imagined to emancipate herself. Indeed, as Tarr has pointed out in relation to *beur* filmmaking, it is via the denigration and humiliation of young men that young women's emancipation and integration is imagined to be possible.[80]

Bellil's narrative is represented by Stoquart as a reassuring story of successful integration. In Stoquart's analysis, it is by telling her story and having it validated by readers that Bellil may overcome her trauma, piece together her shattered self and assume her place in society. She writes:

> Lorsque les violences de son histoire furent extirpées de sa mémoire, imprimées, lues et relues, elle commença à se distancer de son passé et à se pacifier. Tout était dit, hurlé, pleuré. Tout était réfléchi, compris, intégré. Elle avait remis à leur juste place tous les morceaux de sa vie. Tout était trié, rangé, consigné. (*L'Enfer*, 16)

> [Once the violence of her past was extricated from her memory, printed, read and reread, she started to distance herself from it and find some peace. Everything had been said, screamed, sobbed. Everything had been reflected upon, understood, integrated. She had put her life back together again. It had all been sorted, organized and put away.]

However, although Bellil attaches great importance to the therapeutic and emancipatory value of self-expression, and although the book sold on its supposed status as an authentic *cri de cœur*, the author is also dispossessed of her voice. As Stoquart insists, Bellil's feelings and experiences are 'trié, rangé, consigné' during her sessions with Fanny, and tailored by her co-author in line with the demands of the reading public who will judge her. She explains: 'Ecrire avec l'objectif d'être lue, par moi à la séance suivante puis plus tard par un lecteur éventuel, l'a obligée à garder une certaine rigueur et à ne pas "se lâcher" dans une expression spontanée' [Writing with the objective of being read, by me at our next meeting, then later by the reading public, obliged her to maintain a certain rigour and not 'lapse' into spontaneous expression] (*L'Enfer*, 15). Bellil's story, as Stoquart reminds her, must be accessible and palatable to her audience who are predominantly white and middle class. Indeed, in order to gain the approval she desires Bellil must take care not to 'let herself go', but must instead craft and market herself to her readership as the feisty *beurette* they have come to expect. This is not to say that the author does not experience the writing and publishing process as beneficial to her sense of self-worth. Indeed, Bellil claims that writing her story has given her greater self-confidence and has allowed her to come to terms with her appalling treatment. But her sense of self is largely dependent on her collaborator's, and ultimately her readers', approval. She writes:

En me rendant mes écrits éclaircis, restructurés et tapés, la prise de conscience s'amplifiait encore. J'existais, et mon malheur aussi. Josée m'a offert un autre regard sur moi-même, un vrai regard auquel j'ai intuitivement fait confiance. Elle m'a reconnue telle que je suis et m'a donné la valeur que je ne parvenais pas à me donner moi-même. (*L'Enfer*, 303)

[Whenever she gave back what I had written — clarified, restructured and typed up — I would become even more self-aware. I existed and my unhappiness too. Josée offered me another view of myself, a real view that I instinctively trusted. She saw me for who I am and gave me a value that I wasn't able to give myself].

It is Stoquart and the majority-ethnic French readership who are constructed here as the origin of value. Bellil's life-story only achieves meaning in her eyes when it is filtered through Stoquart's *vrai regard*. Just as colonial feminists constructed a maternal relationship to their Muslim others, Stoquart, as a white woman and member of the dominant classes, positions herself as judge and saviour in relation to her vulnerable *protégée* who is only able to recognize herself in her co-author's terms.

However, as Alec Hargreaves observes in his analysis of Bellil's text, parts of the narrative suggest that the author is aware that her personal testimony is vulnerable to stereotyping. As Hargreaves explains, when Bellil is invited to participate in a television show about rape-victims she responds with caution. Although she is at first attracted to the idea of reaching a wider audience, she does not trust the presenter and his crew who, she fears, are motivated by audience ratings alone (*L'Enfer*, 282). She ultimately turns down the invitation for fear of being 'croquée à la sauce voyeur' [a spectacle for consumption] (*L'Enfer*, 285) and 'prise pour une bête de foire' [taken for a circus animal] (*L'Enfer*, 283) — images that, as Hargreaves remarks: 'recall the "human zoos" organized for the entertainment of Europeans during the colonial period'.[81] However, Bellil's caution with regard to the mainstream media does not extend to her relationship with Stoquart whose introduction to Bellil's text appeals directly to the readers' voyeurism, sensationalizes her story and divests Bellil of her individuality to make her representative of the *filles des quartiers* and Muslim women in general.

Stoquart's framing of Bellil's narrative, although it purports to give voice to the author and grant her access to mainstream French culture, may be seen to simultaneously mark her out as distinctly Other and dispossess her of that voice. Despite her desire to 'speak out' and become fully integrated into French society, Bellil in many ways remains the eroticized Other woman for a public and media fascinated by stories of sexual violence in the *cités*, her exoticization becoming the condition of possibility for her right to speak. In other words, while Bellil is on the one hand nominally accepted and held up as a positive example of integration, she is simultaneously positioned as an outsider. Bellil and Stoquart's collaboration is not exceptional, there being a large number of texts co-authored by women of immigrant origin and majority-ethnic French women writers that conform to this model. Aïssa Benaïssa's *Née en France: Histoire d'une jeune beur* [*Born in France: A Beur Woman's Story*], written in collaboration with Sophie Ponchelet, Loubna Méliane's *Vivre libre* [*Live free*] co-authored by Marie-Thérèse Cuny, and Fadela Amara's *Ni putes ni soumises* with Sylvia Zappi are among such examples.

L'Affaire du foulard as Distraction and Diversion

In March 2004, after months of media hysteria and on the recommendation of the vague and rambling Stasi report, a law was passed banning the wearing of ostentatious religious symbols in public schools. As John R. Bowen reports, the law was followed with the same degree of absurdity and confusion that preceded it as teachers fretted over whether the wearing of bandanas was permissible, and other public services, including a number of doctors surgeries, took it upon themselves to exclude veiled women.[82] Most veiled girls agreed to remove their headscarves in order to avoid expulsion but, although this was interpreted as a triumph by prohibitionists, it caused considerable hurt, resentment and humiliation. Those who refused to comply, either of their own volition or under pressure from others, were duly expelled and were either home-schooled or lost out on their education altogether.

But, as the riots of November 2005 dramatically demonstrated, this law did nothing to address the problems of poverty, social exclusion and institutionalized racism that effect the life chances of French Muslim women and their communities far more than a headscarf ever could. Furthermore, it did not address the concerns of ethnic-majority French citizens.[83] According to a survey carried out by the independent research group *TNS Sofres* in March 2004, at the time the law prohibiting religious symbols in schools was passed, the key concerns of the French population were unemployment, the quality of healthcare, pensions, social inequality, the environment and crime. The veil at school did not feature. However, the controversy provided France's political classes with an expedient opportunity to garner public support at little expense. According to Tévanian, the *affaire* offered the centre-right the chance to divert attention away from unpopular reforms such as Raffarin's pensions proposals, while allowing the mainstream left to counter its soft image and show it was able to get tough on issues such as immigration, insecurity and the veil, winning back (largely working-class) support that had been lost to the *Front National*.[84] Above all, the debate's privileging of *cultural* difference, drew attention away from France's failed socio-economic policies. While problems of poverty and discrimination would require imaginative and expensive reforms, 'Arab sexism' simply called for denunciation by means of an inexpensive and cathartic law.

Adrian Favell has pointed to the growing importance of a national consensus on cultural questions as a means of obscuring social and economic antagonisms in society, thus preserving the supposed integrity of the nation. He writes: 'instead of addressing the causes of integration failure — notably poverty, declining welfare and inequality — these states [France and the United Kingdom] promote an increasingly centralized ideological consensus around cultural and value issues'.[85] Nacira Guénif Soulimas sees this tendency to use cultural issues as a smokescreen reflected in nativist feminists' construction of the *beurette* stereotype. By imagining the *beurette* to possess a 'double culture', torn between 'North African' and 'French' values, French society posits that failure to integrate is the result of a failure to break with the culture of origin. This focus on cultural barriers, Soulimas argues, draws attention away from the existence of social and economic barriers which are much more difficult to overcome. She writes:

La question de la double culture se conçoit dès lors non plus comme une
réalité intangible mais comme une construction sociale et idéologique. Elle a
pour fonction de justifier la dissymétrie dans les rapports entre classes sociales,
en utilisant l'argument fictif de cultures étrangères et irréductibles l'une à
l'autre.[86]

[The question of 'double culture' is no longer a tangible reality but a social
and ideological construct. It works to justify the asymmetry of class relations
by using the false argument that foreign cultures are incompatible with one
another.]

Such arguments echo colonial-feminists' emphasis on sexual oppression at the
expense of an account of Muslim women's oppression as colonial subjects. This is
not to say, however, that nativist feminists ignore the social and economic depri-
vation of the *banlieues*. Indeed in the closing pages of *Bas les voiles!* Chahdorrt
Djavann urges the French government to invest in deprived areas and insists on
the (re-)education of all 'immigrants', children and adults alike, with a view to
dissipating their alien cultural practices and integrating them into a 'French' way
of life.[87] However, what this argument (like the cultural argument) does not
consider is the possibility that the French model of integration fails, in part, because
of a profound unwillingness to reconsider the co-ordinates of what it means to
be French. Arguments like Djavann's imagine that, if only economic and social
barriers could be lowered through better access to education, employment and so
on, then cultural differences would be erased as 'immigrant' communities integrate
into a unified vision of French citizenship. The possibility of Islam becoming a
legitimate French cultural reference is taken into account by neither the cultural
nor the socio-economic arguments. This inflexible vision of French identity,
citizenship or indeed womanhood may be seen to represent the hard kernel at the
centre of nativist feminist discourses. From this perspective, the practice of Islam
becomes either a manifestation of radicalism, or is practised by those who 'don't
know any better' — it is never considered a legitimate choice made by bona fide
French citizens and feminists.

During the *affaire du foulard* nativist feminism pursued a colonial logic that did not
so much serve to emancipate French Muslim women as to facilitate the promotion
of a reified notion of French womanhood as an aspirational ideal. Although
references to France's colonial past tended to be suppressed throughout the *affaire*,
nativist feminists' insistence on the 'woman question' as the axis around which
integration would be achieved, their exploitation of *la cause des femmes* as a means of
insisting on French cultural superiority, their maternal tutelage of the *beurettes*, their
eroticization of the Other woman, and their inability to conceive of their cultural
others as anything more than flattering or horrifying reflections of themselves,
all provide clear points of comparison. Furthermore, just as the feminist potential
of colonial women's discourses diminished as they became ever more tightly
harnessed to the imperial project, nativist feminists' professed wish to emancipate
French Muslim women is compromised by their complicity with an uncritical and
reactionary republican ideology. Indeed, despite the debate's supposed privileging
of feminist discourses, the feminism of the *affaire du foulard* was profoundly anti-
feminist. The exclusive focus on sexism within Muslim communities, coupled

with an idealization of a regressive ideal of French 'femininity' as a model of emancipation, not only alienated and excluded French Muslim women but failed to confront the sexism that persists at the heart of French society and is manifest in levels of domestic violence, the endurance of sexist gender norms, the failure to question the traditional division of labour within the family and the continuing under-representation of women in public life. In short, nativist feminism is no feminism at all.

The second part of this book will examine the work of writers and activists who are seeking to move beyond the roles offered to them by nativist feminism by rethinking what it means to be a Muslim woman living in contemporary France and by contesting the assertion of a monolithic notion of French femininity as the unique model of female emancipation.

Notes to Chapter 2

1. <www.marchemondiale.org> [accessed 28 February 2006].
2. <www.saphirnet.org> [accessed 28 February 2006].
3. Le Collectif féministe pour l'égalité, 'Pour les droits de femmes, contre les exclusions, pour un monde plus solidaire' <www.lmsi.net/article.php3?id_article+410> [accessed 22 September 2005].
4. Erwan Le Corre, 'La Marche de TOUTES les femmes?' <www.lmsi.net/article.php3?id_article=227> [accessed 28 February 2006].
5. Ibid.
6. Bernard Stasi, *Laïcité et République: Rapport de la commission de la réflexion sur l'application du principe de laïcité dans la République remis au Président de la République le 11 décembre 2003* (Paris: La Documentation française, 2004).
7. In *Marianne et le Prophète: L'Islam dans la France laïque* (Paris: Grasset, 1998), Soheib Bencheikh usefully explores the issues involved in identifying oneself or others as Muslim. For his purposes, Bencheikh defines the Muslim as 'celui qui reconnaît les grandes vérités de l'islam et essaye de le pratiquer; celui qui ne pratique pas reste musulman s'il ne renie ni la véracité ni l'utilité de la pratique' [one who recognizes the fundamental truths of Islam and tries to practise the religion. A non-practising Muslim remains a Muslim, so long as he does not deny either the truth nor the utility of practice], p. 75.
8. Carrie Tarr quotes figures published by the *Commission Nationale des Droits de l'Homme* in 2000 suggesting that at that time 63% of the 'French' thought there were too many 'Arabs' in France. Carrie Tarr, *Reframing Difference: Beur and Banlieue Filmmaking in France* (Manchester: Manchester University Press, 2005), p. 8. The electoral successes of the *Front National* in 2002 also points to a widespread intolerance of 'immigrants' and their children.
9. See for example, Nick Cohen, 'Controversy unveiled', *The Observer*, 24 December, 2006 <http://www.guardian.co.uk/theobserver/2006/dec/24/features.magazine167> [accessed January 2007]
10. Alain Badiou, 'Foulard', in *Circonstances, 2: Irak, foulard, Allemagne/France* (Paris: Léo Scheer, 2004), pp. 109–25.
11. Cécile Laborde, *Critical Republicanism: The Hijab Controversy and Political Philosophy* (Oxford: Oxford University Press, 2008), p. 25.
12. Rogers Brubaker, *Citizenship and Nationhood in France and Germany* (Cambridge, MA: Harvard University Press, 1992), p. 1.
13. Bencheikh, pp. 16–65.
14. Quoted in, Sharif Gemie, 'Stasi's Republic: The School and the 'Veil', *Modern and Contemporary France*, 12 (2004), 387–97 (p. 387).
15. For an analysis of *beur* identity and the *beur* movement see Alec Hargreaves, *Immigration and Identity in Beur Fiction: Voices from the North-African Community in France* (Oxford: Berg, 1997), and Peter Fysh and Jim Wolfreys, *The Politics of Racism in France* (Basingstoke: Macmillan, 1998).

16. For a discussion of Mitterrand's remarks see Maxim Silverman, *Deconstructing the Nation: Immigration, Racism and Citizenship in Modern France* (London: Routledge, 1992), pp. 95–106.

17. I refer in particular to the Méhaignerie law of 1993 that required children born in France of foreign parents to request French nationality at adulthood rather than being automatically granted it, and the Pasqua laws that restricted residence rights and facilitated expulsions.

18. Tarr, p. 7.

19. Alain Gresh, *L'Islam, la République et le monde* (Paris: Fayard, 2004), pp. 130–31.

20. Tarr, p. 7, Laborde, p. 150.

21. Dounia Bouzar, *L'Islam des banlieues. Les prédicateurs musulmans: Nouveaux travailleurs sociaux?* (Paris: Syros, 2001), p. 107.

22. Quoted in Bouzar, p. 108.

23. Farhad Khosrokhavar, *L'Islam des jeunes* (Paris: Flammarion, 1997).

24. Jeanne-Hélène Kaltenbach and Michèle Tribalat, *La République et l'islam: Entre crainte et aveuglement* (Saint-Amand: Gallimard, 2002), p. 187.

25. Michèle Vianes, *Un voile sur la République* (Paris: Stock, 2004), pp. 234–35.

26. François Dubet and Danilo Martucelli, *Dans quelle société vivons nous?* (Paris: Seuil, 1998), p. 204.

27. Although the term *beurette*, like *beur*, is somewhat dated and has long been rejected by the descendants of North Africans as condescending and more applicable to the 1980s generations, the image of the integrated Maghrebi woman that the *beurette* embodies still has tremendous currency. Bearing these qualifications in mind, I will use the term *beurette* to refer, not to a specific group of women but to an enduring cultural stereotype.

28. Jane Freedman, *Immigration and Insecurity in France* (Aldershot: Ashgate, 2004), p. 107.

29. *Putes* is French for 'whores' while *soumises* literally means 'submissive women'. One possible translation for the name of this organization would be 'Neither Sluts nor Slaves'.

30. Fadela Amara and Sylvia Zappi, *Ni putes ni soumises* (Paris: La Découverte, 2003), pp. 78–79.

31. Collectif les mots sont importants, 'Ni putes ni soumises, ou la parole confisquée: Notes sur une réunion publique du mouvement de Mohammed Abdi et Fadela Amara' <www.lmsi.net/php3?id_article=321> [accessed 5 May 2005].

32. Pierre Tévanian, *Le Voile médiatique* (Paris: Raisons d'agir, 2005), p. 71.

33. Dounia Bouzar and Saïda Kada, *L'Une voilée, l'autre pas: Le Témoignage de deux musulmanes françaises* (Paris: Albin Michel, 2003), p. 75.

34. Ibid, p. 81.

35. Tévanian, p. 25.

36. Ibid, p. 15.

37. Gresh, pp. 262–67.

38. Stuart Hall and others, *Policing the Crisis* (London: Macmillan, 1978), pp. 57–60.

39. Tévanian, p. 4.

40. Ibid, p. 27.

41. Ibid, p. 39.

42. Ibid, pp. 38–39.

43. Ibid, p. 86.

44. Ibid, p. 52.

45. Ibid, pp. 108–09.

46. Fawzia Zouari, *Ce voile qui déchire la France* (Paris: Ramsay, 2004), p. 105.

47. Quoted in Tévanian, p. 71.

48. Amara, p. 44.

49. Ibid, p. 50.

50. Erique Macé, 'Entretien avec Erique Macé: Le Féminisme républicaniste est un pseudo féminisme', <www.oumma.com/article.php3?id_article=1297> [accessed 8 December 2005].

51. For a vigorous critique of 'feminine' neo-feminism in an American context see Ariel Levy, *Female Chauvanist Pigs: Women and the Rise of Raunch Culture* (London: Simon & Schuster, 2006).

52. Since 1969 official busts of Marianne have been modelled on famous French actresses, models and television personalities including Catherine Deneuve (1985) and Laetitia Casta (2000).

53. <http://www.assemblee-nationale.fr/evenements/mariannes.asp> [accessed 28 November 2005].

54. Quoted in Nacira Guénif-Souilamas and Eric Macé, *Les Féministes et le garçon arabe* (La Tour-d'Aigues: Editions de l'Aube, 2004), p. 90.
55. Vianes, p. 230.
56. Badiou, pp. 114–15.
57. Quoted in Tévanian, p. 96.
58. Badiou, p. 117.
59. Vianes, pp. 201–02.
60. Djavann, *Bas les voiles!*, p. 26.
61. Ibid, p. 33.
62. Bouzar and Kada, p. 96.
63. Houria Bouteldja, 'De la cérémonie du dévoilement à Alger (1958) à Ni putes ni soumises: L'Instrumentalisation coloniale et néo-coloniale de la cause des femmes' <www.lmsi.net/article.php3?id_article=320> [accessed 5 May 2005] (para. 29 of 32).
64. Amara, p. 77.
65. Laborde, p. 119.
66. Ibid, p. 130.
67. See for example, Bouzar and Kada, pp. 33–39.
68. Ibid, pp. 130–39.
69. See for example, Gresh, pp. 361–65.
70. As Laborde remarks 'The [Stasi] commission barely took notice of the best sociological works on contemporary French Islam, and gave disproportionate attention to second-rate works castigating Iranian or Algerian Islamism and replicating the *laïciste* enchanted story of Western modernity fighting off the obscurantist forces of essentialized "Muslim societies"', p. 134.
71. Siobhàn McIlvanney provides an introduction to some key themes of *beur* women's writing in 'The Articulation of *beur* Female Identity in the Works of Farida Belghoul, Ferrudja Kessas and Soraya Nini', in *Women's Writing in Contemporary France*, ed. by Gill Rye and Michael Worton (Manchester: Manchester University Press, 2002), pp. 130–41. Carrie Tarr also identifies similar themes in *beur* women's cinema. See Tarr, pp. 86–97.
72. Tarr recognizes similar tendencies in representations of *beur* women in film, Tarr, p. 112.
73. Quoted from back cover of Bellil, *Dans l'enfer des tournantes*.
74. For a discussion of co-authorship between French women writers of Maghrebi origin and majority-ethnic French women writers see Alec Hargreaves 'Testimony, Co-authorship, and Dispossession among Women of Maghrebi Origin in France', *Research in African Literatures*, 37, 1 (2006), pp. 42–54.
75. Bellil refers to herself as a '*caillera*' on p. 22. The term *caillera* is an example of urban street slang known as *verlan*. It is an inversion of *racaille*, a term of abuse literally translated as 'rabble'.
76. Stoquart refers to Bellil in these terms in her preface, p. 16.
77. Amara, pp. 44–45.
78. Literally 'cellar-girls'. In other words, women who have sex or are raped in cellars or other public spaces in the *cité*. It is a term of abuse that, in most cases, could be translated as 'slut'.
79. Quoted in Gresh, p. 272.
80. Tarr, pp. 121–22.
81. Hargreaves, *Testimony, Co-authorship, and Dispossession*, p. 52.
82. See John R. Bowen, *Why the French don't like Headscarves: Islam, the State and Public Space* (Princeton, NJ: Princeton University Press, 2007), pp. 140–52.
83. For a discussion of the widespread rioting involving young men from the *banlieues* see *Quand les banlieues brûlent...: Retour sur les émeutes de novembre 2005*, ed. by Laurent Muchielli and Véronique Le Goaziou (Paris: La Découverte, 2006).
84. Tévanian, p. 17.
85. Adrian Favell, *Philosophies of Integration: Immigration and the Idea of Citizenship in France and Great Britain* (Basingstoke: Macmillan, 1998), p. 252.
86. Nacira Guénif-Souilamas, *Des 'beurettes' aux descendants d'immigrants nord-africains* (Paris: Hachette, 2002), p. 48.
87. Djavann, *Bas les voiles*, p. 68.

PART II

Looking out of the Veil

CHAPTER 3

The Republic's Broken Promise:
Fawzia Zouari's *Ce pays dont je meurs*

While narratives like Samira Bellil's *Dans l'enfer des tournantes* read as success stories that seem to validate the French model of integration, other texts authored by women of Muslim origin break the mould of conventional *beur* women's writing in order to reveal the bankruptcy of the integration process and the artifice of the *beurette* stereotype. Fawzia Zouari's *Ce pays dont je meurs*, a fiction about the fortunes of an Algerian immigrant family in France, is a case in point. While traditional *beur* women's narratives invest hope in the possibility of integration by representing the protagonist's traumatic but emancipatory 'choice' between France and her culture of origin, Zouari's novel insists on the impossibility of making such a 'choice' or, more exactly, that mainstream discourses of integration and emancipation work to create the illusion of such a 'choice' when, in reality, the life-choices available to certain sections of the population are extremely limited. This is not to say that all previous writing by *beur* women conforms to the conventional *beurette* story of emancipation. I do not wish to caricature '*beur* women's writing' in these terms, as many texts that form part of this corpus (even Bellil's) have an ambivalent relationship to dominant ideals of femininity and the French model of integration.[1] However, as we saw in the last chapter, these texts are vulnerable to recuperation by nativist feminist agendas that — by means of the editing and marketing process and by shaping reader reception — tend to overlook these nuances in order to press the story into a familiar pattern. I have chosen to focus on Zouari's text because it explicitly engages with and attacks the naïve optimism that frames the conventional *beurette* narrative revealing the new depths of disillusionment that have followed the dissipation of the *beur* movement and the dream of integration that it embodied.

Fawzia Zouari was born in Tunisia but came to France as a student to study comparative literature. She has since lived in Paris and has become an established journalist and writer, publishing both essays and works of fiction. While, on the one hand, her lack of *beur* credentials leaves her open to criticism from those desiring the supposed authenticity of testimonies such as Bellil's, on the other, her status as an established writer affords her the confidence in her writing ability that Bellil so clearly lacks, and spares her the need to seek validation and approval from majority-ethnic editors. It is this independence that perhaps allows, in part, for Zouari's more critical reading of nativist feminist discourses and stereotyping.

Ce pays dont je meurs was inspired by a *fait divers* that made the headlines in the French press in 1998, when a twenty-six-year-old woman of Algerian immigrant origin was found to have starved herself to death in a flat she shared with her sister. The sister, too, was found to be severely malnourished, but survived. Narrated from the perspective of the surviving sister, Nacéra Touirellil, the novel is a fictional reconstruction of the lives of the two young women and their parents as their hopes and fortunes spiral slowly towards disaster. The story of the Touirellil family's migration to France in many ways conforms to that of the stereotypical Algerian immigrant family. The father Ahmed is hired by a car factory and at first goes to France alone where he lives in a *cité de transit*. A few years later, when he upgrades to a small flat in an HLM (i.e. a council flat), he is joined by his wife Djamila and young daughter Nacéra. A second daughter, Amira, is born on French soil and her pale skin and self-identification as French distinguish her from the rest of the family who see themselves first and foremost as Algerian. Narrated by the elder sister, the story relates the different ways in which the members of the family attempt to negotiate a place for themselves in France, devoting particular attention to Amira, who ardently desires to be accepted as a fully integrated French citizen, yet is unable to fulfil this desire as, time and again, she finds herself blocked by racial, class and gender stereotypes. It is through the figure of Amira, her gradual withdrawal from the world, and her self-starvation, that the narrator conducts her fiercest criticism of a system that promises integration and acceptance to those marked as culturally or racially Other, yet indefinitely postpones the fulfilment of that promise.

The Unwelcome Reader

While Bellil's narrative and Stoquart's paratext place a high value on the approval of future readers which, they imagine, will signal the writer's acceptance into French society and entry into 'la vraie vie', Zouari's narrative strips the readers of their fantasized roles as judges, saviours and guardians of French identity. Zouari's fictional narrator does not lay her experience open to the readers' scrutiny nor does she esteem and fear their *vrai regard*. Instead, she draws attention to the readers' implicit voyeurism and, rather than investing the reader with the power to approve or reject her story, the reader is invoked as an intrusive and unwelcome presence.

Whereas Stoquart's introduction to Bellil's text effectively welcomes readers into Samira's world and invites them to pull up a seat, *Ce pays dont je meurs* opens with a scene of violent forced entry in which armed policemen push their way into the flat where Amira lies dying:

> Je les ai reconnus. Leur pas au cliquetis de ferraille. J'ai deviné la poche arrière de leur uniforme, que gonfle une arme frémissante. Leurs gestes mécaniques. Leurs cils ourlés de soupçons. Ils étaient penchés sur toi, ces policiers devant lesquels mon père a toujours baissé les yeux sans jamais avoir rien à se reprocher.

> [I recognized them. Their iron-toed step. I imagined the back pocket of their uniform, bulging with a shuddering gun. Their mechanical movements. Their suspicious brows. They were bent over you, those policeman, in front of whom my father always lowered his eyes though he had never done anything wrong.]
> (*Ce pays*, 9)

Stoquart constructs the reader of Bellil's narrative as a benevolent judge, but Zouari's text aligns the reader with the more hostile and aggressive forces of law. The arrival of the police, coinciding with the reader's entry into the world of the text, is not a welcome intervention, but is instead experienced as an unwanted intrusion into the sisters' lives and, as the police search the barren flat for some clue to the women's condition, the narrator comments:

> Ils veulent savoir. Mais savoir quoi? Pourquoi se mêlent-ils de notre sort, ces gens qui ne cherchent jamais à nous comprendre? Croient-ils que nous leur livrons la clef de nos existences aussi facilement que celle de nos tiroirs? (*Ce pays*, 10)

> [They want to know. But know what? Why are they meddling in our fate, these people who have never tried to understand us? Do they think that we will give them the keys to our lives as easily as those to our cupboards?]

Like the officers, the readers 'veulent savoir'. They want to know, to find out what happened. They want an explanation for this mysterious suicide. But the narrator draws a distinction between the desire to know and the desire to understand. While 'knowing' seems to imply a straightforward assimilation of facts into existing frames of reference, 'understanding' requires greater openness and flexibility. The policemen want to 'know' but do not seek to 'understand' and as a result, having rummaged through drawers and inspected empty cupboards, they leave none the wiser. Similarly, a reader who seeks no more than a vicarious journey into another's despair that will confirm rather than challenge their own assumptions, needs to look elsewhere.

As the narrator's question implies, the 'key' to the sisters' stories is deliberately withheld, denying the reader easy and immediate access to their interiority. Indeed, the reader is barred from the intimate relationship permitted by confessional narratives like Bellil's, and is instead positioned as an outsider or intruder on a private moment. While confessional narratives tend to address the reader as the primary recipient of the story, Zouari's narrator, Nacéra, instead addresses her ailing sister, 'Rappelle-toi, Amira' [Remember, Amira] (*Ce pays*, 11) and, although the narrator later switches to naming her sister in the third person, she frequently returns to a direct address maintaining this feeling of dislocation. We are not being consulted or asked for approval, rather we are listening in. In this way, Zouari's text subverts the rules of access implicit in more conventional examples of *beur* women's writing — rules of access that, as we have seen, resemble colonial women's fantasized intimacy with their Muslim 'sisters'. While a text like Bellil's promises the reader unlimited access to the experience of the narrator who, in turn, seeks to gain access to dominant society, Zouari's narrator leaves the reader out in the cold. This is not to say that we, as readers, are not made privy to details of the sisters' lives, but that we are positioned differently in relation to them and denied the privilege of judgement. Indeed, Zouari's narrator has, by this time, abandoned any desire to be accepted by French society and, rather than being constructed as the benevolent keepers of the keys to freedom and happiness, members of dominant French culture appear instead as the thuggish doormen to an exclusive club — a club to which the narrator no longer wishes to belong.

Refusing the Confessional Narrative

Colonial feminist discourse imagined that, were Muslim-Arab women free to speak for themselves, they would express a fervent desire to 'be like the French woman'. Nativist feminists appear to realize this fantasy by ostensibly allowing Muslim women to speak on their own terms while, as we have seen, reducing their stories to simplistic narratives of emancipation. The act of speaking for oneself is key to the conventional *beurette* narrative as it is by 'telling her own story' that the *beurette* is imagined to (re-)construct herself and to integrate. This self-construction is also part of the process of healing. Narratives like Bellil's are often framed by psychotherapeutic discourses that see confession as part of a cathartic process beneficial to the development of a secure and well-adjusted sense of self via the exorcism of trauma. Charting the individual's journey from a traumatized, dislocated self to a stable and secure one via the approbation of a sympathetic audience, the confessional narrative may be seen as the ideal expression of the French model of integration whereby the 'immigrant' is supposed to exorcize alien cultural references in order to achieve a secure, socially sanctioned personhood. For Bellil, her course of psychotherapy and the act of writing allowed her to strip away her previously disparaged self as a *fille des cités*, and be born into mainstream French culture as a 'normal' person with a 'normal' life: 'la vraie vie'.

However, in Zouari's novel, the act of confession is not characterized as a universally viable process of self-emancipation, but instead is represented as a culturally specific phenomenon. The very idea of salvation through writing or speaking before an audience is seen to be grounded in particular discourses (such as those of psychotherapy, autobiography and the Catholic tradition of confession) that Zouari's narrator associates with a French or, more broadly, Western cultural model. This specificity is most clearly observed by the Touirellils' Algerian relatives. The following exchange between Djamila and her sister (in which the sister accuses Djamila of being too harsh on her children) is especially revealing:

> Laisse-les tranquilles. Tu ne vas pas faire comme là-bas. Tu crois peut-être que je ne sais pas mais tu te trompes. Je tiens de mon amie Yvonne que les enfants n'ont aucune liberté en France. Tout leur est tracé à l'avance, consigné par les parents, les instituteurs, les surveillants, les éducateurs et Dieu sait quoi encore.
> C'est pour mieux les préparer à leur avenir répondait maman.
> Pour en faire des déséquilibrés oui! Je tiens d'Yvonne que les gosses subissent la visite de drôles de médecins qu'on appelle 'psychiatres' dès l'âge de cinq ans. On les force à tout confesser si tôt que, une fois grands, ils n'ont plus envie de parler. (*Ce pays*, 32)

> [Leave them be. Don't be like them over there. Perhaps you think I don't know, but you're wrong. My friend Yvonne tells me that children have no freedom in France. Everything is planned for them in advance, decided by their parents, teachers, guardians, educators and God knows who else.
> 'It's to prepare them for their futures', Maman said.
> To turn them into screw-ups more like! Yvonne tells me that kids have to visit these strange doctors called 'psychiatrists' from the age of five. They are forced to confess everything from such a young age that, by the time they grow up, they don't want to talk any more.]

To the Algerian aunt, the Western confessional tradition — rooted in Catholicism and given secular form in psychotherapy — appears quite alien. Furthermore, her caricature of French parenting as excessively controlling is suggestive of a French cultural model that demands a high degree of conformity. Indeed, as Bellil's text suggests, the confessional tradition plays a role in this drive towards cultural uniformity, the act of confession consolidating the self in line with dominant norms. But whereas Bellil's text equates the French cultural model with freedom, imagining French cultural norms as the very expression of personal emancipation, the aunt's remarks represent the French confessional tradition (and, by extension, the model of integration that it informs) as repressive.

These comments are later echoed by Nacéra on the subject of French schooling. She observes:

> Le corps enseignant voulait en tout cas que le moule de l'école soit solide et sans aspérité. Afin que tous les élèves en ressortent frappés du même sceau. Une fois adultes, ils pourraient se permettre toutes sortes de déviations, ce n'était plus l'affaire de leur institution. On leur faisait même comprendre que les meilleurs d'entre eux se lanceraient plus tard dans la course à l'originalité, feraient carrière dans la dissidence, sous le label incontestable de leur 'individualité'. (*Ce pays*, 68)

> [The teachers were adamant that the educational mould be solid and watertight, so that all students would be stamped with the same seal. Once they became adults, they would be allowed all kinds of deviations from the norm — that was no longer the business of the school. They were even given to understand that the best of them would throw themselves into the pursuit of originality, that they would make careers of dissent, under the indisputable sign of their 'individuality'.]

However, the 'course à l'originalité' that Nacéra wryly describes, does not constitute true dissent from cultural norms as it is fully incorporated within existing models of power in which conforming and 'being an individual' are one and the same.[2] The aunt's and Nacéra's remarks turn dominant French discourses of individual emancipation, prevalent during the *affaire du foulard*, on their head. Nativist feminists caricatured veiled girls as unthinking conformists, while fantasizing French culture, in particular French education, as the background for individual autonomy. Nacéra's remarks, however, reveal the injunction to conform that underpins such discourses. While the stereotypical *beurette* narrative figures the act of confession as a means of emancipation from oppressive North African cultural norms, Zouari's text suggests instead that confession constitutes the inscription of the self into a new set of (French) cultural matrices that are not necessarily more conducive to the exercise of autonomy.

Furthermore, confession implies a narcissistic individualism that Zouari represents as being in contradiction with Algerian-Muslim cultural norms. The notion that Arab-Muslim culture is somehow resistant to individualistic self-expression is quite a common trope in academic discussion of North African or migrant literature, in particular in relation to autobiography. However, as Debra Kelly argues, this is something of a simplification of Arab-Muslim culture that, though constructing the individual's relationship to the community quite differently to Western culture, is not devoid of notions of individuality and has autobiographical traditions of its own.[3] However, the notion of Algerian culture as resistant to individualism, invoked by Zouari and others, is nonetheless useful for understanding the situation of the migrant whose cultural, familial and affective bonds are threatened by a model of integration that privileges the individual over the community. This situation is poignantly described by Slimane Zéghidour who, in his moving account of North African migration to France, suggests the feelings of alienation experienced by the newly arrived Maghrebi immigrant, '[celui] qui ne disait jamais "je"' [He who never said 'I'], as he learns to define himself as an individual, brutally separated from '[le] magma du clan' [the magma of his clan].[4] Similarly, Nacéra's sense of self is inseparable from other members of her family. Distancing herself from the introspective nature of confessional narratives that suppose an emergent individuality, Nacéra adopts a speaking position that suggests a relational sense of identity. Although Nacéra is both the narrator and a central character in the novel, she rarely speaks directly of her own experience and her name is not divulged until late in the book. Instead, she is the invisible centre around which her family's story turns, narrating the actions of her sister and parents from the position of an observer. In the closing pages, she explains her narrative perspective as follows:

> Peut-on s'attarder sur ses propres blessures, lorsque vos proches en exhibent de plus profondes? Peut-on raconter sa propre vie lorsqu'elle ne tient que par celle des autres? Ai-je eu une vie, privée de parole, de choix, coincée entre vous tous, à vous regarder vous perdre, l'un après l'autre? (Ce pays, 142)

> [Can you linger on your own wounds, when those of your loved ones are deeper? Can you tell the story of your life when it is inseparable from those of others? Have I had a life, denied a voice, choices, caught between you all and losing you, one after the other?]

Nacéra is not so much a repressed subject, struggling to free herself from competing sets of cultural and community values, as somebody for whom the notion of an individual that is independent of community is an impossibility. There is no pre-existing subject that can be extracted, whole and autonomous, from its cultural context and slotted neatly into French society and, as a result, the integration process is experienced as humiliating, agonizing and is ultimately doomed to failure.

Nacéra's relational identity is not, however, only framed in terms of a supposedly anti-individualist Algerian culture in tension with French individualism. In fact, she is not so much a 'pre-modern' subject as a postmodern subject negotiating her situation in the world amongst a plurality of conflicting references. As Laborde remarks in her analysis of the *affaire du foulard*, the French model of integration is premised on a decontextualized notion of the subject that posits the individual as an autonomous, free-floating agent and fails to account for the ways in which a subject is necessarily constituted and constrained by the cultural discourses in which it is immersed.[5] Thus the injunction to simply throw off one's alien cultural references in order to integrate makes impossible and cruel demands of minority groups. The suffering this causes is frequently represented in *beur* women's texts via images of split or doubled bodies, expressing the cultural tug-of-war in which the protagonist feels caught. In some cases, this doubling is represented as a painful but necessary transition as the character projects herself, through role-play, towards the vision of emancipated womanhood to which she aspires. In this case, the protagonist's multiple embodiments come to represent the choices available to her, and her painfully split identity is healed when the protagonist ultimately chooses France over her family.[6] This is not to say that this resolution is arrived at easily however. As Ferrudja Kessas's *Beur's Story* suggests,[7] the seeming triumph of the *beurette* is often at the cost of a painful repression. In *Beur's Story* the protagonist Malika is doubled with her best friend Farida. Both girls struggle to resolve the contradictions in their lives but, whereas Malika makes compromises that allow her to survive, Farida loses hope and ultimately kills herself. Farida is the unacceptable difference that Malika has had to repress in order to integrate and she continues to haunt the protagonist long after her suicide. However, the stereotypical *beurette* narrative of the kind deployed during the *affaire* tends to gloss over these tensions, emphasizing resolution in the form of successful integration.

Zouari's text offers no such happy endings. Repeating familiar tropes of doubling, Amira is frequently described as a part of Nacéra's self. Speaking of their childhood, Nacéra remarks:

> [N]ous jouions ensemble comme des jumelles. Malgré ta peau blanche et la mienne si brune, personne n'aurait mis en doute que nous fussions sœurs. Une baguette invisible soumettait nos mouvements et nos jeux à la même ordonnance. Une forte ressemblance nous unissait, puisant sa réalité, non pas dans une similitude de traits, inexistante, mais peut-être dans l'intuition d'un destin identique. (*Ce pays*, 12–13)

> [We would play together like twins. Despite your white skin and the darkness of my own, nobody would have doubted we were sisters. An invisible baton conducted our movements and games to the same tune. We were united by a strong resemblance that was grounded, not in a physical similarity — there was none — but perhaps in the intuition of an identical destiny].

The double figure Nacéra–Amira does not suggest a possible resolution but works to reveal the impossibility of the sisters being accepted as *des françaises comme les autres* when they are perpetually defined in terms of their difference. Rather than representing a real (if traumatic) choice between Algerian heritage (as embodied in Nacéra's dark looks) or French society (as fetishized in Amira's white skin), each sister locks the other into an *impasse* in which neither can fantasize a full sense of belonging. Amira expresses an urgent desire to pass as French even at the cost of rejecting her family. However, her name, appearance and social class mean that she nonetheless continues to be perceived as different by those she most wishes to resemble, and she fails to escape the cultural stereotypes foisted upon her. Nacéra comments: 'Non, elle ne pouvait avoir un autre corps, ni changer de destin. Sous sa peau blanche coulait le sang de Djamila. Quelle que fût sa complicité avec ses camarades français, sa sœur s'appellerait toujours Nacéra' [No, she could not have another body or change her fate. Beneath her white skin, Djamila's blood flowed. However close she got to her French friends, her sister would always be called Nacéra] (*Ce pays*, 103). Locked in her difference and pushed to the margins, Amira is unable to fantasize herself as an authentic French subject however much she is willing to sacrifice.

However, in Zouari's narrative these margins are not idealized as spaces of freedom and possibility beyond the realm of dominant culture. Other narratives featuring *beur* protagonists, such as Leïla Sebbar's *Shérazade*,[8] lend themselves to readings that celebrate fluid, hybrid selves existing on the fringes of dominant culture. In such readings, the characters' situation between two or more sets of cultural norms allows them to playfully disrupt these norms through parody, mimicry and ironic appropriation, subverting claims to secure cultural identities and carving out spaces of agency.[9] But while Zouari's text disinvests in the notion that there is any such thing as an 'authentic' cultural identity to which one might fully belong, it remains painfully aware of the importance and necessity of *fantasizing* a sense of belonging, *especially* for the excluded, rejected and dismissed.

The Stakes of Identity

Ce pays dont je meurs suggests that one's investment in matters of 'identity' depends greatly upon whether one is positioned as a 'host' or as a 'guest' in a given society. In other words, the ways in which a person negotiates their claim to 'Frenchness' or 'Algerianness' depends upon whether that person is invested with the power to allocate identity, or whether he or she is reduced to outsider status and is obliged to seek validation from others. Whereas nativist feminist discourse implies that it is possible for young Maghrebi women to choose between their 'French' or 'Muslim-Arab' selves, Zouari's novel makes it clear that the stakes of transgressing the cultural identity to which one has been ascribed vary tremendously depending on one's socio-economic status and gender.

Despite their efforts to claim French culture as their own, the Touirellil sisters find that they are repeatedly positioned as 'guests' in France. At school, French culture is to be admired and aspired to but cannot be fully possessed. Nacéra remarks: 'Il y avait les héros de Zola et de Flaubert que nous pouvions aimer sans prétendre nous identifier à eux. Il y avait la beauté des sites et des monuments français qu'il convenait de louer, tout en reconnaissant qu'ils ne nous appartenaient pas' [There were the heroes of Zola and Flaubert that we allowed to admire but not identify with. There was the beauty of French heritage and monuments that we could praise, as long as we recognized that they did not belong to us] (*Ce pays*, 69). Indeed, even perfect mastery of French culture and language is not enough to guarantee belonging and the sisters, despite speaking faultless French, are denied the privileges that their neighbour Pierrot, a *Français de souche*,[10] takes for granted:

> Nous possédons à la perfection leur langue, Amira et moi, pourtant elle ne nous a point donné le privilège de forcer les barrages de ses administrations, ni de prétendre à de quelconque succès. Même Pierrot qui l'écorche, qui l'enroule, pire que maman, qui la salit de son haleine imbibée d'alcool, est persuadé de mieux la parler que nous. Parce qu'il la croit sienne, comme tout le reste... Mais comment faire entendre raison à Pierrot? Comme ma mère, il a sa logique à lui. Sans laquelle il ne serait pas en vie. (*Ce pays*, 140)
>
> [Amira and I speak their language perfectly, but they have never allowed us to play a part in their affairs nor to claim any success in doing so. Even Pierrot

who flays the language, who garbles it even worse than Maman does, who dirties it with his alcohol-breath, is convinced he speaks it better than we do. Because he thinks he owns it, like everything else... But how could Pierrot understand? Like my mother he has his own reasoning, without which he couldn't survive].

Whereas Pierrot has his 'logique à lui' and may fantasize himself as self-identical with a certain notion of 'Frenchness', the Touirellil sisters are denied a narrative in which they might ground their identity. Indeed, according to Nacéra, the French school curriculum fails to account for her family history by erasing the history of North African immigration to France. In her words: 'Il n'y avait rien dans l'histoire française qui coïncidât avec notre propre histoire et pourtant, il fallait y reconnaître toute l'Histoire' [There was nothing in French history that reflected our own history, yet we were expected to recognize it as History itself] (*Ce pays*, 69). The only valid cultural perspective is deemed to be French, but the sisters are positioned outside looking in, stranded in a cultural no man's land.

The impossibility of the Tourellils' fully fantasizing their belonging to either French or Algerian culture means that their every attempt to assert or claim an identity appears partial or inauthentic. Each member of the Touirellil family seems engaged in a series of role plays that emphasize their urgent desire to belong, while simultaneously underscoring the impossibility of realizing this desire. Amira tries to pass for a white French girl, renaming herself 'Marie' and inventing Italian origins to explain her exotic features: 'elle voulut à tout prix convaincre ses camarades de classe qu'elle leur était semblable. Française à cent pour cent,' [she wanted to convince her classmates, at all costs, that she was just like them. One hundred percent French] (*Ce pays*, 70). In her efforts to be accepted as one hundred per cent French, she goes so far as to adopt racist discourses and taunts Nacéra for her dark skin and curly hair: 'signes de sous-développement et de la barbarie' [signs of backwardness and barbarity] (*Ce pays*, 104). But her efforts to assimilate are in vain and her aggressive ultra-Frenchness assumes the dimensions of parody. Similarly, the 'Algerianness' of Nacéra's father Ahmed appears inauthentic when transferred to a French context. Whereas in Algeria, 'being Algerian' was an unquestioned part of everyday life, in France his 'Algerianness' is reconstructed as a defensive reaction to French hostility. Nacéra explains: 'il fallait aussi que papa jouât au père Arabe. Juste pour se rappeler qu'il n'était pas français' [Papa felt compelled to play the role of the Arab father. Just to remind himself that he wasn't French] (*Ce pays*, 38). Ahmed's occasional eruptions of violence or chauvinism are represented as a product, not of some authentic Algerian masculinity, but as a reaction to his sense of emasculation on French soil. The narrator remarks: 'Sous son toit, dans son lit, sur sa femme, il redevenait propriétaire de son destin. Il pouvait commander et se faire obéir' [Under his roof, in his bed, on top of his wife, he was once again the master of his own destiny. He could command and be obeyed] (*Ce pays*, 40). Just as Ahmed performs the role of the Arab patriarch in France, Djamila, on her visits to Alouane, insists that she and her daughters act the part of wealthy French women: 'Jouer aux personnages importants, aux filles riches' [Pretending to be important people, rich girls] (*Ce pays*, 92). Nacéra collaborates in this deception, weaving 'fictions occidentales' [Western fairytales] that transform their lives into a fantasy of wealth and happiness in an endeavour to impress her relatives. The family's performance of 'French' or 'Algerian' identities is always incomplete, partial, verging on parody.

They are, to borrow Homi Bhabha's well-known characterization, *almost the same but not quite*, '[a]lmost the same but not white*' [original emphasis].[11] In *The Location of Culture*, Bhabha describes a figure of colonial discourse that he calls the 'mimic man'. The mimic man is the result of a partial and flawed imitation of the colonizer: a colonized subject that mimes, through dress or behaviour, the authority of his colonial masters. In the context of British colonial rule in India, Bhabha describes him as 'the effect of a flawed colonial mimesis, in which to be Anglicized is emphatically not to be English' (*Ce pays*, 87). Nacéra and Amira are similarly positioned in relation to French society, their partial imitation of French identity excluding them from the benefits of full 'Frenchness'. They are not 'French' but 'Gallicized'. Bhabha sees subversive potential in the figure of the mimic man whose incomplete or parodic image of colonial culture is imagined to reveal the fiction of all claims to 'authentic' cultural identity, undermining the colonizer's authority. Drawing on thinkers like Bhabha, postcolonial literary critics have investigated the subversive potential of these marginal or hybrid identities that are not only imagined to destabilize 'us and them' narratives of cultural belonging, but to allow for the creation of new subjectivities that escape stereotypical subject positions. Mireille Rosello, for example, discusses what she calls 'performative encounters' described as a type of encounter (between individuals, communities or even nations) that 'coincides with the creation of new subject-positions rather than treating pre-existing (pre-imagined) identities as the reason for, and justification of, the protocol of encounter — whether it is one of violence or trust, respect or hostility'.[12] The encounters she describes entail a liberation from pre-existing cultural, historical and social scripts through their imaginative reinvention. In her account this does not so much produce new identities (as these too would run the risk of becoming petrified into stereotypes) as new ways of cohabiting and coexisting. However, as Rosello herself acknowledges, such encounters are 'more likely to be present in the realm of art and literature than in the practices of immigrants and binationals'.[13] Indeed, in Rosello's account, literature appears as a utopian space that allows for encounters that, though not impossible, are severely inhibited in the extra-textual world. As Rosello admits, pre-established relations of power in a given historical and social context and the violence with which they are defended troubles and limits the theoretical possibilities of creative encounters.

Ce pays dont je meurs draws attention to these limits. In Zouari's novel, old histori-cal scripts powerfully reassert themselves, capturing and crushing any potential for felicitous 'performative encounters'. This is made painfully clear in a scene in which Amira insults a black woman in the metro. From the reader's perspective, Amira's partial, imperfect French identity may, in line with Bhabha's observations, be imagined to subvert majority-ethnic claims to cultural authenticity. By performing French identity in a way that does not map perfectly onto supposedly essential and universal models of Frenchness, Amira unwittingly draws attention to the performativity of the 'original' model itself. In other words, 'Frenchness' appears not as an essence but as a repetition of gestures coded 'French'. So far, so troubling. However, within the world of the novel Amira's 'flawed' imitation of French culture does not disrupt but reinforces the cultural boundaries she is seeking to transgress. Insulting a black woman in an attempt to appear white, she fails to convince others of her 'Frenchness' and is exposed as a fake. In the eyes of her fellow passengers, her imitation of 'Frenchness' does not unsettle the boundaries of 'French identity' but instead secures them: if she has failed to convince, it is not, in the eyes of the other passengers, because there is no such thing as 'French identity', but simply because *she* is visibly 'not French'. Although the novel presents notions of authentic identity as fictions, Zouari nonetheless insists on the power of these fictions and the violence with which they are imposed. Amira's insults provoke the black woman to defend her own claim to 'Frenchness' threatening: 'Mais c'est à toi de déguerpir de ce pays, sale bougnole! Ici, c'est chez moi' [You're the one who should fuck off home, dirty Arab! This is *my* country], to which Amira responds: 'Je suis plus française que toi, tu entends, plus française que toi!' [I'm more French than you are, do you hear me, more French than you!] However her protests fall on deaf ears and none of the passengers comes to her aid as the woman begins to rain down blows: 'Après tout, c'était une affaire qui ne les concernait pas' [After all, it wasn't anything to do with them] (*Ce pays*, 105). The passengers' sense of their own 'Frenchness' is not troubled by this scene and they leave it to the black woman and the 'Arab' to fight over the terms of this desired identification. Exposed, humiliated and abandoned by the passengers who do not identify her as one of their own, Amira succumbs to her assailant's kicks and punches.

The playful appropriation and subversive parodying of dominant identity categories often celebrated in postcolonial literary criticism does not only, as Rosello concedes, lend itself more readily to the literary space, it is also a privilege. Whereas Amira's attempts to transgress cultural boundaries are fraught with physical and psychological risk, for integrated members of French society identities may be performed and discarded with great facility. Amira's performance of 'Frenchness' is quite literally a matter of life or death, but for the novel's majority-ethnic characters, role-play and cross-cultural experiments are performed out of amusement or curiosity. In many ways, the behaviour of these characters may be seen to resemble that of colonial travellers who disguised themselves in native costumes in order to vicariously experience indigenous culture. Like these travellers, Zouari's white French characters are able to flirt with the idea of foreignness from the security of a culturally 'superior' French identity. In her essay on cross-cultural dressing during the colonial era, 'On Veiling, Vision and Voyage',[14] Reina Lewis considers the behaviours of European women travellers who experimented with wearing Oriental women's dress and veils. The experience of veiling permitted, she maintains, a vicarious journey into Otherness that temporarily created the illusion of inhabiting the Other's identity. However, she argues, the pleasures of cross-cultural dressing are underpinned by a sense of racialized differentiation. Referring to Gail Low's work on the subject, Lewis argues that, for the Westerner, 'the pleasure of wearing an exotic and splendid "native" costume is enhanced by the knowledge of the white skin underneath the disguise.' When worn by the Western tourist, 'exotic' clothes are a superficial expression of an assumed identity and may always be removed when one has to revert to type and reassert one's racial or cultural superiority. The 'breaking of boundaries' implied by the adoption of the Other's guise is therefore transitory, superficial and, as Lewis concludes, 'predicated on a reinvestment in the very boundaries they cross.'[15] The cross–cultural experiments of Zouari's white, French characters may be seen in a similar light.

The clearest example is that of the sisters' schoolteacher, M. Eccars. On one level, M. Eccars appears as an absurd parody of the inspiring teacher-mentor figure common to many examples of *beur* women's writing.[16] He emphasizes his sympathy for Arab peoples and cultures believing, as a new-age Buddhist, that he was an Arab in a past life. He sees Amira's difference as enriching and, casting Amira in the role of the spirited *beurette*, he treats her as his class favourite encouraging her to study and '"comme les héros de Balzac" [...] à "conquérir Paris"' ['like a Balzacian hero' [...] to 'conquer Paris'] (*Ce pays*, 66). However, he is frustrated by Amira's refusal to conform to the role of enthusiastic protégée, and is outraged by her provocative questions: 'Ne trouvez-vous pas, que les Arabes manquent de civilization?' [Don't you think the Arabs are uncivilized?] (*Ce pays*, 70). As Amira senses, M. Eccars's flirtation with difference does not represent any real transgression of cultural boundaries but instead serves to strengthen them. His claim to share in Amira's supposed cultural heritage exoticizes Amira and marks her as Other to a 'normal' model of Frenchness. But whereas Amira finds herself trapped by stereotypes of Arab identity, M. Eccars is able to discard his assumed 'Arabness' and reassert himself as a native Frenchman. Just as colonial ladies were able to throw off their veils to end their masquerade, Eccars can revert to type and reassert himself as a member of the dominant order whenever it is convenient to do so. For example, as an educated member of the French middle class, Eccars allows himself to pose as an authority on Muslim-Arab culture and when Ahmed (angered by Eccars's interest in Amira) pays him a visit, he responds as follows:

> L'enseignant répliqua que notre paternel ne comprenait rien à l'Histoire, encore moins aux mystères de la Réincarnation.
> D'ailleurs, conclut-il, amer, à notre intention, pour que votre père accorde si peu d'importance à la sympathie que j'éprouve envers le peuple Arabe, c'est qu'il doit être un 'harki'. (*Ce pays*, 67)

> [The teacher replied that our father knew nothing about history, and even less about the mysteries of reincarnation.
> 'What's more,' he concluded with bitterness, 'if your father attaches so little importance to the esteem in which I hold the Arab people, it must be because he is a "harki".']

M. Eccars, as a member of the 'host' society, is invested with the power to name and condemn, to judge and exclude. As such, he asserts his own authority on the nature of both French and Muslim-Arab culture and brands Ahmed a traitor, a *harki*, neither a 'true' Algerian nor a 'true' Frenchman.[17] As it happens, Ahmed, unlike some of his friends and co-workers, is not a *harki*. However, Ahmed refuses to judge his colleagues, leaving such condemnation to 'professionals' like Eccars: 'L'ancien berger répugnait à juger. Il laissait les détenteurs de diplômes et les professionnels de l'accusation faire leur travail' [Judging others was repugnant to this old shepherd. He left that job to the diploma-holders and professional accusers] (*Ce pays*, 67). Whereas M. Eccars uses language as a weapon to name and frame others, Ahmed prefers silence. Another French character who flirts with Otherness is Amira's boyfriend Nicolas. Nicolas is twice Amira's age and the editor of a political journal. He impresses her with his political rhetoric, grand ideals and apparent desire to defend the dispossessed. However, at home he treats Amira like a domestic and sexual slave. Nacéra comments:

> Quelle ironie du sort! Alors que ma sœur n'aspirait qu'à une chose, être française jusqu'à la pointe de ses pieds, son Nicolas n'avait qu'une envie: trouver en elle l'Arabe obéissante, une langoureuse houri qui céderait à ses caprices et comblerait ses fantasmes. Même au pire de nos harems d'antan, je ne pense pas que les nôtres eurent à subir ces amours perverses. (*Ce pays*, 103)

> [What a twist of fate! While my sister had one desire, to be French from head to toe, Nicolas's one wish was to reduce her to the obedient Arab woman, to the celestial virgin who would yield to his every caprice and fulfil his every fantasy. Even in the most depraved of our harems of yesteryear, I don't think our women ever had to submit to such perversion.]

For Nicolas, Amira's perceived Otherness is part of a fantasy of power in which he allows himself to play the part of the Arab patriarch or the white male colonizer. Like M. Eccars, Nicolas constructs cultural Otherness as part of a fantasy scenario that may be assumed or discarded at will.

Zouari's awareness of the social, economic and cultural inequalities that affect one's level of conscious investment in discourses of identity may be seen to provide a critique of postmodern assertions that we are *all* nomads, inevitably at odds with ourselves in today's world and irretrievably separated from any stable sense of self. An example of this thinking is found in Julia Kristeva's *Etrangers à nous-mêmes* [*Strangers to Ourselves*],[18] in which the author argues that the preoccupation with sociological analyses of indigenous populations' relations to foreigners has prevented us from paying attention to the universal psychic dynamics that shape those relations. Analysing relations with foreigners in terms of a 'foreignness within', Kristeva imagines a world in which the acceptance of our own internal difference would help bring about a transformation of subjectivity (not dissimilar to that imagined by Rosello) that would permit greater tolerance of others' alterity. However, Winifred Woodhull's analysis may be more apposite in its insistence that '[b]y focusing on foreignness within and dissociating it from social inequalities, Kristeva ends by ignoring the foreigners whose foreignness, unlike her own, sparks hostility and violence in France'.[19] The stakes of defining and coming to terms with difference vary depending upon whether one is, like Kristeva, an integrated European intellectual living and working in Paris or, like members of the Touirellil family, an economic migrant living on the fringes of society.

Mariannes manquées

Whereas nativist feminist discourses tend to privilege cultural difference as a means of glossing over socio-economic divides, Zouari's text highlights the socio-economic inequalities between women. Zouari's narrator undermines the imagined solidarity between French Muslim women and majority-ethnic French women that is an important feature of many examples of '*beur* women's writing'. Soraya Nini's *Ils disent que je suis une beurette* [*They say I'm a beurette*] and Ferrudja Kessas's *Beur's Story* both depict a productive and emancipating relationship between the protagonist and a female teacher, while Samira Bellil and Aïcha Benaïssa establish similar relationships with female editors and psychotherapists. Carrie Tarr detects the same patterns in films like *Marie-Line* and *Chaos*.[20] In such cases, the female mentor, echoing colonial feminist concerns, develops an intimate maternal relationship with her protégée who is gradually pressed into the mould of French 'femininity' producing a solidarity that appears to transcend race and class.

However, no such solidarity exists in Zouari's text. With the exception of Nacéra's friend and colleague Geneviève, relations between French and migrant women are ones of power, determined by socio-economic status. This is clearest in the relationship between Djamila and her employer Mme Sentini. After Ahmed's death, Djamila is forced to find work as a cleaning lady in order to make ends meet. Djamila is from a well-respected, middle-class Algerian family where the women are expected to perform domestic and maternal duties in the home while the men go out to work. Consequently, the move to France entails a shift from middle to working class, and the necessity of going out to earn a living is experienced as humiliating rather than emancipating. Nacéra remarks: 'Elle avait l'impression de mendier. De lacérer le corps de Fattoum [her mother], depuis longtemps silencieux. De dénuder son corps et son âme' [She felt like she was begging, lacerating the body of her mother Fattoum, who had fallen silent long ago. Stripping her body and her soul] (*Ce pays*, 86). Mme Sentini exhibits racist views and exploits Djamila's economic vulnerability by employing her illegally, paying in cash and imposing long hours. There is no sense of sisterhood or mutual understanding, rather their relationship is defined by the race and class divides that separate them.

Although the *beurette* stereotype appears to promise integration and acceptance, the social and economic barriers that stand between young Muslim women and the vision of French femininity promoted by nativist feminism are, in Zouari's account, insurmountable. The suffering endured by the Touirellil women as a result of their poverty and low social status in France is highlighted by Zouari's recycling of stereotypical images of the Muslim woman as 'oppressed'. Whereas images of Muslim women as sequestered, veiled and denigrated are a staple ingredient of nativist feminist discourse, Zouari's representations of Muslim women recast nativist feminist imagery to point to Muslim women's oppression at the hands of the French system. To begin with, the Touirellil women's sequestration and isolation are not so much the result of Muslim-Arab patriarchy as a consequence of their material poverty. Djamila, for example, is forced to stay in the apartment, not because her husband prevents her from leaving, but because she has bad legs, cheap shoes and lives in a high rise apartment block with a broken lift. Similarly, Amira is described as isolated, not in a harem but 'dans un minuscule bureau' [in a tiny office] (*Ce pays*, 118), where she is sexually harassed by her French boss. Furthermore, whereas nativist feminist discourse encourages women to emancipate themselves by throwing off the veil in favour of lipstick and jeans, dressing like a French woman does not liberate Djamila but, like Fanon's newly unveiled woman, alienates her from her body: 'Quelques centimètres en moins de la gandoura traditionnelle et elle n'était plus elle-même. Un autre voile, d'étrangeté celui-là, venait d'être jeté sur elle' [A few centimetres shorter than the traditional gandoura and she wasn't herself anymore. Another veil, a foreign one, had just been thrown over her] (*Ce pays*, 20). In this instance, Zouari's use of veil imagery attributes the oppressive qualities usually associated with the Muslim veil to Western dress codes. Zouari also reinvents the image of the tattooed Algerian woman. Djamila's forehead is marked with traditional blue tattoos and her hands are often painted with henna. However, after months working for Mme Sentini, Djamila's hands are scrubbed free of henna and are instead 'tatou[ées] de détergents' [tattooed with detergents] (*Ce pays*, 107).

Zouari's relocation of the vocabulary and imagery that usually define Muslim-Arab women as victims of a repressive patriarchy underscores the ways in which such women also suffer as a result of their socio-economic situation in France. The nativist feminist opposition 'oppressed Muslim woman / emancipated French woman' is destabilized, undermining the claim that French womanhood represents a universal ideal accessible to all. Indeed, in Zouari's text, the fantasy of the emancipated and integrated *beurette* exists as a tantalizing mirage that reinforces a perverse logic of integration that forces ethnic-minority women into a permanent position of debt vis-à-vis French society.

Silence and Sequestration

Unable to fantasize a secure sense of identity from which to speak, the sisters are consigned, and consign themselves, to oblivion. Indeed, the sisters' response to their seemingly inevitable reduction by others to racial and cultural types is not to justify their presence or loudly claim their right to acceptance, but to fall silent. To attempt to justify their existence on French soil is simply to continue to play the game that keeps them subject to French approval. Nacéra describes her family's contact with the French authorities in the following terms:

> Chaque démarche nous obligeait à justifier de nouveau de notre identité, de nos sources de revenus, de la bonne marche de notre foyer [...]. Je voyais, quant à moi, voler en éclats l'illusion que nous caressions de passer pour des gens d'ici. De nous mettre dans la perspective du regard aimant de la République. (*Ce pays*, 78)

> [At each step we had to justify ourselves all over again; our identities, our sources of income, the wholesomeness of our household [...]. As for me, I saw our cherished illusion shatter into tiny pieces. Our illusion that we might one day pass for locals, that the Republic might cast a benevolent eye upon us.]

Their response is ultimately to withdraw into themselves and say nothing at all. The therapeutic value of Bellil's confessional narrative is expressed through a certain verbosity and investment in language, but silence is a strong motif throughout Zouari's novel. Although on one level their silence makes them complicit in their own exclusion, on another it refuses the logic whereby people of immigrant origin are denied representation in French society, yet are expected to continue to demand acceptance. Although the Touirellils are in many ways victims of the French system, they are not entirely passive.

As the novel progresses and the family lose hope of integrating successfully, the Touirellil women leave the apartment less and less frequently until they have entirely imprisoned themselves. Nacéra and her sister are no longer willing to participate in a game they know they cannot win and, despite Geneviève's efforts to encourage Nacéra to claim benefits and insist on her rights vis-à-vis the French state, Nacéra has the impression that to do so would simply reduce her to a beggar:

> [J]e n'étais plus armée pour ces démarches. Comme maman en son temps, j'aurais eu l'impression de m'abaisser à mendier [...]. Je tremblais à l'idée d'être regardée de haut par le personnel des services sociaux. Je répugnais à répondre aux questions, à élucider le mystère des factures et des avis d'échéance, à fournir des attestations qui garantiraient mon honnêteté [...]. Par fierté je ne pouvais pas réclamer, solliciter, contester, même auprès de destinataires anonymes. (*Ce pays*, 130)

> [I was no longer strong enough to deal with the procedures. Like Maman when she was alive, I would have felt like I was lowering myself, begging [...]. I shuddered at the thought of being looked down upon by the social-workers. I was repelled by the idea of answering questions, of explaining the mystery of the unpaid bills and unheeded warnings, of providing references that would prove my honesty [...]. Out of pride I couldn't bring myself to plead, solicit, dispute, even anonymously.]

The sisters' withdrawal from French society and their refusal to accept the role that has been assigned to them infuriates their neighbour Pierrot. He exclaims:

> Je ne comprends pas! Vous refusez toute aide sans raison. Vous vous enfermez alors que personne ne vous veut de mal. Et après, on dira qu'en France on meurt de misère. On dira même que c'est par racisme que nous vous avons laissées périr. C'est ça ce que vous voulez, n'est-ce pas, c'est ça? (*Ce pays*, 133)

> [I don't understand! You refuse all help for no reason. You shut yourselves away when nobody means you any harm. And then they say that people die of poverty in France. They even say that we've let you die because we're racists. That's what you want, isn't it? That's what you want.]

Pierrot's disgust, it seems, arises from the sense that the sisters have upset the rules of hospitality that govern France's relationship to its immigrant Others by ungratefully refusing their role as guests. Indeed, for Pierrot, the Touirellil family are not casualties of the French system, rather they are outsiders; intruders who have 'entaché[es] l'honneur de la France' [tarnished the honour of France] (*Ce pays*, 148). Like the policemen who desire to 'know' but do not care to 'understand', Pierrot is unable to assimilate the sisters' behaviour to his own prejudices and assumptions and so responds with violent outrage.

The sisters' refusal is embodied in the starving figure of Amira. Having failed
to pass as French, Amira destroys the body that she feels has betrayed her. Though
she cannot control the way in which others perceive her, she can control what she
consumes, and her anorexia (it is diagnosed as such) is explained as an expression
of her desire to refuse both her culture of origin, and the society that rejects her:
'Elle ne connaissait pas assez la culture et la langue de ses origines pour y trouver
un refuge. Et la France ne lui ouvrait pas les bras. Alors elle vomissait tout. Le passé
de ses parents et son propre avenir' [She didn't know the culture and language of
her origins well enough for them to give her refuge. And France did not open its
arms to her. So she vomited everything. Her parents' past and her own future] (*Ce
pays*, 108). Destroying her body seems to be the only way of claiming ownership
of it and refusing to subscribe to the false promises of integration in which she had
previously invested. Indeed, Nacéra observes that ultimately Amira 'savait regarder
mieux que nous' [was more lucid than the rest of us]. She is represented as the most
clear-sighted of the Touirellil family as, unlike the others, '[e]lle avait vue l'impasse'
[she had seen the hopelessness of the situation] (*Ce pays*, 107) and had understood
that she would never belong. Although Amira, born on French soil, should have
been the better adjusted of the two sisters, she is in fact the most vulnerable as she
is prevented from identifying fully with either Algeria or France, ultimately sliding
into oblivion. Nacéra comments:

> Finalement, la plus Algérienne de nous tous, c'était elle. Quel était ce paradoxe?
> Ni nos parents, ni moi-même, nous ne voulions nous rebeller contre ce pays
> d'adoption. Nous nous efforcions seulement d'y trouver une place. D'y passer
> des jours tranquilles. Mais Amira, c'était différent. Parce qu'elle est née ici. (*Ce
> pays*, 107)

> [Ultimately, she was the most Algerian of all of us. How can this paradox
> be explained? Neither our parents, nor myself wanted to rebel against our
> adoptive country. We were only concerned to find our place and get by, to live
> peacefully. But for Amira it was different. She was born here.]

For Amira, death is the only way out of this *impasse* and marks a perverse victory,
avenging 'le peu d'amour que la France lui portait, le peu de place qu'elle lui
concédait' [the little love that France had shown her, the little room it had made
for her] (*Ce pays*, 107)

Whereas nativist feminist representations of the *beurette* imagine the protagonist
to be torn between two clearly identified cultures, becoming whole only when she
chooses to conform to a reified vision of French femininity, Zouari's novel suggests
that full, successful integration remains beyond the reach of many of France's cultural
Others, however much they may desire it. Whereas the fiction of authentic cultural
belonging may be experienced as truth by those who, like Pierrot, are positioned
as 'hosts', it remains an unrealizable dream for those existing on the margins.
Although Pierrot is temporarily troubled by the sisters' seemingly incomprehensible
behaviour, his position of relative privilege allows him to reassert 'sa logique à lui'
and the final image we have of him is one of self-assured 'Frenchness', his grotesque
complacency contrasting sharply with the pained, emaciated figure of Amira:
'Pierrot caresse son ventre. Il se cale dans son fauteuil et de sa gorge remonte un

renvoi de vin acide et de foie gras' [Pierrot rubs his belly. He wedges himself in his armchair and belches up an acid trace of wine and foie gras] (*Ce pays*, 144–45).

The final point I shall make looks towards some of the issues I will explore in the next chapter. Zouari's novel emphasizes that the Touirellil family's suffering is not so much the responsibility of specific racist individuals, but is instead the result of a complex web of prejudice and poverty that appears inescapable. Furthermore, the banality of the family's problems means that they are not perceived by French society as exceptional or worthy of intervention, but are instead tolerated as an inevitable part of the system. Amira remarks:

> Si au moins nous avions des motifs clairs pour militer, ou revendiquer des droits surtout [...]. Nous n'avons même pas un frère tombé sous les balles des flics, par erreur. Poussé dans la Seine, par mépris. Nous aurions bénéficié d'une solidarité, même chez les Français. (*Ce pays*, 116)

> [If we had only had some clear reasons to fight back, or to claim our rights above all [...]. We didn't even have a brother who had been accidently gunned down by the police or spitefully pushed into the Seine. Then we would have felt some solidarity, even from the French.]

Indeed, unless they are prepared to assume the stereotype of the victimized Algerian woman, there is no place for them at all: 'Il aura fallu des victimes algériennes pour acheter le bon voisinage de Pierrot. Amira a dit qu'on nous aimait morts ou martyrs. Le passeport de la douleur ou rien. Faire compatir pour exister' [We would have had to have been Algerian victims to buy Pierrot's sympathies. Amira said that they liked us dead or as martyrs. The victim-ticket, or nothing. Surviving on pity] (*Ce pays*, 118). The next chapter will consider two texts by Zahia Rahmani, *Moze* and '*Musulman' Roman*, in which the protagonists, like the Touirellil family, are disempowered and reduced to the status of outsiders or beggars by a sinister French bureaucracy. Rahmani's novels, however, have a broader scope than *Ce pays dont je meurs* and invite a consideration of the ways in which a modern democracy like France is able to tolerate the existence of citizens within French territory who, like the Touirellils, do not fully benefit from the rights and privileges supposedly guaranteed by citizenship.

Notes to Chapter 3

1. See, for example, Anissa Talahite's analysis of *beur* women's texts that construct alternative discourses of identity that challenge essentialist definitions of ethnicity and gender in 'Constructing Spaces of Transition: 'Beur' Women Writers and the Question of Representation', in *Women, Immigration and Identities in France*, ed. by Jane Freedman and Carrie Tarr (Oxford: Berg, 2000), pp. 103–19.
2. As Sivagami Subbaraman remarks in an article about the role of dress codes in the production of identity, ethnic identities have acquired fashionable status amongst Western consumers and may be playfully worn and discarded. But, although consumerism counsels a constantly updated individualism, this remains resolutely at the level of style and does nothing to undermine a fundamental conformity to dominant cultural models. Sivagami Subbaraman, 'Catalog-ing Ethnicity: Clothing as Cultural Citizenship', *Interventions*, 1 (1999), 572–89 (p. 583).
3. Debra Kelly, *Autobiography and Independence: Self and Identity in North African Writing* (Liverpool: Liverpool University Press, 2005), pp. 16–37.

4. Slimane Zéghidour, *Le Voile et la bannière* (France: Hachette, 1990), p. 140.

5. Laborde, p. 140.

6. See, for example Soraya Nini's protagonist Samia who identifies with the fictional heroines of the novels she reads. Soraya Nini, *Ils disent que je suis une beurette* (Paris: Fixot, 1993).

7. Ferrudja Kessas, *Beur's story* (Paris: L'Harmattan, 1994).

8. Leïla Sebbar, *Shérazade, 17 ans, brune, frisée, les yeux verts* (Paris: Stock, 1981).

9. See for example Anne Donadey, *Recasting Postcolonialism: Women Writing Between Worlds* (Portsmouth, NH: Heinemann, 2001), pp. 95–141.

10. *Français de souche* literally means a Frenchman of French stock. It might be translated as 'a born and bred Frenchman'.

11. Homi K. Bhabha, *The Location of Culture*, 2nd edn (London: Routledge, 2003), p. 89. First published in 1994.

12. Mireille Rosello, *France and the Maghreb: Performative Encounters* (Gainesville: University Press of Florida, 2005), p. 1.

13. Ibid, p. 36.*f*

14. Reina Lewis, 'On Veiling, Vision and Voyage: Cross-Cultural Dressing and Narratives of Identity', in *Feminist Postcolonial Theory: A Reader*, ed. by Reina Lewis and Sara Mills (Edinburgh: Edinburgh University Press, 2003), pp. 520–41.

15. Ibid, p. 528.

16. Both Soraya Nini's *Ils disent que je suis une beurette*, and Ferrudja Kessas's *Beur's Story* feature French teachers who encourage and inspire their pupils. Samira Bellil and Aïcha Benaïssa may also be seen to have a relationship of tutelage with their editors Josée Stoquart and Sophie Ponchelet respectively.

17. The term *harki* refers to Muslim Algerians who served as auxiliaries with the French army during the War of Independence. The term is also used as a derogatory expression within Algeria and amongst some of the Franco-Algerian community to mean 'collaborator' or 'traitor'. I will investigate the specific situation of the *harkis* and their families more closely in the next chapter.

18. Julia Kristeva, *Etrangers à nous-mêmes* (Paris: Fayard, 1988).

19. Winifred Woodhull, *Transfigurations of the Maghreb: Feminism, Decolonization and Literatures* (Minneapolis: University of Minnesota Press, 1993), p. 92.

20. Tarr, pp. 153–66.

CHAPTER 4

Homo sacer and the Muslim Pariah: Zahia Rahmani's *Moze* and *'Musulman' Roman*

During the *affaire du foulard*, those in favour of the ban appealed to republican democratic principles in order to bolster arguments that effectively denied certain citizens their democratic rights. Whereas some French citizens were endowed with the authority to speak in the name of 'France' and its cultural and philosophical heritage, others, despite their citizenship status, were marked as undesirable in their non-conformity to a certain notion of 'Frenchness'. In her two novels *Moze* and *'Musulman' Roman*, Zahia Rahmani investigates the ways in which modern democratic discourses of human rights and citizenship may, in certain circumstances, betray themselves by working in the service of nativist notions of cultural identity that protect the rights of some, while denigrating and excluding others on supposedly humanist grounds. More specifically, she investigates what she sees as democratic societies' production of pariahs or what she calls *hommes bannis*: human beings who are forced to live beyond the 'normal' functioning of the law, existing on the margins of democratic notions of humanity and citizenship.[1] Like Zouari's protagonists, Rahmani's characters do not conform to dominant notions of French identity and citizenship, and are forced to contend with cultural, social, economic and juridical institutions that mark them as outsiders. But whereas Zouari focuses on the texture and minutiae of oppression, Rahmani's texts address the larger structures of political power that govern France's, and more generally the West's, relationships to its cultural others. In particular, her construction of *l'homme banni* as a figure of exception and exclusion exposes the ambiguities and failures of democratic rights-based discourses and the institutions that sustain them.

Moze and *'Musulman' Roman*, though not autobiographies in the conventional sense, both draw explicitly and profoundly on the writer's personal experiences, combining prose, poetry and dramatic dialogue to create a collage of dreams, reflections, anecdotes and memories that explore the sensations of loss, shame and revolt experienced by the author, her family and, by implication, the many others like them who exist on the margins of French society. Published in 2003, *Moze* is offered as a testimony to the life and death of the author's father, Moze, who killed himself on Remembrance Day 1991, after visiting the local war memorial. Moze was a *harki*; a Muslim Algerian recruited to fight for the French during the War of Independence. When Algerian forces began to massacre the *harkis* following France's defeat, Moze and his family were forced to seek refuge in a Red Cross refugee camp (where Zahia was born) and were later transferred to a camp for *harkis* at St-Maurice de l'Ardoise. The story of Moze, as told by his daughter, is that of *l'homme banni*; a man banished from his country of origin and abandoned by his country of adoption. Moze and his family are seen as traitors in Algeria, but feel betrayed by a France that forces them to live on the edges of society. In her novel, Rahmani incorporates a series of real and imagined dialogues with members of her family and government officials, that investigate and condemn what she calls 'la fabrique du paria' [the fabrication of pariahs],[2] the production of 'undesirable' men and women who are relegated to the margins of history, society and politics.

Whereas *Moze* focuses specifically on France's failure to live up to its self-image as the *pays des droits de l'homme* in its treatment of the *harkis*, Rahmani's second book *'Musulman' Roman* is firmly situated in a post-9/11 context, and takes into account the ways in which global politics impact on the lives of Muslims and other denigrated or excluded populations worldwide. As the inverted commas of the title indicate, *'Musulman' Roman* explores the meaning of the term *Musulman* [Muslim] as a generic, politically loaded identity label, the fictionalized characterization of which is suggested by the second part of the title: *Roman* [Novel]. The diffuse action of the story, narrated through a series of fragmented anecdotes, dialogues and dreams, is played out against a surreal dystopian landscape patrolled by nameless soldiers and government officials who repeatedly hunt down, imprison and interrogate the narrator, and force her to assume identities and stereotypes that are not of her making. In opposition to this narrative of persecution is a tentative narrative of self-creation, whereby the narrator relearns her mother tongue, Berber, and investigates her Algerian cultural and religious history in an attempt to find a voice of her own. The difficulties of finding a voice with which to bear witness to excluded and marginalized experience is explored in both texts but, as I shall argue in the concluding section of this chapter, this is balanced by a belief in the political necessity of testimony however fragmentary, partial or inadequate.

I will read Rahmani's novels in relation to the Italian philosopher Giorgio Agamben's understanding of modern Western power. Agamben's enduring interest in the status of individuals who fall outside the boundaries of dominant notions of the human being or citizen, yet whose fate is nonetheless tied to the powers that have excluded them, makes him the obvious critical partner for Rahmani. Both writers explore the relationship between the human being and the citizen, the living body and the state and imagine, in their own ways, a biopolitical dystopia at the heart of modern Western democracy. But there are also significant differences in focus. As I shall explain, Agamben imagines the Nazi concentration camps' separation of human beings endowed with rights from those who can be stripped of their rights and reduced to vermin, as paradigmatic of modern power. Camps also play a crucial role in Rahmani's work, but the camp model that Rahmani evokes is not so much the Nazi death camp as the *camps de regroupement*, created by the French during the Algerian war, and the *cités de transit* where migrant workers were housed on arrival in France. As previously mentioned, Rahmani spent her early years firstly in refugee camps then in a *cité de transit* and, like Agamben, the camp environment provides her with a key frame of reference. However, whereas the purpose of the Nazi camps was ultimately to reduce their inhabitants to the status of non-humans and exterminate them, the camps that Rahmani refers to, though they were the cause of atrocious suffering, were officially represented as humane initiatives and were, in some cases, underpinned by humanitarian concerns.

In his detailed study of the *camps de regroupement*, Michel Cornaton reveals the disastrous effects of this policy on the Algerian population. The term *camp de regroupement* refers to a variety of differently organized enclosures, camps and centres used during the War of Independence to round up, survey and control the Algerian population in an effort to isolate militants. During the war, the French army herded people into trucks and forcibly relocated them, obliging them to abandon their homes and leave their farms to ruin. Conditions in these centres were often cramped and sometimes nothing was provided for the inhabitants who were left to die of hunger and cold. As a result, the camps had the unintended effect of increasing support for the FLN amongst the native population. So, between 1959 and 1961 French policy shifted towards a more humanitarian approach in a bid to win the hearts and minds of the Algerian people. 'La politique des mille villages' [The 1000 villages initiative] was intended to transform the *centres de regroupement* into functioning villages with the necessary facilities and services. However, as Cornaton reports, a combination of poor organization and lack of motivation meant that humanitarian concerns were short-lived and were often never applied.[3] Although these centres were represented by the French authorities as places of refuge to which Algerians turned voluntarily, Cornaton is quite clear that any mention of 'regroupement volontaire' is entirely inappropriate given that people only came to the camps by military force or by force of circumstance.

As a *harki*, Rahmani's father and his family were forced to take refuge in camps provided by the Red Cross and the French state at the end of the war. But, despite the ostensibly benevolent purpose of these camps, Rahmani sees a cruel dynamic at work that she implicitly identifies as paradigmatic of France's (and more broadly the West's) relationship to its cultural others. While the logic of the Nazi camps sought to reduce its inhabitants to non-human vermin to be destroyed, Rahmani's camps are embedded in French colonial and postcolonial contexts that insist on the humanist, inclusive, assimilationist nature of their projects. However, as I shall seek to show, Rahmani's camp inhabitants are kept under the constant threat of social, civic and political annihilation and kept on a knife-edge between assimilation and exclusion. As we have seen with regards to colonial and neocolonial feminist discourses, this tension between exteriority and interiority, sameness and otherness is a hallmark of colonial power. Before moving on to a consideration of the texts, however, it would be useful to sketch out some of the key dimensions of Agamben's thought.

Giorgio Agamben and the Dynamics of Modern Power

In *Homo Sacer: Sovereign Power and Bare Life*,[4] Agamben combines Michel Foucault's analyses of biopower with Hannah Arendt's investigation of totalitarian structures and the Nazi concentration camps to produce an enquiry that situates itself at the intersection of biopolitical and juridico-institutional models of power. Foucault argues that a fundamental characteristic of the modern era is the inclusion of bare life (the simple fact of living) in the mechanisms of state power, transforming politics into what he calls biopolitics. Whereas in pre-modern society the sovereign ruler could assert power over his people by torturing or destroying their bodies at will, modern forms of power work in a more diffuse way, regulating the private lives of its subjects from cradle to grave by subjecting them to discourses of health, happiness and personal fulfilment. Power, in Foucault's terms, is productive and the state produces amenable citizens, not by violently disciplining their bodies, but by granting them the right to pursue the fulfilment of their desires. As Agamben explains, the rights of the individual — as first consecrated by the *Déclaration des droits de l'homme et du citoyen* [Declaration of the Rights of Man and of the Citizen] — make of the individual citizen not only a subject but an object of state power:

> [T]he spaces, the liberties and the rights won by individuals in their conflicts with central powers always simultaneously prepared a tacit but increasing inscription of individuals' lives within the State order, thus offering a new and more dreadful foundation for the very sovereign power from which they wanted to liberate themselves.[5]

In modern biopolitics, the citizen, that is to say the bearer of rights, can only be constituted as such by inscribing her body into the state order. In other words, the acquisition of rights and liberties supposedly guaranteed by citizenship also makes the individual dependent on the institutions that grants these liberties, and 'bare life', while supposedly achieving emancipation, is simultaneously placed under the care, control and scrutiny of the state. In this way, 'bare life' becomes what Agamben calls 'qualified life' — human life with rights guaranteed by citizenship.

In Agamben's analysis, the state's investment in the natural lives of its citizens constitutes both the making and unmaking of modern democracy. Although modern democratic society imagines itself to be diametrically opposed to totalitarian forms of power, Agamben argues that in fact, modern democracy and totalitarianism share fundamental similarities in their distinction between bare life and qualified life creating the possibility of a human being who, stripped of citizenship, is socially and politically dead while remaining biologically alive. This thought is most clearly articulated in Agamben's notion of *Homo sacer*. *Homo sacer* is a figure of ancient Roman law that refers to a man, judged on account of a crime, yet whose existence is deemed so worthless that he is unfit for sacrifice and may be killed without his killing constituting homicide. Although he is a living being, his life is so devoid of human value that its extinction would amount to neither sacrifice nor murder. Existing outside both human and divine law, *Homo sacer* cannot be killed in conformity with the procedures sanctioned by society (i.e. executed or sacrificed), but may instead be killed with complete indifference, as one might crush a louse. For Agamben, this particularity of ancient Roman law, far from being an antique relic, may provide a model for understanding the ways in which modern societies continue to produce human beings who are excluded from approved notions of humanity and are consequently deprived of any workable notion of human rights.

In Agamben's analysis, the separation of bare life from qualified life that makes *Homo sacer* possible is inscribed in modernity from the outset. Indeed, the founding document of modern democracy, the *Déclaration des droits de l'homme et du citoyen*, provides not only the blueprint for a democratic organization of power but also the conditions for modern totalitarianism, in that it introduces the notion of the citizen as independent from the concept of man. Agamben notes the 'striking fact' that 'at the very moment in which native rights were declared to be inalienable and indefeasible, the rights of man in general were divided into active rights and passive rights.'[6] Women, children, the insane and prisoners, among others, were excluded from full, active citizenship and only granted passive rights. Thus, citizens were separated out into a hierarchy whereby the citizenship of some functioned more fully than that of others. The end point of this 'logic of separation' is *Homo sacer*: a human being with no human rights.

Nazism represents, in Agamben's view, the extreme conclusion of this 'logic of separation' that distinguishes the political life of the citizen from bare life. Nazism maps the question 'what is/is not German?' onto the question 'what is/is not human?' and life considered to have worth is separated from life deemed to have no human value at all. Indeed, as Agamben observes, it is significant that the Jews were denationalized before being deported, as it represented the camps' radical separation of the rights of man from the rights of the citizen; or to be more exact it revealed that the only enforceable rights were enshrined in citizenship, so that a man with no national status was extremely vulnerable to abuses of power. To emphasize this point, Agamben refers to Hannah Arendt's essay on the problem of refugees, 'The Decline of the Nation-State and the End of the Rights of Man' in which she argues that the very figure that should embody the rights of man *par excellence* — the refugee — instead signals the concept's radical crisis. He quotes:

> The conception of human rights based upon the assumed existence of a human being as such, broke down at the very moment when those who professed to believe in it were for the first time confronted with people who had indeed lost all other qualities and specific relationships — except that they were still human.[7]

In Agamben's analysis, modern discourses of human rights unwittingly make a person's humanity dependent upon her rights, creating the possibility of a person who, stripped of her citizenship is effectively stripped of her humanity.

States of Exception

This inner solidarity between fascism and modern democracy makes the tipping point from one to the other frighteningly precarious. In *Homo Sacer* Agamben writes: 'Today politics knows no value (and, consequently, no non-value) other than life, and until the contradictions that this fact implies are dissolved, Nazism and fascism — which transformed the decision on bare life into the supreme political principle — will remain stubbornly with us'.[8] In the modern world, the slippage between democracy (and its supposed protection of human rights) and totalitarianism (with its violation of them) is facilitated by the declaration of a state of emergency, or what Agamben calls a 'state of exception',[9] whereby the normal functioning of democracy is 'temporarily' suspended and executive and legislative bodies granted exceptional powers in the interest of defending a nation's integrity and security.

For Agamben, the 'state of exception' found its most extreme manifestation in the biopolitical dystopia that was the Third Reich, but has been repeated in various ways throughout the twentieth and twenty-first centuries. In Agamben's opinion, the most obvious recent example of a 'state of exception' allowing the production of *Homo sacer* was President George W. Bush's creation of a continuous state of emergency (on the grounds of a perceived threat to national security) in the name of which he authorized the indefinite detention at Guantánamo Bay of non-citizens suspected of terrorist activity. His order to detain so-called 'unlawful combatants' radically erased any legal status of the individual, producing a legally unnameable and unclassifiable being. The inhabitants of Camp X-ray were neither prisoners-of-war (protected by the Geneva Conventions), nor accused persons (with a right to trial) but simply objects of pure de facto rule.

Although Agamben does not consider the treatment of those at Guantánamo to be of the same scale or gravity as the treatment of Jews in the Nazi death camps, he compares the two in order to draw attention to the power of states (both totalitarian and democratic) to reduce populations to pure biological existence: 'The only thing to which it [Guantánamo] could possibly be compared is the legal situation of the Jews in the Nazi *Lager* [camps], who, along with their citizenship, had lost every legal identity, but at least retained their identity as Jews.'[10] Agamben's comparison of Guantánamo to the Nazi camps is not intended to imply that democracy and totalitarianism are one and the same thing, but rather to draw attention to the ways in which, given particular circumstances, modern democracies may integrate and tolerate mechanisms of power associated with totalitarian rule.

Like the inhabitants of the Nazi camps or the detainees at Guantánamo Bay, the *harkis* were created during an official 'state of exception' beyond the boundaries of 'normal' democracy. In April 1961, faced with the increasing difficulty of containing nationalist uprisings in Algeria, De Gaulle invoked Article Sixteen of the Constitutional Act of 1940, granting the Head of State the power to take all necessary measures to defend the integrity of the Republic against imminent threat. Under this 'state of exception', acts committed were no longer subject to juridical rule and it was this suspension of democracy that, in the words of Rahmani's narrator, allowed the French state to 'fabriquer une armée de soldatmorts sans se soucier qu'ils étaient des hommes' [produce an army of dead-soldiers without worrying that they were men] (*Moze*, 20).

In Rahmani's work, the figure of the *harki*, with no nation, people or language to which he can be said to belong, provides a clear example of *Homo sacer*. Moze forfeited his Algerian nationality by fighting for the French, but was not granted the same rights and privileges as a French citizen and soldier when the French were finally defeated. In Rahmani's account, the *harkis* were not treated as French soldiers whose freedom could be negotiated in an exchange of prisoners of war, but instead were abandoned and many of them massacred, before France reluctantly granted them asylum. She describes Moze's time in the refugee camp in terms that are strikingly resonant with Agamben's description of Guantánamo:

> Moze n'était plus français et les autorités algériennes l'avaient assigné comme 'Etranger à la nation'. Ils l'ont interné. Mis dans un camp. N'est-ce pas encore une folie que d'être un détenu sans titre, sans nationalité et sans pays? Jusqu'à la durée de son enfermement qu'il ignorait. Durant toute sa détention on ne lui a pas dit ce pourquoi il était là. Il n'a pas été jugé. Ni même condamné. On l'a détenu, juste détenu! *Quid* des prisonniers de guerre et de la convention de Génève? *Quid* des accords d'Evian et de la France des droits de l'homme? *Quid* des Français musulmans emprisonnés? Ils n'étaient que des chiens. [Original emphasis] (*Moze*, 44–45)

> [Moze was no longer French and the Algerian authorities had labelled him a 'foreigner to the nation'. They imprisoned him. Put him in a camp. Is it not madness to be a detainee without a title, nationality or country? He had no idea how long his imprisonment would last. Throughout his whole time in detention nobody told him why he was there. He was not tried. Not even condemned. They detained him, just detained him! What happened to the Geneva conventions on prisoners of war? What about Evian and France the home of human rights? What about the French Muslims in prison? They were no more than dogs.]

With no legal or political existence, and living beyond the protection of either French or Algerian law, the *harkis* were 'unsacrificable' yet could be killed, or left to die, in great numbers, hence the epithet *soldatmort*. Politically and legally dead, though biologically alive, the *harkis* could be casually disposed of without the intervention of the justice system. As Rahmani insists: 'Ils furent abandonnés pour être tués' [They were abandoned to their deaths].

Reduced to bare life, the *harkis*, in Rahmani's account, become the pure objects of power: 'Il y a eu des milliers de corps perdus. Et aussi 100 000 voire 150 000 corps tués' [There were thousands of lost bodies. Also 100 000 to 150 000 killed bodies] (*Moze*, 20). They are no longer subjects endowed with rights, but 'corps', pure objects that do not benefit from the state order but are entirely subject to it, constituted by it and bound to it. As a *harki*, Moze is figured as a passive object of state power as he is shunted relentlessly from one institution to the next.

> Moze n'a pas été tué.
> Il fut arrêté, torturé, interné, vendu, déplacé, recelé, acheté, déplacé. Il ne fut pas tué.

> Durant cinq années, il fut interné, transféré, frappé, négocié, racheté, emprisonné, torturé, recelé, déplacé, frappé, vendu, racheté. (*Moze*, 22)

> [Moze was not killed.
>   He was arrested, tortured, interned, sold, moved on, received, bought, moved on. He was not killed.
>   For five years, he was interned, transferred, beaten, negotiated, bought back, imprisoned, tortured, received, moved on, beaten, sold, bought back].

Stripped of any effective notion of nationality or citizenship, he is a human being beyond the law: a human being with no meaningful human rights.[11]

The State of Exception as Norm

Although governments justify a declared state of emergency by arguing that it is a short-term necessity in response to extreme circumstances, Agamben observes that all too often this 'state of exception' penetrates the mainstream political order to become the norm. In Agamben's view, rather than appearing as an historical anomaly or aberration, the camps provide a paradigm of modern democratic institutions which have entered a process of dissolution by which the 'state of exception' is increasingly becoming the rule, allowing the state to differentiate between human beings endowed with human rights and those whose human rights may be diminished or entirely suspended. What is perhaps most disturbing about Rahmani's notion of *l'homme banni*, is the way in which the 'state of exception' which permitted the creation and abandonment of the *harkis* extends beyond its official duration to permeate, in more subtle ways, the 'normal' functioning of democracy. However, the situation of Rahmani's characters maps more closely onto the French *camps de regroupements* than the Nazi model. While the Nazis deprived the Jews of their citizenship and with it their 'humanity', French colonial power did not ostensibly figure its subjects as non-human. Instead, French colonial racism, as we have seen, operated through a dual movement of assimilation and exclusion by which natives were made to wait at the threshold of approved humanity and citizenship, potentially assimilable, but never fully assimilated, and therefore in possession of only a partial and unstable 'humanity'.

Rahmani's characters inhabit what Agamben would call a 'zone of indistinction' that is neither fully inside, nor fully outside the functioning of state power.[12] They are entirely subject to state power, yet dispossessed of the rights that would make the state accountable to them, and this situation endures beyond the context of the Algerian war. Moze and his family are granted asylum and subsequently French citizenship, yet even after they have left the refugee camps they remain, in many ways, camp inhabitants. Moze may no longer be killed with impunity as he and his family are officially protected by French law, yet they cannot fully enjoy the privileges of French nationality as, even once the official state of exception has passed, they continue to be the objects of suspicion and scrutiny. Like Zouari's Touirellil family, they are repeatedly placed in a position of debt vis-à-vis their 'host' country and, despite having fought for a country he saw as his motherland, Moze is forced to make an official plea for French citizenship:

Il a dû plaider sa cause, convaincre le juge, dire combien il aimait ce pays, cette France qu'il avait servie. Il a insisté sur ses faits d'armes, il a presenté ses papiers. Il a dû se convaincre lui; étouffer sa douleur et son amertume; dire qu'il n'avait agi qu'en ce sens, que pour ce pays qui ne le voulait pas. Dire au juge, je serais mort pour vous, croyez-moi, gardez-moi, vous verrez que je le mérite. (*Moze*, 47)

[He had to plead his case, convince the judge, say how much he loved this country, this France that he had served. He insisted on his military service, he showed his papers. He had to make himself do it: bite back his pain and bitterness; say that he had done his duty, for this country that did not want him. Say to the judge, I would have died for you, believe me, keep me, you'll see that I have earned it.]

His request for citizenship is at first turned down; a rejection that is experienced as a crippling humiliation that undermines his very humanity: 'Moze avait été rétrogradé au rang de non-existant au fichier national. Humilié comme le chien qu'il a depuis toujours été' [Moze's national status had been downgraded to the rank of non-existent. Humiliated like the dog he had always been] (*Moze*, 48). But even once he is granted citizenship, he does not benefit from the rights to which he believes himself to be entitled as an ex-soldier. As a result, he writes obsessively to the state and its officials demanding recognition of these 'rights'. The narrator tells the official sent to investigate Moze's death that '[i]l n'était qu'un réclamant' [he was nothing but a claimant] (*Moze*, 53). He does not demand money but rather his 'droit de réclamer' [right to claim] (*Moze*, 51). It is the rights supposedly guaranteed by citizenship that would allow Moze to fully exist as a human being and without the security of these rights, Moze and his family have the impression that they barely exist. Moze possesses a 'citoyenneté inachevée' [incomplete citizenship] (*Moze*, 61), while the narrator explains that: 'Il y a comme un trou dans ma citoyenneté et c'est difficile à vivre' [It is as if there is a hole in my citizenship and it is hard to bear] (*Moze*, 115).

Even as a French citizen Moze remains the passive object of a state order that continually processes and manages him without ever granting him the recognition that would make him a full subject. The text is structured around a series of interviews, court hearings and interrogations, and is interspersed with copies of official documents and letters, which appear to be genuine, creating a Kafkaesque labyrinth of institutional and judicial power through which Moze and his family are continually processed. The disorienting effect of the following paragraph provides one example:

Pas de questions. Des mesures. Mesure, mesure. Etat qui prend des mesures maximales: couture et bûcheron pour les enfants de harkis. On prend en charge les tickets de bus, deux timbres et une paire de souliers par an. Toutes les factures sont à photocopier en quatre exemplaires et à adresser par lettre recommandée avec accusé de réception au ministère des Affaires sociales et de la santé, secrétariat d'Etat à la solidarité nationale, service des familles en difficulté; au ministère de la Défense, service des soldats des départements d'outre-mer, section soutien aux harkis et à leurs descendants; au ministère de l'Education nationale, secrétariat d'Etat à l'insertion professionnelle et aux

minorités historiques et au secrétariat d'Etat aux rapatriés, service des aides et du soutien scolaire qui se trouve dans la Nièvre, à Plouc exactement!
  Ne dites jamais que c'est de la discrimination négative, non dites, Ouah, ouah! Merci! (*Moze*, 55).

[No questions. Just measures. Measure after measure. State that takes maximum measures: sewing and woodcutting for the children of *harkis*. Bus tickets taken care of, two stamps and one pair of shoes a year. Four photocopies made of all bills and sent special delivery to the Ministry of Social Affairs and Health, the Office for National Solidarity, the Service for Families in Difficulty; Ministry of Defence, Service for Overseas Soldiers, Section for the Support of *Harkis* and their Children; the Ministry of Education, the Office of Recruitment and Minorities and the Office for the Repatriated, the Service for Learning Support that is situated in la Nièvre, in Nowheretown to be more precise!
  Never cry discrimination. No, say wow, wow! Thank you!]

Harkis and their families are not invited to question their situation: 'Pas de questions.' They are not subjects endowed with effective rights but objects of incessant 'mesures' imposed upon them by a system whose impersonal bureaucracy means that 'reclamants' are perpetually processed from one institution to the next without anybody taking responsibility for their fate. It is in this sense that they find themselves outside of the system while remaining deeply entrenched within it. Although the apparatus of human and democratic rights seems to be in place, the long list of offices, bureaus and services does nothing to help Moze or his family and terminates in 'la Nièvre, à Plouc exactement' — nowhere.

  The situation of Moze and his family as objects of a state power that is not accountable to them, resembles that of Muslim Algerians under French colonial rule. The *senatus-consulte* of 1865 stipulated that all indigenous Algerians were French nationals subject to French laws but citizenship was restricted to those who renounced their Muslim religion and culture. As Azzedine Haddour has argued, this 'established the formal structures of a political apartheid encouraging the existence of 'French subjects' disenfranchised, without any rights to citizenship, treated as objects of French law and not as citizens.'[13] Although Moze's family, unlike Muslim Algerians, are officially granted French citizenship, a mixture of institutionalized racism and socio-economic exclusion denies them the privileges of belonging.

The *Muselmann* and the Impossibility of Testimony

Embodying a painful history that France would rather forget, Moze and his family are relegated to the margins of citizenship and struggle to make their voices heard. The difficulty of representing marginal or repressed experience is explored through the figure of Rahmani's father. Moze's lapse into silence and his subsequent suicide represent the traumatic core of Rahmani's work that is itself an attempt to narrate and come to terms with this trauma.

  The problem of bearing witness to indescribable pain is explored by Agamben through the figure of the *Muselmann*. In this context, the German word *Muselmann* should not be confused with its literal translation, 'Muslim'. In the language of the Nazi camps, the term *Muselmann* was not a religious designation, but was used to refer to a specific kind of camp inhabitant found at the very bottom of the hierarchy of life determined by Nazi biopolitics.[14] In *Remnants of Auschwitz: The Witness and the Archive*,[15] Agamben quotes camp survivor Jean Améry's description of the *Muselmann*:

> The so-called *Muselmann*, as the camp language termed the prisoner who was giving up and was given up by his comrades, no longer had room in his consciousness for the contrasts good or bad, noble or base, intellectual or unintellectual. He was a staggering corpse, a bundle of physical functions in its last convulsions.[16]

The *Muselmann* is a figure of pure limit representing the melting point at which the defining concepts of human existence break down. He hovers between life and death and, though his body still functions, his subjectivity is shattered leaving him with no place from which to speak and bear witness to his suffering.

Like the *Muselmann*, Moze is described as a living corpse, 'Vivant il était mort' [Living, he was dead] (*Moze*, 19), who loses his ability to speak and cannot testify to his trauma. Indeed, the narrator marks the time of Moze's 'death' at the moment he falls silent. She writes: 'Une nuit, après avoir crié si fort et si longtemps, il s'est soudainement tu pour toujours. La mort le rappelait [...] Il n'était que ce débordement sans voix. Un râle, à la manière sourde d'une bouche ouverte' [One night, having screamed so hard and for so long, he suddenly fell silent forever. Death called him [...] He was no more than a voiceless excess. A muffled death rattle from an open mouth] (*Moze*, 19). Without a voice he is reduced to simple, suffering flesh, unable to bear witness to that which 'killed him': 'De ce qui l'a tué, de ce qu'il a compris, il n'a rien dit' [He said nothing of that which had killed him, of that which he understood] (*Moze*, 20). In Primo Levi's accounts of Auschwitz, the *Muselmann* is described as he who has seen the Gorgon; in other words, he who has witnessed the full face of horror and has simultaneously been destroyed by it. In Agamben's terms, the *Muselmann* has witnessed the 'impossibility of seeing', producing an instant liquidation of his subjectivity or selfhood. He writes:

> If to see the Gorgon means to see the impossibility of seeing, then the Gorgon does not name something that exists or that happened in the camp, something that the *Muselmann* and not the survivor would have seen. Rather, the Gorgon designates the impossibility of seeing that belongs to the camp inhabitant, the one who has 'touched bottom' in the camp and has become a non-human.[17]

As a 'non-human' human, the *Muselmann* marks a point of ethical crisis at which human beings, consumed by trauma, slip beyond the criteria used to define humanity. Moze's psychological collapse prompts the narrator on several occasions to question the nature and validity of his humanity. An exchange between the narrator and her sister, in which they discuss whether or not they should claim compensation after Moze's death, is particularly revealing in this respect. The narrator is the first to speak:

> — Je leur dirai qu'on indemnise pas des cadavres vivants. Ils sont partout. Dois-je te rappeler nos suicidés? Nos fous?
> — Je sais que ce sont des hommes sans vie. J'entends qu'on ne puisse indemniser ce survivant-là. Mais un homme dans cet état reste un homme!

— Payer un demi-mort? Quelle farce! Il faut vouloir le sauver, le réparer.

— Il n'est pas revenu de l'horreur, il n'en est pas sorti. On ne l'en a pas libéré. Il est l'horreur, l'horreur qui dure. Il faut l'en sortir! Ce sont des hommes morts qu'on est en droit de rappeler. On les réveillera s'il le faut.

— Ce n'est pas un survivant! Il n'en a pas la légitimité. (*Moze*, 92–93).

['I will tell them that the living dead cannot be compensated. They are everywhere. Must I remind you of all our suicides? Those who have lost their minds?'

'I know that these are lifeless human-beings. I understand that such survivors cannot be compensated. But a man in that state is still a man!'

'Pay a man who is half-dead? What a joke! They have to want to save him, to heal him.'

'He didn't come back from the horror, he didn't escape it. He wasn't released from it. He is the horror, the horror that endures. He must be saved! They are dead men that we must revive. We will wake them if we must.'

'He's not a survivor! He has no legitimacy.']

Like the camp inhabitant who has 'seen the Gorgon', Moze 'n'est pas revenu de l'horreur'. Indeed 'Il est l'horreur'; indistinguishable from that which destroyed him; fully engulfed by his trauma and unable to bear witness to it. If he has slipped beyond the bounds of the human it is, as the narrator implies, because '[i]l n'en a pas la légitimité', again suggesting the troubling link between citizenship and humanity. If Moze is not *legitime*, it seems, he is hardly human.

But if Moze 'est l'horreur', it is not only because he is entirely consumed by his trauma. It is also because he embodies national traumas that neither Algeria nor France wishes to recognize. In particular he represents a traumatic episode in French national history that threatens France's self-image as *le pays des droits de l'homme*. Indeed, Moze's slide into oblivion is represented in terms of a collapse of concepts used to define the nation, along with ethical concepts used to define humanity. The narrator exclaims:

Vous voulez le savoir ce que c'est que cette mort, cette douleur? C'est d'une telle violence une mort comme ça. Dans le geste de Moze tout est pris, saisi et confondu. Tout hurle. Le Mal, la Justice, le Meurtre, la Vengeance, la Raison, le Tort, la Nation, le Peuple, l'Honneur, la Trahison, le Frère et le Pardon hurlent. Ces mots hurlent! Cette mort vous tient à la gorge. Le Frère, la Nation, la Trahison, se vident en vous. Ils vident votre corps de leur poids qui vous tue. (*Moze*,79)

[Do you want to know this death, this pain? A death like that is so violent. In Moze's final gesture, everything is taken, grasped and thrown together. Everything screams. Evil, Justice, Murder, Vengeance, Reason, Wrong, Nation, People, Honour, Treason, Brother, Forgiveness, scream. These words scream! This death grasps you by the throat. Brother, Nation, Treason, the words empty themselves inside you. They empty your body of their weight that is killing you.]

Terms like 'Justice', 'Reason' and 'People' dissolve into a meaningless welter of words; the defining concepts of humanity and nation — good and evil, dignity and honour — melting into one pained, animal cry. Significantly, Moze kills himself on Remembrance Day. France is unwilling to remember its treatment of the *harkis* as this would pose too great a threat to national consciousness, and as a result, this trauma is fully assumed by Moze and destroys him. Rahmani presents her text as an attempt to recover her dead father's voice and oblige France to confront its crimes so that it might renew its professed commitment to human rights. I will return to this matter soon, but first I will consider how Rahmani deals with matters of voice and testimony in her second novel, *'Musulman' Roman*.

'Musulman' Roman: The Muslim as Pariah

Moze focuses on the situation of the *harkis*, produced during an official 'state of exception', and considers the ways in which this 'state of exception' persisted beyond its official duration to penetrate 'normal' French democracy and create *hommes bannis* within the boundaries of French law and society. In *'Musulman' Roman*, Rahmani investigates the production of *hommes bannis* under a different, more pervasive, 'state of exception': that produced in the name of the War on Terror. The War on Terror, as articulated by Western leaders may be seen to have produced an unofficial 'state of exception' whereby a perceived threat to national and international security has been used to justify actions in contravention of international human rights legislation; the detention of 'unlawful combatants' at Guantánamo being a case in point. As discussed in earlier chapters, since 9/11 the focus of the immigration/integration debate in the West has switched from 'immigrants' in general to 'Muslims' in particular, and people who were previously defined by their racial identity have come to be perceived in terms of their presumed religion. In *'Musulman' Roman*, the Muslim protagonist confronts what she perceives to be a new world order in which Muslims are designated as the scapegoats and enemies of 'the West'; the new *hommes bannis*. Rahmani's text distinguishes itself from many other examples of autobiographical or semi-autobiographical work by French women of Muslim origin, in that its dual focus on intimate personal narrative and sweeping critique of the global political and economic order, emphasizes the ways in which the lives of Muslims are increasingly disrupted by the shockwaves of international affairs. Furthermore, in extending its scope beyond France's borders, Rahmani's text is suggestive of the ways in which French Muslims, rather than simply aspiring to a French identity or retreating into notions of a Maghrebian cultural essence, are instead cultivating transnational identifications with Muslims and other oppressed peoples around the world.

Like *Moze*, the camp environment in *'Musulman' Roman* comes to represent the paradigm of a modern state order that divides the population into 'citizens' and *hommes bannis*, only this time the action is played out on a global scale. *'Musulman' Roman* is shot through with references to concentration camps past and present, but the description of the camp in which the narrator is interned tallies with familiar media images of Camp X-ray (kneeling prisoners, orange jumpsuits, metallic cages), making Guantánamo Bay the dominant reference. The prevalence of camp imagery in *'Musulman' Roman* works as a metaphor firstly for the logic of separation that the narrator perceives to have divided the world into Manichaean structures, separating the 'West' from its 'enemies', and secondly for her own sense of being trapped in Western stereotypes of 'the Muslim' which distort her perception of herself and of her religion. Indeed, the imposition of the label 'Muslim' is experienced as a condemnation. She writes: '[C]ontre la meute on ne peut rien. Elle vous condamne sans sommation. "Musulman tu as été, musulman tu es!" Ainsi elle me nomma. De ce seul nom de "Musulman", je devais répondre' [You are helpless in the hands of a mob. A mob condemns you outright. 'Muslim you have been, Muslim you are!' That's how they labelled me. I was to respond to the name Muslim alone] (*Musulman*, 15). The 'Muslim' that her persecutors see in her is not the Muslim she perceives herself to be, but instead serves to confirm the image of Islam that suits, what the narrator sees as the expanding global power of the 'West'. As the narrator notes in the opening lines of the novel: 'Sur moi s'est abbattue une entente entre des hommes. Je suis devenue, redevenue "Musulman"' [An agreement amongst men fell upon my shoulders. I became, or became once more, a 'Muslim'] (*Musulman*, 13). As a Muslim woman she becomes an unwilling pawn in political power struggles. Indeed, the roles assigned to the Muslim woman in Rahmani's text are not dissimilar to the *voilée/beurette* dichotomy identified in previous chapters. She is either expected to conform to the role of the 'enemy' — the West's negative opposite and dangerous double — or to that of the female martyr whose perceived suffering justifies political or military intervention. She writes: 'je suis pour l'un l'ennemi et pour l'autre le témoin, je suis brutalisée, maltraitée, méprisée et assignée' [For some I am the enemy, for others the witness, I am brutalized, mistreated, scorned and labelled] (*Musulman*, 45–46). In both cases, she is crushed beneath the symbolic weight of the Muslim Woman. She writes: 'Du "Musulman", de nous, ils ne veulent rien. Rien. C'est une volontaire certitude quant à notre nature dangereuse qui a suffi à leur pouvoir' [They don't want to know anything about the 'Muslims' that we are. Nothing at all. All their power needs is confirmation of our dangerous nature] (*Musulman*, 17).

Trapped in stereotypes that alienate her from herself and from her religion, the narrator attempts a rediscovery of her culture of origin. In a section entitled 'Ma langue ne veut pas mourir' [My language does not want to die], she describes the rediscovery of her mother tongue, Berber, as a positively emancipatory experience. She writes: 'La nuit je suis partie. Je suis loin. Je pars avec ma langue. Et dans cette tôle où on veut m'éteindre, je la fais encore rouler. Une langue ça parle toujours' [At night I escape. I am far away. I escape with my language. Even in this prison where they want to extinguish me, I can still speak my language. A language speaks forever] (*Musulman*, 75). This characterization of the Berber language as emancipatory reverses a common cliché of *beur* women's writing whereby the narrator feels oppressed by her parental language and culture and seeks emancipation through Western literature. Whereas many heroines of *beur* women's texts seek emancipation through identification with the female characters in Western literature, Rahmani's narrator instead takes Kabyl poets and musicians as her guides and role models.

> À l'époque j'étais convaincue d'être autre chose et que de cette autre chose mes papiers ne tenaient pas compte. Il me fallait chercher. Dans ma langue je décidai de m'enfoncer [...] Casque sur les oreilles, je reprenais dans mon grenier

les poésies rythmées en langue kabyle de Aït Menguellet, Slimane Azem et Idir. Est-ce en raison de ces conditions d'apprentissage? Pareille à une résistante qui se doit de taire son activité, je me voyais comme en dissidence avec le monde. Dans mon isolement, ces troubadours étaient pour moi des maîtres. Ils étaient affranchis du pouvoir et libres à l'égal des grands hommes. Je voulais être de ceux-là (*Musulman*, 86–87).

[During this time, I was convinced that I was something else; something that my official papers didn't account for. I had to find myself. I decided to throw myself into my language [...] Earphones on, in my attic, I studied the rhythmic Kabyl poetry of Aït Manguellet, Slimane Azem and Idir. Was it a result of the conditions in which I was learning? Like a resistant who must conceal her activity, I saw myself in conflict with the world. In my isolation, these troubadours became my guides. They were powerful and as free as great men. I wanted to be like them].

This rediscovery of her mother tongue is treated with some ambivalence however, and is not figured as wholly satisfactory. As the above passage suggests, it is her situation as an outsider in France that pushes her towards an identification with her 'origins'. As such it appears, to some extent, as a romanticized escapist fantasy in response to a culture that incarcerates her in stereotypes. Against the hard contours of the language that imprisons her, she pitches the living, flexible and fluid language of her ancestors.

But she is careful not to make another prison for herself by retreating into a fantasy of origins. Instead, her investigation of her cultural roots allows her to renew her relationship to the world, and she does this first and foremost through a rediscovery of her religion. First of all, this means casting off the Western stereotypes of Islam as hostile, despotic and oppressive that had previously coloured her view. She writes:

Et l'Islam, cette religion qui était commune à ceux de ma langue et aux Arabes, je le concevais volontiers autrement qu'eux. En raison même de l'idée toute fausse que je me faisais en ce temps-là du savoir et de la liberté, je digérais, non sans intérêt et sans peur, toute la boue qu'on servait à leur sujet. Ils ne savent pas penser, pas lire, pas s'émanciper, ils ne savent pas vivre, me disais-je des Arabes [...] D'eux, je ne retenais que des mots négatifs et régressifs entendus derrière les portes de gens qui, à mon égard, se voulaient bienveillants. (*Musulman*, 87–88)

[And Islam, that religion that was shared by my people and Arabs, I imagined it in an entirely different way. As a result of the utterly false idea I had of knowledge and freedom, I swallowed (not without a certain curiosity and fear) all the filth served up on the subject. They don't know how to think, or read, or emancipate themselves. Arabs don't know how to live, I was told [...] I only heard negative and regressive words, muttered behind the doors of people who thought themselves well-intentioned.]

To these reductive notions of Islam as obscurantist and oppressive, Rahmani opposes a vision of Islam as transcultural and inclusive. The narrator recounts the story of Islam and of the Prophet Mohammed as one of continual adaptation, transformation, interpretation and transferral. She writes:

Lire le Coran, lire ce livre qui défie l'entendement, c'est comprendre qu'il nous est venu par les langues de l'étranger, en partageant ses histoires, en remplaçant certaines versions par d'autres, en les donnant ensuite à ceux qui les ignoraient, dont ceux qui ne parlaient pas l'Arabe, mais aussi à celles et ceux qui n'ont jamais pu lire, leur offrait pour un temps un plus vaste monde. Un récit sans fin. [...] L'Islam n'a pas contraint la langue des hommes. (*Musulman*, 30)

[To read the Koran, to read this book that defies understanding, is to understand that it has come to us via foreign languages, in the sharing of stories, in the replacement of some versions with others, in then passing these on to people who were unaware of them, some of whom did not speak Arabic, but also to those men and women who could not read, offering them, for a while at least, a wider world. An story without end [...] Islam has not constrained the language of men.]

Rahmani imagines Islam as a flexible, living discourse that resists ossification. Like the Berber language, 'il ne veut pas mourir'. The Koran, in her description, 'défie l'entendement'. It cannot be reduced to a single, monolithic interpretation, but is characterized by its open-endedness. In a similar fashion, Islam is imagined in terms of its inclusive, hybrid character, offering a striking contrast to the reductive terms within which the narrator is confined as a 'Musulman', and to her internment in the imaginary camp. As we shall see in the next chapter, thinking of Islam as an inclusive and flexible religion and conducting re-interpretations of Islamic texts offer Western Muslims an important means of negotiating their various cultural commitments and is an important critical tool for Muslim feminists.

However, in *'Musulman' Roman*, the narrator's attempts to resist stereotyping and recover a voice she might claim as her own are not always successful. In the prison camp, Rahmani's narrator's sense of identity becomes disoriented and, despite her resistance, the narrator at moments assumes the characteristics that are foisted upon her. In a series of interrogations and interviews, the narrator is constantly forced to justify herself before Western officials and soldiers, who demand repeatedly: 'Qui est-tu?' [Who are you?]. The narrator protests: 'Je n'en veux pas de ce qu'on fait de moi' [I want nothing to do with what they are turning me into] (*Musulman*, 111), but at certain moments she transforms into the image of a radical Islam that the West both fears and desires. Mimicking Islamic extremist characterizations of the West as the Great Satan, the narrator rants: 'Fils du diable, voilà ce que vous êtes. Des comme toi il y en a pas mal sur terre. Toi et tes frères, vous tous frères de vermines je vous exècre.' [Sons of the devil, that's what you are. There are plenty of your type on earth. You and your brothers, all of you vermin, I abhor you] (*Musulman*, 113).

'Musulman' Roman stages the struggle to fantasize a secure sense of identity when one's existence either fails to be recognized or attracts the wrong kind of recognition. The narrator responds in various ways; retreating into a romanticized fantasy of her 'origins', rediscovering her religion as a way of re-engaging with the world, and defensively assuming the stereotypes forced upon her. But despite the difficulty of finding a place from which to speak, she does not abandon hope altogether. Indeed, although both *'Musulman' Roman* and *Moze* reveal the ways in which supposedly humanist discourses of human rights, justice, freedom and democracy may be transformed into tools of oppression, Rahmani's efforts to expose the failings of these discourses do not signal her loss of faith in the principles

of human rights per se. Her narrator claims that the Algerian war exposed serious flaws in France's professed commitment to human rights arguing that '[e]n Algérie, la République Française s'est fourvoyée. Elle n'avait de république que le nom' [The French Republic lost its way in Algeria. It was republican in name only] (*Moze*, 117). But, as the quotation suggests, Rahmani's critique of France's abuses of its humanist legacy is, as we shall see, conducted in the name of that legacy. In particular, the narrator invests hope (albeit fragile) in the power of testimony.

The Need to Bear Witness

As the *Muselmann* is deprived of his voice and subjectivity, camp survivors must speak in his stead as 'pseudo-witnesses', seeking to provide some account for his missing testimony, however inadequate. Primo Levi acknowledges this lacuna at the heart of testimony in *The Drowned and the Saved*. He writes:

> '[W]e, the survivors are not the true witnesses... We survivors are not only an exiguous but also an anomalous minority: we are those who by their prevarications or abilities or good luck did not touch bottom. Those who did so, those who saw the Gorgon, have not returned to tell about it or have returned mute, but they are the Muslims [*Muselmänner*], the submerged, the complete witnesses, the ones whose deposition would have a general significance'.[18]

This impossibility of knowing or seeing what the *Muselmann* saw means that, in Agamben's words, 'to bear witness to the *Muselmann*, to attempt to contemplate the impossibility of seeing is not an easy task'.[19] In *Moze* and '*Musulman*' *Roman*, Rahmani takes up this challenge by attempting to represent her father's experience, her text functioning as Perseus's reflective shield in which France might confront its own Gorgons.

Agamben argues that the mass trauma of the Holocaust is an event without witnesses 'in the double sense that it is impossible to bear witness from the inside — since no one can bear witness from the inside of death, and there is no voice for the disappearance of voice — and from the outside — since the 'outsider' is by definition excluded from the event'.[20] Rahmani's narratives, however, work to a slightly different model. As products of colonial or postcolonial power, Rahmani's narrators are caught between interiority and exteriority; assimilation and exclusion; they nominally 'belong' but there are holes in their belonging. They are not reduced to the absolute incoherence of the *Muselmann* or of Moze, rather they inhabit an intermediate zone between language and silence. In both *Moze* and '*Musulman*' *Roman*, silence and self-annihilation constantly waver on the horizon, threatening to engulf the narrator's testimony. Indeed, suicide is a strong theme in both books and the silence of death seems, at moments, to offer the narrator of '*Musulman*' *Roman* a welcome release from the language of others that injures and imprisons her. Contemplating suicide, she comments: 'Je ne serais pas qu'une exilée, une immigrée, une Arabe, une Berbère, une musulmane ou une étrangère, mais plus' [I would no longer be just an exile, an immigrant, an Arab, a Berber. I would not longer be anything at all] (*Musulman*, 93). However, whereas Zouari's character Amira chooses death, Rahmani's narrator, though she constantly teeters on the brink of silence and self-destruction, ultimately chooses life and the regenerative power of language.

The theme of losing and regaining language is key to both of Rahmani's texts, and although the narrators never entirely lose the capacity to narrate, they frequently identify themselves with characters that have passed the point of no return. Moze, as we have already seen, loses the capacity to articulate and is reduced to incomprehensible animal cries. Similarly, the narrator herself, on learning of her father's death, slides towards a trauma which seems to temporarily plunge her into psychosis:

> J'ai pleuré longtemps.
>> J'ai pleuré ta mort. Ton malheur.
>> J'ai pleuré bruyamment. Je t'ai pleuré en tremblant.
>> Et puis ma voix est partie ailleurs. Ma bouche s'est collée à la vitre.
>> J'étais soudainement devenue une mouche collée à la vitre de la lucarne.
> J'étais un insecte. Une petite chose. Mes pattes s'accrochaient vainement, je n'entendais plus rien, tout était sourd, le monde s'était réduit.
>> Je glissais inexorablement vers le bas. J'ai poussé un cri.
>> Ma vie s'arrachait à toi.
>> Ma mort était imminente.
>> La tienne était trop grande.
>> J'ai fait ce jour-là une chute vertigineuse. (*Moze*, 16)

> [I cried for a long time.
>> I cried over your death. Your unhappiness.
>> I cried loudly. I wept for you, trembling.
>> And then my voice left me. My mouth was glued to the glass.
>> Suddenly I became a fly stuck to the glass of the window. I was an insect. A tiny speck. I clung on in vain, I couldn't hear anything, everything was muted, the world had shrunk.
>> I slipped inexorably to the bottom. I cried out.
>> My life tore itself away from yours.
>> My death was imminent.
>> Yours was too big.
>> That day I made a vertiginous descent.]

In this passage, the narrator tells of her loss of speech and reduction to a suffering animality. Language appears to collapse around her and, as the world falls silent, the only sound to reach her ears is that of her own howls. This passage stands outside the main body of the text, appearing before the prologue on unnumbered pages. As such, this moment of trauma, existing beyond the normal boundaries of language, subjectivity and humanity, is also isolated from the conventional structures of narrative. It exists at the margins of the novel, just as the characters inhabit the borderlands of society. It is neither inside nor outside the text, just as the narrator and her father are neither inside nor outside the French system. The narrator teeters at the edge of trauma, slipping in and out of silence.

Rahmani feels a duty to bear witness to her father's unnarratable trauma by attempting to write *Moze's* experience while remaining aware of the limits of her enterprise. She writes: 'Par l'écriture je sais que je l'expose et le réduis [...] Mais je rappelle, étant sa fille, que je suis aussi ce qui est venu par lui et qui le continue.

Un legs. Une exécution testamentaire...' [I know that I am exposing and reducing him through writing [...] But, being his daughter, I also remember that I have come from him and am a continuation of him. A legacy. A enactment of his will] (*Musulman*, 24). The narrator does not seek to bestow some mystical prestige on the 'unsayability' of horror, rather she invests in the ethical imperative to remember. Whereas Zouari's character Amira entirely loses faith in language and retreats into silence altogether, in *Moze*, Rahmani's protagonist insists on the political necessity of testimony. The narrator may not be able to fully bear witness to her father's life and acknowledges that her attempts to do so inevitably constitute a form of betrayal but, as she remarks in a dedication at the end of *'Musulman' Roman*: '*parfois il fallait trahir*' [sometimes betrayal was necessary] (*Musulman*, 147).

Testifying to Moze's life is, for the narrator, a necessary means of persuading the French state to remember and acknowledge its treatment of the *harkis* and the role it played in the creation of 'une armée de soldatmorts'. In a chapter entitled 'LA JUSTICE', the narrator visits the *Commission nationale de réparation* not to claim compensation but to deliver Moze's story to the officials present. The commission, insisting that they are not a court of law, claim that they wish to hear Moze's story 'dans la transparence et l'équité' [in an open and fair manner] (*Moze*, 108). However, the narrator's account of her father's life and death does not conform to their expectations. Indeed, the narrator insists on putting the French state on trial for its abuses of its own humanist legacy. Rather than give up on the ideals of justice and equity supposedly enshrined in citizenship, the narrator instead revalorizes and appropriates them.

The president of the commission advises her that her approach is inappropriate: 'C'est un autre procès! [...] Vous ne pouvez pas demandez cette justice-là' [That's another trial! [...] You can't ask for that kind of justice] (*Moze*, 117). *She* is not entitled, it seems, to hold the state to account. But she pursues her accusations. Like Zouari's characters, Rahmani's narrator refuses to participate in the perverse logic that seeks to reduce her to the status of a simple 'réclamant', but rather than opt for silence, Rahmani's narrator instead invests hope in the power of testimony to redress the wrongs of the past and their legacy. Whereas the commission hopes to be able to compensate the narrator and bury Moze's legacy, she insists that her father's story does not belong to an exceptional error situated in the past, but is an ongoing truth at the heart of French society. She insists: 'Nous voulons de la politique. L'histoire qui nous concerne n'est pas close. Tout est vif, il faut agir' [We want politics. This episode in history is not over yet. It is an open wound. We must act now] (*Moze*, 126).

As the 'trial' progresses, the narrator compares France's treatment of the *harkis* to other human rights abuses around the world, including South African apartheid and the Nazi Holocaust, undermining France's self-image as *le pays des droits de l'homme*, guarantor of freedom and equality for all. However, the members of the commission are unwilling to listen, and interpret her anger as simple ingratitude 'Vous insultez l'Etat qui vous accueille!' [You are insulting the state that welcomes you!] (*Moze*, 123). The state is only capable of dealing with her either as an object of extreme suspicion, or as a depoliticized victim who can be compensated and ultimately the officials walk out. As their remarks make clear, the narrator remains a 'guest' in the country, and the balance of power between the 'host' country and those designated as its 'guests' remains undisturbed. Nonetheless, by redefining the terms by which justice is distributed, the narrator creates the opportunity to make a passionate plea for a new politics in which no man or woman could be reduced to the status of *l'homme banni*:

> Vous faites de la justice. Vous êtes les juges et la loi. Si la dignité de la France souffre d'une telle requête, vous trouverez l'argument qui lui épargnera le ridicule. Ce pays a fait cet homme. Et il vous revient à vous, vous les magistrats du monde, d'en proscrire jamais l'existence. Plus un homme ne sera un banni. Plus un! Imaginons qu'aucune loi, qu'aucune politique ne pourront justifier cet homme. Jamais plus! Jamais plus un homme ne sera un banni! (*Moze*, 127).

> [You make the law. You are the judges and justice itself. If the dignity of France is threatened by such a request, you will certainly concoct an argument that will spare the country ridicule. This country made this man. And it falls to you, you the law-makers of the world, to stop this from happening again. To say, never again shall a man be a pariah. Never again! Let us imagine that no law, no policy could ever justify the existence of such a man. Never again! Never again shall a man be a pariah!]

Rahmani's evocation of *l'homme banni* not only describes the situation of the *harkis* or Western Muslims, but also resonates powerfully in a global context. Indeed, the often surreal and non-specific nature of her narratives, along with her narrators' tendency to cite or evoke international human rights abuses invite readings that are not limited to national or European contexts. In particular, Rahmani's construction of *l'homme banni* as a human being who is entirely subject to state powers but dispossessed of her rights, resonates with the situation of migrant and trafficked peoples, refugees and asylum seekers forced to inhabit a political and legal no-man's-land. These contemporary examples of *Homo sacer* are not simply the discarded objects of national state orders, but products of the increasingly unjust and dangerous disparities of wealth and power between the global North and South that create a frontier between what Etienne Balibar calls the humanity of 'consumption' and that of 'destitution' that is irreducible to national boundaries.[21] The camps that this 'humanity of destitution' is forced to inhabit are sometimes created and regulated by the state (the detention centres for failed asylum seekers at Heathrow airport for example) and sometimes they are created by migrants themselves (such as those in Calais). But these 'camps' are also invisible or mobile, slipping under the radar of national and international law in the form of sweatshops, brothels, the holds of ships and the undersides of lorries. Rahmani's evocation of *l'homme banni* through the figure of her father speaks volumes about the suffering of those who, because they have no political or legal status or because this status is not properly recognized, have no workable human rights.

However, for Rahmani, the issue is not to sweep away the foundations of human rights discourses themselves, rather it is to criticize their abuses. Although her work reveals a profound disenchantment and disappointment with the French Republic in its treatment of the *harkis* and of Muslims in general, she sees this as a deviation from, and betrayal of, republican principles, not their inevitable outcome. Her characterization of *l'homme banni*, like Agamben's *Homo sacer*, reveals the troubling inconsistencies in the ways in which discourses of human rights are applied, but it does not undermine the notion of human rights themselves. Indeed, the narrator's protests before the commission, her investment in a language that resists the violently reductive language of the French state, and the author's decision to publish her novels, are all enacted in the name of the human rights that she believes her father and her family were denied.

In the final chapter I will consider the ways in which contemporary French Muslim women activists criticize what they see to be the distortions and abuses of republican and feminist principles, in order to develop an understanding of a citizenship that, rather than recognizing the legitimacy of some while confining others to the waiting-rooms of history, provides a common space that allows all citizens to participate in the public and civic life of a country they may recognize as home.

Notes to Chapter 4

1. 'hommes bannis' may be translated as 'banished' or 'excluded' men or women. Interview with Zahia Rahmani, <www.swediteur.com/auteur_3326.html> [accessed 1 September 2005].
2. Ibid.
3. Michel Cornaton, *Les Regroupements de la décolonisation en Algérie* (Paris: *Les Editions ouvrières*, 1967), pp. 61–67.
4. Giorgio Agamben, *Homo Sacer: Sovereign Power and Bare Life*, trans. by Daniel Heller-Roazen (Stanford, CA: Stanford University Press, 1998).
5. Agamben, *Homo Sacer*, p. 121.
6. Ibid, p. 130.
7. Quoted in *Homo Sacer*, p. 126.
8. Agamben, *Homo Sacer*, p. 10.
9. Giorgio Agamben, *State of Exception*, trans. by Kevin Attell (Chicago, IL: University of Chicago Press, 2005).
10. Agamben, *State of Exception*, p. 4.
11. It is also important to acknowledge clear differences between the situation of prisoners at Guantánamo and that of the *harkis*. Whereas the former suffer directly at the hands of the American government, the *harkis* were not murdered by the French but by their fellow Algerians. Nonetheless, by failing to offer protection to the *harkis* in the immediate aftermath of the war, the French government may also be seen to be complicit in their fate.
12. Agamben, *Homo Sacer*, p. 10.
13. Quoted in Kelly, p. 43.
14. Several tentative explanations exist as to the origins of this term though none is deemed satisfactory by historians. For a discussion of the possible origins of the term, see Gil Anidjar, *The Jew, The Arab: A History of the Enemy* (Stanford, CA: Stanford University Press, 2003). Rahmani never refers explicitly to the *Muselmann* as such, although the title of her second novel *'Musulman' Roman*, with its frequent camp imagery and characterization of Muslims as outcasts, might be seen to be playing on the word's dual meaning: Muslim and camp inhabitant.
15. Giorgio Agamben, *Remnants of Auschwitz: The Witness and the Archive*, trans. by Daniel Heller-Roazen (New York: Zone Books, 1999).
16. Ibid, p. 41.
17. Ibid, p. 54.
18. Quoted in *Remnants*, p. 33.
19. Ibid, p. 54.
20. Ibid, p. 35.
21. Etienne Balibar and Immanuel Wallerstein, *Race, Nation, Class: Ambiguous Identities* (London: Verso, 1991), p. 44.

CHAPTER 5

Rereading the Republic:
Muslim Women's Activism in France

Though largely ignored or actively marginalized by the mainstream media, French Muslim women are exploiting the platforms at their disposal to develop new representations of French Muslim womanhood that reject the 'with us or against us' logic of the *beurette/voilée* pair, and instead seek to identify themselves as Muslims while simultaneously inscribing themselves into a participative understanding of French citizenship. This model of the French Muslim woman, who does not need to be *less* Muslim in order to be *more* French (or vice versa), but who is instead fully and actively engaged with both her society and her religion, resists both patriarchal Muslim and nativist feminist claims that Islam is fundamentally incompatible with feminism and, by extension, that 'France' and 'Islam' are irreconcilable with one another. But the discourses of French Muslim feminists do not only resonate locally; rather, they are part of a global conversation about the status of minority groups in the West and the situation of Muslim women worldwide. This concluding chapter will consider how the activities of French Muslim feminists suggest new models of belonging that both reinvigorate the French context and transcend it.

The mobilization of French Muslim feminists was galvanized by the *affaire du foulard*, which saw the emergence of a number of groups promoting inclusive or alternative feminisms in opposition to nativist feminist discourses which, as previously discussed, excluded veiled Muslim women. These groups include Christine Delphy's *Collectif féministe pour l'égalité* (CFPE), Saïda Kada's *Femmes Françaises et Musulmanes Engagées* (FFEME), *Femmes Plurielles*, *Femmes Publiques*, *Les Indigènes de la République*, and a feminist collective based at *Sciences Po* in Paris, *Les Sciences-potiches se rebellent*.[1] With the exception of FFEME, these groups do not identify themselves as specifically Muslim, but they all pursue a policy that is open to veiled and unveiled Muslim women and they all either count Muslim women amongst their number or have forged direct collaborations with them. In particular, all of these groups participated in the umbrella organization *Une école pour tou(te)s* which, as mentioned earlier, mobilized a campaign against the headscarf ban. In May 2006 I visited Paris and Lyons to conduct interviews with a number of women representing several of these organizations. The interviewees included practising and non-practising, veiled and non-veiled Muslim women, but also non-Muslim French feminists who work alongside Muslim women on issues of common concern. While some of the organizations represented have a feminist bias (such as *Le Collectif féministe pour l'égalité*), others tend to privilege issues of race and class (such as *Les Indigènes de la République*). I also interviewed two independent commentators, the writer and sociologist Dounia Bouzar and the documentary-maker Sonia Kichah.

The diverse agendas of these groups and the fact that they (again with the exception of FFEME) do not identify themselves as exclusively Muslim, mean that it would be misleading and reductive to speak of a clearly identifiable French Muslim feminist movement that has a unified agenda and works in isolation from other feminisms in France. French Muslim women activists participate in a variety of organizations, and there are plenty of differences and disagreements amongst them in terms of aims and strategies. However, within this diversity, it is also possible to identify a certain coherence. This chapter will suggest that French Muslim feminists frequently look beyond France's borders for political inspiration and bring these influences into dialogue with French republican discourses. Drawing on Anglo-American queer culture, Islamic feminisms and the anticolonial spirit of transnational feminist movements, French Muslim feminists seek to destabilize a nativist feminism grounded in falsely universalizing republican ideals. However, this does not entail a rejection of republican ideals themselves. Rather, these activists explicitly base their arguments on an embrace of revised notions of *laïcité*, *liberté*, *égalité* and *fraternité*, and a de-ethnicized vision of French citizenship. In this way, they make a specifically French contribution to global debates. As we shall see, their faith in French humanist traditions steers them away from the problematic relativism of multicultural models and the isolating tendencies of identity politics, towards a practical idealism that emphasizes solidarities within differences.

Above all, French Muslim feminists stress the compatibility of feminism, French citizenship and their religion, and this demands the de-ethnicization of all three. Rather than imagine Islam, feminism and republicanism to be easily reducible to stable sets of cultural norms, they imagine them both as critical tools and texts that are open to perpetual reading and rereading. The activists I met were concerned by what they saw as a tendency to reduce Islam, feminism and republicanism to uncritical dogma or false sites of consensus grounded in ready-made cultural identities. The tendency of mainstream media discourses to represent Islam as the preserve of Arab peoples alone or to caricature it in terms of specific cultural traditions and practices, along with the nativist feminist assimilation of feminist values to a nativist ideal of 'French femininity', makes feminism and Islam seem irreconcilable. By figuring Islam and feminism as constituent parts of what Edward Said calls 'nativist cultural identities',[2] it becomes difficult either to engage with Islam from a French cultural perspective or to identify oneself as both a feminist and a practising Muslim, but this is precisely the challenge that these activists are hoping to meet.

It is possible to identify two key ways in which French Muslim feminist activists are seeking to rescue both feminism and their religion from those who would reduce them to cultural property. The first of these is via an 'Islamic feminism' that resists both patriarchal Muslim traditions and nativist feminist caricatures of Islam as inherently patriarchal, by conducting feminist readings of the sacred sources. The second is via a 'féminisme pluriel'[3] that includes Islam as a legitimate reference in the construction of a French feminist subject. Although I have separated these two strands for the sake of clarity, in reality they frequently function alongside each other, depending on the specific concerns of individual activists or groups. However, before considering these feminist initiatives, I shall situate the emergence of Muslim feminist activism in relation to broader attempts to rethink the French model of integration on the part of young French Muslims.

Rethinking the Model of Integration.

As discussed earlier, the experience of young French Muslims of immigrant descent differs from that of previous generations. The first generation of immigrants accepted their status as 'guests' as they did not perceive themselves to be *chez eux* in France and hoped to return to their homeland. Consequently, the practice of their religion was a private matter and was intimately linked to the cultural traditions of their country of origin. Their children, on the other hand, were born and educated in France and demanded equality in the name of republican values insisting, above all else, that they were *des Français comme les autres*. Politically speaking, this generation was defined by the *beur* movement of the 1980s and was mobilized by a sense of shared exclusion over and above a sense of religious or cultural identity. Indeed, they often spurned their parents' religion that continued to be perceived in relation to the 'country of origin' from which they sought to distance themselves. However, according to Bouzar, today's young Muslims, in contrast to the disidentification with France and Islam characteristic of immigrants and their children respectively, seek instead to integrate Islam as an important part of their identity as French citizens. In other words, young Muslims are now seeking to free themselves from both the ghettoization of the first generation and the de-Islamization of the *beur* movement in order to claim an identity that is neither split between France and a 'country of origin', nor abandons all religious references in an attempt to integrate, but is instead both fully French and fully Muslim.

The situation of Muslims living in the West is explored by the Swiss Muslim scholar Tariq Ramadan whose (sometimes controversial) work has had an important influence on younger generations of Western Muslims seeking to reconcile their status as Western citizens with their religious beliefs.[4] In *Western Muslims and the Future of Islam*,[5] Ramadan emphasizes the privileged position of Western Muslims who, as citizens of democracies, may have greater freedom to interpret and practise their religion than Muslims living in so-called 'Islamic' countries, where only a specific and often oppressive interpretation of the sacred texts may be tolerated.[6] These beliefs are echoed, in a French context, by Soheib Bencheikh who argues that the republican separation of religious doctrine and state rule 'permet l'emergence au sein de l'islam en France de tendances réformatrices' [allows the emergence of reforming instincts at the heart of Islam in France]. For both Ramadan and Bencheikh, politicized, institutionalized Islam is fundamentally 'unislamic' as it suppresses the principle of interpretation that, in Bencheikh's words 'assure à l'islam une extrême souplesse' [makes Islam so flexible].[7] Ramadan refers to this principle as *ijtihad*. *Ijtihad*, according to Ramadan, is the independent reasoning that guides the believer's interpretation of the Islamic sources: the Koran (believed to be the direct word of God) and the Sunna (the way of the Prophet based on authenticated sayings and doings of the Prophet, reported by scribes and scholars), and describes the individual believer's dynamic intellectual and moral relationship to them. *Ijtihad* demands the continual intellectual and moral engagement of its followers as they seek to do God's will, not in the sense of unthinkingly following prescribed laws, but by critically engaging with both Islamic teachings and the world around them in order to make moral decisions.[8] For both Bencheikh and Ramadan, *ijtihad* and Islamic reform is most achievable within a Western democratic context that grants Muslims greater freedom to interpret and debate the meaning of Islam and thus to enter into a more authentic relationship with the texts.

This understanding of Islam as a religion that is in keeping, not in conflict, with Western democratic ideals necessitates a fundamental rethinking of the model of integration. For Ramadan, the notion of integration is problematic when it means that a 'minority' is perceived as having to make concessions in order to 'fit in', instead of participating in society as an equal partner. He argues that such an understanding of integration is limited for the following reasons:

> First of all, because it is built on a dualistic vision of two universes that do not mingle and that make compromises at their boundaries or in the limited area where they intersect, it assumes that it is Muslims, being in the numerical minority, who must adapt by force of circumstances. This approach also implicitly carries the idea (even if the discourse says the complete opposite) that Muslims must think of themselves as a minority, on the margin, in their societies, which will continue to be the societies of 'the Other' and in which they will live somewhat as strangers, their belonging at best being confined to symbolic 'acts': expressions of solidarity, voting, for example. And finally, and perhaps most serious, the vision that undergirds this approach is clearly the concern only that Muslims should integrate into their new environment, and not that they should contribute.[9]

Ramadan and Bencheikh both propose an alternative definition of integration based on a de-ethnicized understanding of Islam and a model of citizenship as equal participation.

For Ramadan and Bencheikh Islam is a universal, ethical way of life, rather than a cultural phenomenon linked to Arab ethnicities and nations. In Ramadan's analysis, the term 'Islamic' does not exclusively refer to practices and concepts produced in the Arab world or by Muslim peoples, but instead describes everything in human experience that conforms to the universal principles that sustain Islam. For example, Ramadan counts social justice and gender equality amongst these universal principles and so, in his analysis, any act that respects these values may be considered, by Muslims, to be 'Islamic'. This may also include acts that are performed by non-Muslims or undertaken in a non-Muslim environment. In Ramadan's words, 'all that is not in opposition to an Islamic principle (or a recognized prohibition) on the level of human and social affairs is to be considered Islamic.'[10] As such, there is no contradiction between contributing to one's society as a Muslim and as a citizen.

This renewed model of integration requires not only a de-ethnicization of Islam but a de-ethnicization of French citizenship. Although the model of the republican citizen is imagined to transcend ethnic and religious affiliations, in practice this ideal demands conformity to dominant cultural norms. Ramadan and Bencheikh, along with political philosopher Cécile Laborde, seek to reassert the ideal neutrality of the republican citizen, not by excluding difference from the public space, but by giving all citizens an equal stake in it.[11] This does not, however, mean fragmenting the public space into separate communities. Rather than place a premium on the official recognition of separate ethnic and cultural identities, in the style of British multiculturalism, commentators like Ramadan, Bencheikh and Laborde instead subordinate the recognition of cultural and ethnic identities to a political identity of citizenship articulated through equal participation in social and civic structures. A global understanding of Islam in conjunction with a de-ethnicized understanding of citizenship opens the way for Western Muslims' full participation in their societies, as it allows them both to disassociate the practice of Islam from a specifically Arab cultural heritage, and to interpret and practise their religion as French citizens.[12] Ramadan writes:

> While our fellow citizens speak of this 'integration' of Muslims 'among us', the question for the Muslims presents itself differently: their universal principles teach them that wherever the law respects their integrity and their freedom of conscience and worship, they are at home and must consider the attainments of these societies as their own and must involve themselves, with their fellow-citizens, in making it good and better.[13]

Such notions of integration allow Western Muslims to escape the false choice between withdrawing from society in order to practise their religion, or abandoning their religion in order to fit in — in Ramadan's words either 'living in the West out of the West' or 'becoming Muslims without Islam'.[14]

Ramadan and Bencheikh's rethinking of integration is shared by Muslim feminists Saïda Kada and Dounia Bouzar. Bouzar argues that the common understanding of integration in terms of assimilation places young Muslims in constant debt with regard to French society that demands they perpetually *prove* their Frenchness. However, the Muslim concept of the *umma*, or worldwide community of believers, she argues, transgresses national and cultural borders, making it possible to identify oneself as both French and Muslim. This is because, in Bouzar's interpretation, the *umma* refers to a community united, not by cultural or ethnic norms, but by their faith in the universal principles of Islam. She explains:

> Il s'agit dans ce cas de figure d'une notion strictement religieuse qui permet, grâce à sa dimension universelle — de 'désethniciser l'islam': il n'y a plus besoin d'être algérien ou marocain pour être musulman. On peut se concevoir français et musulman. C'est paradoxalement le passage par l'islam qui leur permet alors de s'inscrire sur le territoire français en tant que français.[15]

> [In this case, we are dealing with a strictly religious notion that, thanks to its universal dimension, allows Islam to be 'de-ethnicized': there is no longer a need to be Algerian or Moroccan to be Muslim. One can see oneself as French and Muslim. Paradoxically, it is via Islam that one is able to exist in France as a French citizen.]

Furthermore, young Muslims increasingly consider the ability to openly practise their religion as a true sign of integration. Rather than thinking of integration in terms of their ability to conform to dominant cultural norms, many young French Muslims instead perceive their liberty to practise their religion as, not only consistent with, but a crucial expression of their identity as citizens. Sofian, a young man interviewed by Bouzar, explains this as follows:

> Mon père, il n'osait pas sortir en djellaba, parce qu'il ne voulait pas choquer les voisins. Il se comportait comme un invité. Mais moi, quand j'ai envie de mettre ma djellaba pour faire le marché, je ne me pose pas de questions. Et les voisins, qu'est-ce qu'ils pensent? Que mon père était intégré, et que moi je ne veux pas m'intégrer! C'est exactement le contraire! Vous voulez que je m'intègre à quoi? C'est mon pays la France![16]

> [My father didn't dare leave the house in his *djellaba*, because he didn't want to shock the neighbours. He behaved like a guest. But for me it's different. If I want to wear my *djellaba* to the market, I don't hesitate. And what do the neighbours think? — that my father was integrated and that I don't want to integrate! The exact opposite is true! What am I supposed to integrate into anyway? France is my country!]

French Muslim feminist activists are amongst the most vocal proponents of this alternative understanding of integration as it allows them to rethink the nativist feminist *beurette/voilée* binarism whereby Muslim women are expected to 'choose' between abandoning religious and family ties in order to 'integrate' or accepting the oppression that (in the eyes of nativist feminists) is associated with wearing the veil. Indeed, Sofian's 'Vous voulez que je m'intègre à quoi?' is a recurring question amongst young French Muslim women who are exasperated by the tendency of fellow French citizens to constantly refer them back to their supposed 'cultural origins'. In *Identités voilées* [*Veiled Identities*], a documentary film by the independent filmmaker Sonia Kichah, veiled Muslim women are given the opportunity to present their own views on the subject of veiling and to vent their frustration with the *beurette* stereotype. One interviewee, Nassima, complains that she cannot relate to the *beurette's* sense of split identity as, whereas the *beurette* has one foot in North Africa and one in France, she has both feet firmly planted on French soil. Her views are echoed by all the interviewees who each reject the term 'integration' on the grounds that it should not apply to those who, like themselves, consider France to be their only home, and have never questioned their identity as citizens. As Khadîdja puts it: 'Si dans mon pays on m'empêche de vivre ce que je suis, où est-ce que je vais aller pour vivre alors?' [If I can't be myself in my own country, then where can I be myself?].[17]

Muslim Feminist Activism in France: Islamic Feminism and *féminisme pluriel*

Rather than express a sense of split identity or *double culture* typical of the *beurette* stereotype, French Muslim feminists are instead cultivating an image of the French Muslim woman who, far from being torn between two opposed cultures, seeks instead to live her religion and her citizenship in mutually enriching ways. Furthermore, French Muslim feminists are 'global citizens' who identify with other oppressed or excluded peoples around the world and situate themselves in relation to transnational feminist and anti-racist discourses. Looking beyond France to other histories, struggles, and intellectual traditions, French Muslim feminists identify similar problems and opportunities. Houria Bouteldja of *Les Indigènes de la République*, for example, frequently articulates her organization's demands with reference to colonial history, the Palestinian struggle and the history of the American civil rights movement, while Saïda Kada and Dounia Bouzar situate themselves in relation to traditions of Islamic feminism that have been influential in Iran. Radical feminists like Christine Delphy of CFPE identify with the transnational feminist concern to resist the cultural imperialism of Western women, while Anne Souyris of *Femmes Publiques* draws on Anglo-American gender and queer theory in her efforts to dismantle nativist feminist norms of femininity and emancipation. But these feminists are also aware of that too great an emphasis on transnational affiliations can create difficulties in the French context. As discussed earlier, nativist feminists are quick to suppose that French Muslim women are manipulated by pernicious foreign influences and tend to characterize the *voilée* as the embodiment of a cultural and religious difference that is stubbornly resistant to integration and actively hostile to 'French values'. As a result, Muslim feminists have an interest in framing their arguments in a national context. By making their demands in terms of French citizenship they can more easily avoid accusations of mental manipulation or social segregation.[18]

There are two key ways in which French Muslim women are forging a feminist agenda. Firstly, they propose feminist readings of Islamic sources, a practice I refer to as 'Islamic feminism'. Secondly, they articulate what I have called a 'féminisme pluriel'. Both of these strands borrow discourses and practices from beyond France and bring them into dialogue with French republicanism.

Islamic feminism

Many French Muslim feminists assert women's right to interpretation, or *ijtihad*. The practice of rereading the sources from a feminist perspective is broadly known as 'Islamic feminism' and in recent years it has emerged both as a site of transnational feminist resistance to Islamic fundamentalism and as an alternative to dominant 'Western' feminist discourses.[19] Transnational feminist networks working to advance the human rights of women in Islam, for example *Women Living Under Muslim Laws* (WLUML) and the *Sisterhood Is Global Institute* (SIGI), encourage independent readings of the Koran, Hadith and Islamic laws with a view to raising awareness of the misapplication of Islamic law in the Muslim world and the un-Islamic nature of sexist cultural traditions. This kind of activism can have real effects at local and national level, especially in societies, like Iran, where national law is inseparable from interpretations of Islamic Shari'a law.[20] Furthermore, 'Islamic feminism' has become a topic of great academic interest, and in October 2005, the world's first international conference on Islamic feminism took place in Barcelona bringing together various women's associations (both Muslim and non-Muslim), intellectuals from around the world, organizations involved in cultural diversity and immigration, NGOs working in countries with a Muslim majority, and members of the public. However, despite the scale and energy of Islamic feminist practices, the term 'Islamic feminism', coined by Western Muslim and non-Muslim academics, is frequently contested. While some object to the word 'feminism' as they fear that in certain contexts it may alarm and threaten a Muslim patriarchy that, by associating feminism with Western influence, may further repress feminist activism,[21] others object to the term 'Islamic' as they feel that it implies a false separation from 'Western' feminism and ignores the fact that Muslim women participate in a broad range of feminist activity.[22] As we shall see, both of these concerns are relevant to French Muslim women. Bearing these objections in mind, I will use the term 'Islamic feminism' to refer specifically to the practice of rereading and interpreting the sacred sources from a feminist perspective, and will use the term 'Muslim feminism' to refer to Muslim women's activism in a broader sense, for example their involvement in the creation of a *féminisme pluriel*.

The association of feminism with Western influence has been re-enforced by the West's instrumentalization of 'women's rights' discourses to demonize the Muslim world and justify imperialist action against it. As a result, Muslim feminists run the risk of being perceived as cultural traitors. Furthermore, as Aili Mari Tripp argues through an analysis of several case studies, overtly feminist agendas can be counter-productive resulting in defensive patriarchal responses and an even more severe repression of women's freedoms.[23] However, Islamic feminism, whether it announces itself as such or not, can be used to sidestep such accusations of betrayal on the grounds that it draws inspiration from Islam. Like Muslim feminists elsewhere in the world, French Muslim feminists are aware of the potential benefits of Islamic feminism. Indeed, according to Bouzar, these benefits partially explain the appeal of Islam to young women who, in her account, made up between sixty-five and seventy per cent of the turn out at recent Muslim conferences in France.[24] In particular, speaking through an Islamic framework facilitates dialogue within the family. In Bouzar's words:

> Elles sont passées par la religion pour combattre la tradition. C'est à dire que, pour ne pas avoir l'air de trahir le groupe d'origine, l'islam quelque part fait lien avec la famille. Elles sont passées par l'islam pour pouvoir revendiquer de nouvelles valeurs extérieures à leur famille et du coup elles ont beaucoup renvoyé les arguments de leurs parents à ce qu'elles appellent des traditions. C'est à dire qu'elles ont dit à leurs parents: 'Ce que tu présentes comme une valeur sacrée n'est que le produit de la tradition de ton petit village et ce n'est pas sacré'.[25]

> [They are resisting tradition through religion. That is to say that, so as to avoid giving the impression of betraying their origins, they maintain a link with the family via Islam. They claim new values — ones that are external to the family unit — through Islam, and as a result they have been able to show that many of their parents' arguments are simply founded in tradition. That is to say that they have said to their parents: 'What you are telling me is a sacred value is in fact only a local village tradition, and it is not sacred.']

Bouzar and Kada's research provides many case studies of women who have managed to initiate change within their families by insisting on their right to study, work, choose their husband and so forth, within an Islamic frame of reference.

A typical example is provided by Sofia, a member of a Muslim association in Northern France:

> Plus j'étudiais mon islam, plus je me rendais compte que mon père n'était pas vraiment musulman mais plutôt macho. Je n'arrêtais pas de dire à maman qu'elle s'était fait avoir... Rien de ce que lui imposait mon père n'était marqué dans le Coran! Il fallait qu'elle se rende à l'évidence, il s'agissait juste des traditions de leur petit village... Et comme j'argumentais chaque propos par un verset ou un hadith, mon père a été obligé de céder... Pas sur tout... ils ont leurs habitudes... Mais sur les choses essentielles, on a gagné![26]

> [The more I studied my Islam, the more I realized that my father was not really Muslim, just macho. I kept telling Mum that she was getting a raw deal... Nothing that my father insisted upon was actually prescribed by the Koran! My mum needed to face facts, it was just a matter of village traditions... And because I grounded my arguments in a verse or hadith, my father had to give in... Not on everything... old habits die hard... But we won the important battles!]

As we saw in the second chapter, nativist feminists tend to be dismissive of Muslim women's efforts to emancipate themselves through Islam. In particular, they characterize the choice of some Muslim women to wear the headscarf as a mere strategic compromise intended to placate Muslim men. Fadela Amara, for example, describes the situation of women who wear the veil 'comme une armure' [like armour][27] in their own neighbourhoods, but remove it as soon as they venture out of the area, risking violent reprisals if they are ever caught out. Amara is not wrong to claim that the veil offers advantages in terms of mobility and protection from the male harassment that is a very present reality for many young Muslim women, nor is she wrong to claim that some women wear the veil as a defensive strategy. Saïda Kada and Dounia Bouzar also give an example of a young woman, Houria, who takes up the veil partly out of religious conviction but above all to escape her bullying and violent elder brother. Houria explains that as soon as she began to veil, men who previously harassed and insulted her instead showed her respect, and that her brother also ceased to be violent and controlling. For Houria, veiling is a tactical compromise: the best of a bad set of choices. She explains:

> Le pire, c'est que tout le monde a oublié les agissements de mon frère. Tout ce qu'ils ont retenu, c'est que moi, je suis rentrée dans 'le droit chemin' le jour où j'ai porté le voile, comme si ç'avait été moi le problème! Mais je me tais parce que je suis devenue libre grâce à Dieu. Tous les jours, je prie que ça continue. Maintenant, je me concentre sur ma formation professionnelle et je rentre à n'importe quelle heure, c'est cela qui compte. Sortir du cauchemar et construire sa vie.[28]

> [The worst thing is that everyone has forgotten how my brother behaved. All they remember is that I got back onto the 'straight and narrow' the day I started wearing the veil — as if I had been the problem in the first place! But I keep quiet because God has allowed me to be free. Every day I pray that it will last. Now I am focusing on my professional training and I come home any time I want. That's what counts. Leaving the nightmare behind me and leading my life.]

As for Houria, wearing the veil or adopting Islamic feminist practices may, in some circumstances, be no more than strategic. But nativist feminists like Amara *are* mistaken to conclude that it is therefore not a genuine expression of agency. Women of all backgrounds constantly negotiate their freedoms within existing social and cultural contexts and continually make compromises, bargaining with patriarchy as best they can in order to enhance their freedoms. This often includes conforming to gender specific dress codes, for Muslim and non-Muslim women alike. Furthermore, nativist feminists are wrong to assume that Muslim women do not value the veil in itself. Although it may be a tactical manoeuvre for some, others such as Saïda Kada, Ismahane Chouder and Samia Saïd of CFPE, and Sonia Kichah's interviewees, value the positive benefits of the headscarf in terms of their relationship to God,[29] their affective relationship to their family and community, the sense of dignity they feel when wearing it, and as a sign of their personal and feminist embrace of Islam.[30]

There is however a danger in imagining Islamic feminism as a cure-all. In particular, enthusiasm for the benefits of Islamic feminism on the part of outside observers risks reducing Muslim women to their Islamic or Muslim identity alone, as if Islamic feminism were the only culturally appropriate practice for Muslim women. This enthusiasm can be a problematic feature in writing by British and American Muslim and non-Muslim feminist academics for whom the notion of Islamic feminism has particular appeal in a political environment that is increasingly hostile to Islam and Muslims. As Haideh Moghissi complains in her book *Feminism and Islamic Fundamentalism: The Limits of Postmodern Analysis*,[31] Western intellectuals, in their anxiety to rescue Islam from its bad reputation as regards the treatment of women and to protect Muslim minorities in the West, have invested tremendous hope in Islamic feminism as a legitimate and culturally authentic alternative to 'Western feminism'. As Moghissi points out, the exuberant response to Islamic feminism conforms to the postmodern trend of seeking out local, specific forms of feminist resistance as opposed to insisting on a one-size-fits-all metanarrative of emancipation. I do not wish to deny the importance and necessity of questioning feminist metanarratives, and have devoted much of this book to doing so but, as Moghissi argues, too much insistence on Islamic feminism as an *alternative* to 'Western' feminism can be unduly limiting.[32]

In particular, emphasis on Islamic feminism as a culturally appropriate choice ignores the multiplicity of women's cultural affiliations in a globalized world. Improvement in levels of women's education and more widespread access to the internet and other communication platforms allows women to transcend geographical limits and draw on a plurality of cultural references and models of resistance, as well as form transnational alliances, in this cosmopolitan public space. As Tripp rightly points out, such opportunities are not always available to the world's poorest, producing a 'digital divide' amongst women from differing socio-economic backgrounds,[33] but, bearing that important qualification in mind, it is still possible to say that many women in the Muslim diaspora do not simply identify with one cultural model. This is certainly true of Muslim women living in the West. A number of the women I interviewed were keen to remind me that

French Muslim women are not only Muslim but French and, as such, have inherited a long tradition of French feminist history and practice. For them, it is unhelpful and inappropriate to oppose 'Western' or 'French' feminisms to 'Islamic' feminism as if Islamic feminist practices were happening in isolation from the other social and cultural influences to which French Muslim women are exposed. Indeed, in the same vein as Ramadan and Bencheikh, Ismahane Chouder of CFPE emphasizes that it is the fact of living in a democracy in which women have access to education and are guaranteed a certain freedom of expression that enables French Muslim women to re-invigorate their relationship to Islam. She explains:

> Je suis persuadée qu'en Europe, en tant que femmes, on dispose d'un espace de liberté que l'on n'a pas dans beaucoup de pays arabo-musulmans. C'est pour ça que peut-être ça nous a servi comme tremplin pour faire un retour dans les sources, pour les relire dans un autre contexte, en disant [...] qu'il n'est pas possible de les lire de manière tellement rigide, et de façon aussi instrumentalisante. C'est une chance ici [en France], dont on a conscience, et qu'on a parfaitement intégrée parce que ça fait parti de notre histoire, on est né ici. [34]

> [I am convinced that, as European women, we benefit from freedoms that other women are denied in many Arab-Muslim countries. That is perhaps why we are able to go back to the sources on our own terms and read them in another context [...] saying that it is not possible to read them in such a rigid manner, or to instrumentalize them. France gives us a real opportunity of which we are well aware and that we have fully internalized because French tradition is part of what we are. We were born here.]

Chouder's status as a French woman and her experience as a Muslim are not in contradiction, but are inseparable from one another. As we shall see in the following section, French Muslim feminist activism is by no means limited to Islamic feminism alone. Rather, Muslim women are becoming increasingly involved in a range of feminist groups and activities that seek to promote a 'féminisme pluriel'

Féminisme pluriel

Many of the feminist activists I interviewed, both Muslim and non-Muslim, characterized the mainstream feminist institutions in France, headed up by the *Comité National des Droits des Femmes* (CNDF), as exclusive, hierarchical and unwilling to accept women who do not conform to a specific and limited notion of French womanhood. Indeed, as mentioned earlier, the CNDF excluded Christine Delphy's organization *le Collectif féministe pour l'égalité* from a number of their petitions and marches on the grounds that some of CFPE's members wore headscarves. Delphy interpreted their reasoning as follows:

> Elles [members of the CNDF] défendent une certaine idée de la libération. Il y a une seule voie et qu'il n'y en a pas d'autres. C'est une idée très impérialiste, assez classique en Occident: 'Nous, on a trouvé la bonne réponse, maintenant les autres doivent faire pareil. Il n'y a pas trente-six réponses, il y en a une. Et maintenant vous vous alignez sur notre position.'[35]

> [Members of the CNDF defend a certain idea of women's liberation. There is one path to follow and no others. It is a very imperialist approach, quite classic

in the West: 'We have found the right answer, now everybody else must follow our lead. There is only one way to skin this cat, and you will do it our way.']

However, Muslim feminists and their supporters are breaking open the exclusive and repressive model of women's emancipation promoted by nativist feminist discourses by creatively imagining new feminist identities that are not only shaped by specific religious or cultural affiliations, but also accommodate alternative sexualities and histories. This is not to say that the activists I interviewed idealize what Sonia Kruks calls a 'multiple-difference feminism' that privileges differences between women over similarities and potential solidarities.[36] As mentioned above, these activists are keen to remind others that they are inheritors of a French republican cultural heritage that values solidarity. By identifying solidarities within differences and forming strategic alliances on issues of common concern these feminists propose a *féminisme pluriel* that escapes both the false universalism of nativist feminism and the potentially paralysing relativism of multiple-difference feminism.

I shall first consider the ways in which French Muslim feminists and their allies are seeking to diversify dominant narratives of emancipation. We have already seen how some French Muslim women bring their religion into dialogue with their feminist convictions and their French citizenship, but Muslim feminists are also concerned with matters of race, class and sexuality. Indeed, Houria Bouteldja of *Les Indigènes de la République* insists on multiple analyses of women's experiences. In a situation that she openly characterizes as neocolonial it is, she claims, impossible to conduct an authentic feminist analysis in isolation from issues of race, culture and class. For Bouteldja, it is imperative to conduct 'une analyse "féministe-raciale"' [a race-oriented feminist analysis][37] in order to counter what she sees as the manipulative strategies of nativist feminists who, like their colonial predecessors, highlight sexism as a means of stigmatizing certain communities and in particular of vilifying young Arab men. Her feminist association *Les Blédardes* was, in fact, integrated into *Indigènes de la République* (a mixed organization) in order to be seen to be in solidarity with the young men who are so frequently demonized. She explains:

> Notre problème, en tant que femmes, c'est que évidemment on cherche à combattre le sexisme dans nos propres milieux, mais que si on dénonce ce sexisme-là, on finit par jouer le jeu d'Elisabeth Badinter. C'est pour ça qu'il faut qu'on insiste sur la question de race. On fait une réflexion sur les questions féministes mais jamais sans une analyse de race. C'est-à-dire qu'on reste solidaire avec les hommes contre le racisme. Le racisme qui les construit comme des sauvages sexuels, débridés etc. Le premier acte c'est de dire: on est solidaire avec les hommes de chez nous, contre le racisme, mais par ailleurs on va lutter contre eux, contre le sexisme, mais jamais contre eux tout simplement. On ne peut pas tout simplement être féministe.[38]

> [Our problem, as women is that *obviously* we want to fight sexism within our communities, but that if we denounce this sexism we risk playing into the hands of Elisabeth Badinter. That's why we insist on the issue of race. We conduct feminist analyses, but never in isolation from the matter of race. That is to say, we remain in solidarity with the men against racism. The racism that constructs them as sexual savages with no self-control and so on. We need to

say: we are in solidarity with the men against racism, but at the same time we will fight sexism. However, we will never just fight *them*. We cannot simply be feminists].

The assertion that 'on ne peut pas tout simplement être féministe' is also echoed by lesbian Muslims whose sexuality, along with their religion, excludes them from the heteronormative model of desirable femininity. In a fascinating article on lesbians 'of colour' in France, Nathalie Paulme and Paola Bacchetta discuss the activities of members of *le Groupe du 6 novembre: lesbiennes issues du colonialisme, de l'esclavage et de l'immigration* [The Group of the 6th November: Lesbians descended from colonialism, slavery and immigration] from a queer perspective.[39] According to Paulme and Bachetta organizations like *Le Groupe* look beyond France for political inspiration. In particular, they look to Anglo-American queer culture and anti-racism for the critical tools with which to destabilize normative representations of non-white women as either wives and mothers (guardians of tradition and gateways to neocolonial domination), or as sexualized objects of the male gaze. However, as Paulme and Bachetta report, their activities (and those of similar groups) tend to be met with hostility from dominant feminist organizations that accuse them of fragmenting the feminist sisterhood. For *Le Groupe* a degree of separation from mainstream feminism is indeed crucial in order to resist the assimilationism that has rendered them invisible for so long, but rather than retreat into a narrowly identitarian politics, they instead forge alternative solidarities across differences in national, cultural, religious and racial origins and express support for other marginalized groups.[40] For example, *Le Groupe* includes veiled and non-veiled Muslim women amongst its number and, as Paulme and Bachetta reveal, members of the organization participated in the demonstration organized by *Une école pour tou[te]s* on 14 February 2004, to show their solidarity with the veiled schoolgirls. The organization of *Le Groupe* reveals an important aspect of contemporary modes of resistance. As Winifred Woodhull has argued, it is important to pay attention to the ways in which subjected peoples enter into dialogue with each other rather than considering them simply in relation to centres of power; in other words, paying attention to 'relations of margin to margin' rather than 'drawing on the centre–periphery model'.[41] Although *Le Groupe* may, on some level, have alienated mainstream French feminism, they are bridging the distance between different subjected groups opening up supportive and constructive conversations that do not confine them to what Woodhall calls 'a 'tête-à-tête' with 'French' identity.[42]

In this vein, French Muslim feminist activists have attracted support from other women's groups who identify with their marginalization. Anne Souyris, founding member of *Femmes Publiques*, claims that one of the key reasons her organization joined *Une école pour tou(te)s* was to demonstrate its resistance to the narrowness of acceptable models of womanhood. *Femmes Publiques* defends the rights of female sex workers in France who, like Muslim women, are not seen by mainstream feminists to conform to a 'normal' notion of femininity and are frequently excluded from debates that concern them. In particular, the presumed sexual modesty of the *voilée* and the promiscuity of the prostitute are seen to threaten the acceptable organization of female desire and pleasure which, as Souyris points out, is encapsulated in the name of the organization *Ni putes ni soumises*. The ideal 'femininity' is neither too overtly sexual (she is not a *pute*) nor does she renounce or conceal her sexuality (as the veiled woman, the *soumise*, is presumed to do). Prostitutes who claim to have sex for money out of choice are disturbing because they have separated sexuality from desire. Similarly, Muslim women who choose to veil create confusion because they have opted out of a mainstream vision of female sexuality as overtly and publicly alluring. Consequently, both groups of women are excluded from public debate as they are seen to fall outside the acceptable parameters of 'normality' and presumed to hold extreme or unrepresentative views. *Femmes Publiques* identified these similarities and lent their support to the anti-prohibitionists. Souyris explains: 'l'affaire du voile nous est apparu comme en parallèle. De nouveau, on essayait d'exclure un certain nombre de femmes. On voulait savoir pourquoi, une certaine minorité féminine était exclue du mouvement féministe. Pourquoi certaines femmes n'ont pas le droit à la parole?' [the headscarf affair resonated with our own experience. Once again there were attempts to exclude a certain number of women. We wanted to know why a minority of women had been excluded from the feminist movement. Why did some women not have the right to speak?].[43]

The tendency of these activists to look beyond France to Anglo-American queer culture, pluralist feminisms and transnational Islamic feminisms has been interpreted by nativist feminists as a rejection of French republicanism, along with an idealization of a British-style multicultural model. As Anne Souyris reports, mainstream feminist institutions feel 'clashé' [threatened] by the emergence of multiple feminist identities that appear to split the feminist sisterhood. Indeed, Caroline Fourest, in the mould of Samuel Huntingdon's notorious 'Clash of Civilizations',[44] imagines a 'clash of feminisms' engineered by Tariq Ramadan who, in her words, 'incite à inventer un "féminisme islamique" pour s'opposer au féminisme occidental' [seeks to invent an 'Islamic feminism' that would oppose Western feminism].[45] However, the model of feminist activism promoted by these groups — what Christine Delphy calls a *féminisme pluriel* — differs from the potentially fragmentary politics of multiple-difference feminism by drawing on republican principles. Indeed, it is by drawing a respect for differences together with a republican belief in solidarity as citizens that these feminists make a specifically French contribution to a global conversation.

In *Retrieving Experience: Subjectivity and Recognition in Feminist Politics*, the feminist philosopher Sonia Kruks argues that the naïve and ideological appeals to sisterhood typical of early second-wave feminism has given way to a concern with differences amongst women, giving rise to a politics of identity that demands respect for difference as opposed to integration into a 'universal' humanity. As Muslim feminist responses to nativist feminism demonstrate, an emphasis on the plurality of women's experience is an important means of exposing the limits of the supposedly 'universal' feminist subject. But, as Kruks argues, too great an emphasis on difference can undermine notions of shared and communicable experience that can form the basis of feminist solidarities. In particular, Kruks points to the danger of an identity politics that degenerates into a 'commodification of identities', substituting demands for official recognition for demands for legal and institutional change.[46] The inadequacy of identity politics in a French context is underlined by Laborde. Identity politics sits more comfortably with a multicultural model that publicly recognizes group difference and seeks to combat discrimination through a mixture of affirmative action and a celebration of cultural difference. However, French republicans, in Laborde's view, are rightly suspicious of the validation of ethno-cultural difference as a policy of citizenship for two reasons. Firstly, like Kruks, they are concerned that the promotion of cultural difference may come at the expense of a focus on socio-economic inequalities, and secondly they positively value the trans-ethnic and trans-cultural solidarities that are crucial if citizens are to partake in wider society.[47] For Laborde and Kruks, there is no need to choose between a falsely universalizing feminism and an isolating politics of multiple-difference. Instead, solidarities may be grounded in what Kruks (following Sartre) calls *praxis*; organized projects and actions amongst individuals existing in the same or overlapping practical, material fields. Laborde calls this citizenship.

The activists I interviewed, though they wish their differences to be respected, ground their solidarities in shared experiences as women within the broad frame of citizenship. Unlike the essentializing tendencies of nativist feminism or multi-difference feminism, the *féminisme pluriel* promoted by organizations such as *Femmes Publiques* is based on collective action with a view to realizing shared objectives and agendas. These organizations resist being categorized as segregationist and instead focus on 'le commun', that is, shared interests and empathies that allow them to establish partnerships and set up dialogues with other feminist groups. *Femmes Publiques*' support for the veiled schoolgirls on the grounds that Muslim women, like sex-workers, should have the right to speak for themselves is one example of two very different groups of women establishing solidarity as citizens. For Kada, these kinds of collaborations are crucial if Muslim women are to resist being reduced to speaking from a purely identitarian or religious standpoint, and are to succeed in forging a place for themselves in public debate. She writes:

> La femme musulmane doit participer aux grands débats de société, pour être présente, montrer qu'elle existe pour ensuite présenter ce qu'elle est, pour casser cette vision aliénante des banlieues, pour porter ses revendications en tant que femme issue de la société et non des cités, refusant du coup d'être reléguée au rang de subalterne du mouvement féministe [...] Elle ne doit pas s'auto-censurer, en acceptant des sphères d'actions étroites délimitées par ceux qui inventent pour nous des espaces d'actions dans lesquelles on est censée s'enfermer.[48]

> [Muslim women must participate in key social debates, be present, show they exist and who they are in order to destroy the alienating image of the *banlieues*, to make their claims as women and members of society, rather than as inhabitants of the *cités*, and to refuse to be relegated to the status of subalterns within the feminist movement [...] Muslim women must not self-censor by accepting limited spaces of action circumscribed by those who would keep us enclosed in them.]

However, the *féminisme pluriel* articulated by French Muslim feminists also has its limitations. Firstly, its focus on citizenship (however thoroughly revised) fails to account for the situation of those who lack or are denied status as French citizens. As Rahmani's work suggests, those who are not recognized as citizens are vulnerable to the worst kinds of exploitation and abuse. France, like other Western nations, has an invisible population of migrant workers whose situation in France is extremely precarious and for whom discourses of emancipation that are reliant on citizenship have little meaning. That is not to say that French Muslim feminists and their allies are unaware of, or indifferent to, the plight of some the most vulnerable women on French territory. Groups like *Les Indigènes de la République* express solidarity with the *sans-papiers* [those without official papers] and Anne Souyris's *Femmes publiques* is concerned by the specific difficulties faced by women trafficked into prostitution. Nonetheless, these most vulnerable women have little to gain from discourses of emancipation through citizenship. Secondly, there exists a whole underclass of women who, due to poverty and poor literacy, do not have access to the technological platforms that, as previously mentioned, facilitate participation in the public and political sphere. New feminist collaborations in France and elsewhere are exploiting the opportunities offered by global electronic communication networks to form local and transnational affiliations and to generate new forms of collective action. However, participation in this cosmopolitan public space requires some degree of technological expertise and literacy that is not available to the most excluded and isolated; for example older generations of immigrant women who are more cut off from mainstream French culture than their children.

Bearing these important limitations in mind, it is fair to say that *féminisme pluriel* nonetheless provides a productive means of interrogating and renewing the Republic's proclaimed commitment to humanist and feminist ideals. Part of the problem with nativist feminist discourse is, as we have seen, its tendency to produce an abstract defence of these ideals that does not account for real imbalances of wealth, power and opportunity in French society and amongst French women. By contrast, the activists I interviewed advocate what might be called a practical idealism that does not give up on republican idealism, but interrogates it in relation to existing structures of domination. The ways in which these activists are reinterpreting the founding principles of the French Republic will be the subject of the final part of this chapter.

Rereading the Republic

As we have seen, Muslim feminists see Islam, not as a cultural possession to be owned and interpreted by a few, but as a universal ethical model that can and should be interpreted by all believers, regardless of their nationality, gender, class or ethnic origin. In their view, Islam is not the exclusive property of Arab peoples or synonymous with particular national identities, but instead conveys a universal ethical message that transcends cultural and national boundaries. In his posthumously published collection of lectures and essays *Humanism and Democratic Criticism*, Edward Said applies a similar logic to the tradition of humanism. Said proposes a de-nativized vision of modern democracy and Enlightenment humanism which, in his view, are all too often considered to belong exclusively to the Western world. Just as, in Ramadan's analysis, Muslim fundamentalists seek to reduce Islam to a rigid set of interpretations that serve a specific political agenda, in Said's analysis, there is a danger that the tradition of humanism is similarly exploited to serve what he calls the nativist cultural fundamentalisms of the Western world that reduce the humanist principles of, for example, 'Freedom and Democracy' to nationalist slogans that repress dialogue and debate. French Muslim feminists do not only identify with Islam but also with the republican humanist traditions that they have inherited and, as French citizens, they argue not only for a rereading of the Islamic sources but also a rethinking of republican and feminist values in order to revitalize them as what Said calls a 'technique of trouble'.[49]

The case for rereading the founding principles of modern democracy and Enlightenment humanism is persuasively argued by Said in *Humanism and Democratic Criticism*. Although his essays focus on American society and academic institutions, his key ideas are also applicable to Western democratic societies in general. Said describes his project as 'an extended meditation on the useable scope of humanism as an ongoing practice and not as a possession',[50] advocating humanism as a critical tool and useable practice rather than cultural furniture reserved for the dominant classes. Said does not see humanism only in terms of essentializing, totalizing trends, but instead as a 'process of unending disclosure, discovery, self-criticism and liberation' that is not confined to academia but instead 'is directed at the state of affairs in, as well as out of, the university [...] and that gathers its force and relevance by its democratic, secular and open character'.[51] What needs to be confronted and rejected is not humanism itself, but its widespread abuses. He writes:

> I still believe that it is possible to be critical of humanism in the name of humanism and that, schooled in its abuses by the experience of Eurocentrism and empire, one could fashion a different kind of humanism that was cosmo-politan [...] in ways that absorbed the great lessons of the past [...] and still remain attuned to the emergent voices and currents of the present, many of them exilic, extraterritorial and unhoused, as well as uniquely American.[52]

For Said, the abuse of humanism discredits some of its practitioners, not humanism itself.

Like French Muslim feminists, Said brings Islamic intellectual traditions into dialogue with Western humanist ones. Said understands humanism not as a reclusive intellectual practice, but as a common enterprise shared with others and, to illustrate this point, he draws on the Islamic notion of *isnad*. Said explains that since, for Muslims, the Koran is the word of God, it is therefore essentially impossible for the human mind to fully comprehend, and requires readers to try to understand its meaning whilst also remaining profoundly aware of preceding interpretations. The presence of other readers over time constitutes a community of witnesses, a chain, each reading depending to some degree on an earlier one. The term *isnad* describes this system of interdependent readings, whose common goal is to approach the principle of the text, its *usul*. The personal effort and commitment involved in this process is, as mentioned previously, known as *ijtihad*. Like the Islamic principles of *ijtihad* and *isnad*, Said's humanism is inscribed within the community and public, political sphere and involves the humanist in motions of both reception and resistance; receiving and understanding the foundational texts of humanity in a profound awareness of their context and complexity, and resisting essentializing or totalizing readings of them. As Said's reference to Islamic practices suggests, he does not believe humanism to be an exclusively Western or intellectual tradition, but instead a common enterprise that may be undertaken by all.

It follows that, for Said, political dissent and activism fall within the humanist horizon. The activists and public intellectuals mentioned in this chapter and the organizations they represent may be seen to fit Said's model of the engaged intellectual in their commitment to rereading feminist, republican and Islamic narratives. These activists not only stress the importance of the right to interpret Islamic sources, but also the need to reinterpret the humanist sources of the French Republic and, like Said, understand humanism in terms of democratic critique. In concrete terms, this means reconsidering the application of the principles of *laïcité*, Liberty, Equality and Fraternity as well as re-evaluating the role of French education, in order to build an inclusive, understanding of French identity that undermines 'nativist cultural fundamentalisms'.

Starting with laïcité, Muslim feminists do not seek to destroy the principle of state secularism, but instead to criticize its perceived abuses. As John R. Bowen explains, recent republican discourses have tended to represent *laïcité* in terms of a secularized public space that is hostile to religion. However, this understanding of *laïcité* is contentious. As Bowen makes clear, there has never been agreement about the role religion should play in public life in France and the meaning of *laïcité*, far from being a constant value, has always been a site of contestation and debate.[53] In *Marianne et le prophète*, Bencheikh returns to the sources to conduct a scrupulous reading of the history and fluctuating signification of *laïcité* and challenges the recent tendency to conflate *laïcité* with atheism. In Bencheikh's view, understanding *laïcité* as an atheist ideology is to betray its spirit. *Laïcité* is a principle of neutrality and as such cannot favour non-believers over believers.[54] Indeed, properly understood, *laïcité* is a crucial tool in the promotion of *égalité*. Drawing on the spirit of the 1905 law intended to guarantee freedom of conscience, Muslim feminists argue for a *laïcité* that respects the free exercise of organized religions while constraining the state from conferring preference on any one set of beliefs. In this way, *laïcité* provides a neutral framework within which people from different religious and cultural backgrounds may enter into dialogue as equals and as citizens. One leader of a Muslim association, interviewed by Bouzar, explains how rethinking the notion of *laïcité* allowed him to see Islam as compatible with the French Republic. He explains:

> Notre évolution est en lien direct avec la compréhension de la laïcité française. Pour nous, laïque signifiait contre Dieu, contre le religieux. Puis on a découvert que ce n'était pas ça, mais que la laïcité avait été instaurée pour permettre la pluralité: c'était un cadre qui permettait à toutes les religions de vivre ensemble, sans supériorité de l'une sur l'autre. Nous n'avions donc plus besoin de 'faire la guerre', même si ça ne restait que dans le domaine symbolique. La France était un pays favorable pour être musulman, pour être respecté. La compréhension de la laïcité nous a finalement apaisés et redonné espoir.[55]

> [Our development corresponds to our understanding of *laïcité*. For us, *laïque* meant against God or religious people. Then we discovered that this wasn't the case at all, but rather that *laïcité* had been created to allow for plurality: it was a frame within which all religions could exist together, without one

being privileged over another. So we no longer needed to 'wage war', not even symbolically. France was a country in which it was good to be a Muslim, in which one could be respected. This understanding of *laïcité* reassured us and gave us hope.]

In a similar spirit, Dounia Bouzar calls for an open public debate on *laïcité* that would re-engage with what she sees as the essentially pluralist nature of the secular principle. Like Bencheikh, she believes that this would not involve a perversion or adaptation of the 'true' sense of republican sources but, rather, a return to them, uncluttered by nativist notions of French identity. She writes:

> Cette démarche permettrait de retrouver le sens profond de nos principes universels: la laïcité a été établie afin d'unir les hommes au-delà de leurs différences. Le Conseil d'Etat précise à quel point la laicité tend à défendre la pluralité et non à l'éradiquer: 'Les valeurs laïques sont destinées à apprendre aux élèves le respect des convictions d'autrui, à substituer la communication aux caricatures réciproques: ces valeurs s'appellent connaissance, esprit critique, réflexion personnelle'. Il s'agit peut-être tout simplement de revenir, nous aussi, à nos textes.[56]

> [This approach allowed us to rediscover the deep sense of our universal principles: *laïcité* was established with the aim of uniting people beyond their differences. The *Conseil d'Etat* is explicit about *laïcité*'s defence of plurality rather than its eradication: 'The values of *laïcité* are meant to teach pupils to respect others' beliefs, to substitute communication for mutual caricaturing. These values are knowledge, critical thinking, self-questioning.' Perhaps we also need to return to our texts.]

French Muslim feminists and their supporters also emphasize the need to rethink dominant notions of *liberté*. As discussed in the second chapter, nativist feminist discourses limit Muslim women's freedoms by unjustly denying the legitimacy of their choices. Although nativist feminists are right to question the nature of women's choices on the grounds that women can internalize patriarchal norms that limit their autonomy, their claims, as previously argued, are not only vastly overstated in the case of the decision to veil but, by singling out veiling as an instance of false consciousness, they fail to interrogate the ways in which the choices of non-Muslim women are also influenced and constrained by dominant gender norms. While nativist feminists fantasize a free-floating autonomous subject capable of simply choosing between 'tradition' and 'emancipation', Muslim feminist activists show a greater awareness of the ways in which an individual's freedoms are constrained (but may also be creatively enhanced) by a host of cultural, religious, economic and affective factors. Rather than imagine a naïve ideal of autonomy, these activists emphasize their agency in relation to their existing commitments as Muslims, feminists and French citizens. As Bouzar insists: 'La première liberté d'une démocratie est celle qui est donnée à l'individu de choisir ses références pour se construire librement. Ce droit n'est effectivement pas donné aux femmes issues de l'immigration maghrébine et africaine' [The first freedom of democracy is to allow the individual to choose their own references in order to construct themselves in their own manner. This right is effectively denied women of Maghrebi or African immigrant descent].[57] Furthermore, these activists do not simply demand respect for their religious difference. Rather they imagine their religious references to be in constant dialogue with their identity as French citizens. Islam, in Kada's words, is 'une référence supplémentaire qui rejoint les autres en les renforçant. Ce raisonnement place l'islam au même niveau que les autres références qui fondent l'identité française' [a supplementary reference that works with and reinforces others. This reasoning places Islam at the same level as other cultural references that make up French identity].[58]

Furthermore, Muslim feminists and their supporters are critical of nativist feminists' neocolonial efforts to force 'emancipation' on their Muslim sisters. For Delphy, feminism is first and foremost a process of self-emancipation. She insists: 'On ne peut pas être émancipé par autrui, ni de force' [One cannot be emancipated by others nor by force].[59] Indeed, as Laborde has argued, one cannot be forcibly emancipated, only given the tools with which one might seek to ensure one's own liberty and this, as nativist feminists would agree, is the job of national education.[60] By excluding veiled girls from school, nativist feminism fails on its own terms. But its ideal of liberty also fails because, as previously discussed, it only imagines one model of emancipation to be possible and this is not a model that all women can identify with. In particular, mainstream feminist discourses place considerable emphasis on female emancipation in terms of a certain notion of sexual liberation. This can create problems for veiled Muslim feminists who, by projecting an outward sexual modesty, are often seen by nativist feminists as sexually oppressed. Saïda Kada takes issue with this, arguing that, although self-emancipation may take many forms, too often 'la liberté se mesure au nombre de relations sexuelles' [freedom is measured in terms of the number of sexual relationships].[61] This tendency to judge the 'emancipation' of women by the visibility of their sexuality, she argues, reinforces the stereotype of veiled Muslim women as being sexually controlled by their husbands, fathers and brothers. But these activists do not simply argue for the need to respect forms of emancipation that have emerged from other religious and cultural traditions. They also see potential for these alternative emancipations to challenge dominant models of 'emancipated' femininity. For Delphy, veiled women are so troubling precisely because they challenge the notion that 'true' femininity should have overt sexual appeal. The veiled woman 'met mal à l'aise parce que sa seule présence met en relief ce qui passe chez nous pour la "libération sexuelle": l'obligation pour toute femme, à tout moment, d'être "désirable"' [makes people uncomfortable because the simple fact of her presence draws attention to what passes for 'sexual liberation' in France: the injunction that every women be 'desirable' at all times].[62] In a culture that fantasizes norms of desirable femininity as the pinnacle of women's emancipation, Muslim women present an opportunity to question these norms.

These activists imagine liberty in terms of the right to negotiate one's own cultural references in order to maximize one's autonomy, but this does not mean that they idealize a multicultural model that allows communities the freedom to do as they will, so long as they respect the rule of law. Instead, in the spirit of French republicanism, these activists do not so much desire freedom from the state as freedom through the state. It is the role of civic education to develop the critical faculties necessary for autonomous decision-making, while beyond school freedom can be most fully realized through participation in the civic and political sphere as equal citizens. *Liberté*, then, is not a cultural treasure to be defended, nor is it simply curtailed by the state, rather it is continually worked out through citizens' engagement with the public sphere. Full participation as peers in civic, social and political life is also, for these activists, the meaning of *Fraternité*, solidarity. It is in this respect that the exclusion of veiled girls from schools and the marginalization of Muslim women in public debate was a travesty of republican values.

In true republican spirit, Muslim feminist activists grant a central role to national education in the formation of citizens. But education too needs to be revised in fundamental ways. Said advocates an education that would expose students to a catholicity of vision that acknowledges non-European traditions, perspectives and processes, 'not in their essence or purity but their combinations and diversity, their countercurrents, the way they have had of conducting a compelling dialogue with other civilizations.'[63] In particular, this would involve a rereading of national history to provide a counter-memory that resists the reification of history as a national treasure and the entrenchment of Eurocentric or orientalizing historical narratives in the public consciousness. In Said's words, 'there can be no true humanism whose scope is limited to extolling patriotically the virtues of our culture, our language, our monuments' in order to turn them into 'instruments of veneration and repression'.[64] In the same vein, Muslim feminist activists argue for a thorough revision of French national history that will restore the voices of North African, Muslim and migrant experience to France's cultural memory. The historical question is of paramount importance to the descendants of immigrants whose lack of cultural memory contributes to their sense of isolation and exclusion. Kada, Bouzar, Bouteldja, Chouder, Kichah and Delphy all complain that young French Muslims are often unable to recognize themselves in official French history that has erased the stories of their ancestors from its pages. Kada protests that, although the objective of national history classes is to 'souder des citoyens d'une même nation autour d'une histoire commune' [unite the nation's citizens around a common history], instead,

> [O]n continue à raconter l'histoire de France comme si l'islam lui était complètement étranger. Silence sur l'apport de la civilisation arabo-musulmane au siècle des Lumières dans les manuels scolaires. Silence sur le sacrifice de nos arrière-grands-parents pour défendre la France! Silence sur les colonisations! Or nous sommes cinq millions de Français de confession musulmane à attendre aux portes de l'histoire de la France.[65]

> [We keep teaching French history as if Islam were completely foreign to it. In schoolbooks there is nothing on the contributions of Arab-Muslim civilization to the Enlightenment. Nothing on the sacrifices made by our great-grandparents in the name of France! Nothing on colonialism! Today there are five million French Muslims waiting at the doors of French history.]

In Christine Delphy's view, revising history is not only necessary in terms of understanding France's past, but also as a means of understanding contemporary problems. In her opinion, it is necessary to open up a thorough investigation of

France's colonial practices in order to recognize and resist contemporary discourses rooted in a colonial logic. She writes:

> Cet antagonisme à l'islam, qui est le substrat jamais dit parce que consensuel de toutes ces affaires, il faudra bien un jour le regarder en face: regarder sa consubstantialité avec le racisme lié à notre histoire coloniale, à la guerre d'Algérie, à l'exploitation du travail immigré en France. C'est ce racisme qui a crée en France le sentiment — fondé — d'exclusion des descendants d'immigrants maghrébins [...] Il nous faut faire la généalogie de ce racisme; il nous faut démonter et corriger les mécanismes d'une discrimination systèmatique (de tout le système).[66]

> [This hostility with regard to Islam, that is the unsaid (because consensual) foundation of all these controversies, must one day be acknowledged. We must look at its inner complicity with a racism rooted in our colonial past, with the Algerian War, with the exploitation of immigrant labour in France. It is this racism that has created this (justified) sense of exclusion felt by the descendants of Maghrebi immigrants [...] We must trace a genealogy of this racism; we must dismantle the machine of systematic discrimination (that has permeated every part of the system).]

Indeed, this perspective is shared by Bouteldja's *Indigènes de la République*, an organization that describes itself as anticolonialist and draws attention to what it sees as a 'continuum colonial'[67] that continues to structure France's relationship to its 'immigrant' population. In Bouteldja's view, a reassessment of French history is critical to an understanding of contemporary racism and discrimination, and part of the *Indigènes*' agenda involves calling on the French government to officially recognize disavowed aspects of French colonial history. The call to reconsider French history is coupled with a call to include religious education on the national teaching syllabus. This would not constitute religious instruction, but rather a consideration of world religions as legitimate objects of study. Bencheikh insists that, by omitting religious education from the syllabus, schools are neglecting an important area of knowledge and that a proper study of religious phenomena, within the frame of *laïcité*, would be beneficial in terms of improving understanding and relations between religious and secular citizens. In his words 'la laïcité n'est pas l'ignorance'.[68]

Many of the feminist activists interviewed agreed that the government's response to the *affaire du foulard* was a missed opportunity to revise and renew republican principles. On the state's response to protests that resisted the ban, Delphy writes:

> On aurait pu le souhaiter différent, très différent: on pouvait imaginer une France retrouvant ses esprits, reconnaissant le bien-fondé de la révolte, se rendant compte qu'elle a violé tous ses principes, commençant à redresser ses torts, décidée à éliminer les discriminations et à emprunter, pour difficile qu'il soit, le chemin de l'égalité républicaine. On pouvait imaginer en particulier une réponse positive, conforme aux lois de 1905 sur la liberté de conscience, à la demande légitime, légale, que l'islam soit traité sur un pied d'égalité avec les autres religions, croyances et philosophies. Mais l'ensemble de la classe politico-médiatique en a décidé autrement et a répondu par la négativité et par la répression.[69]

[We might have imagined it working out differently, very differently: One might have imagined a France waking up to itself, recognizing the justified grounds for revolt, realizing that it had violated all its principles, starting to repair its wrongs, committed to eliminating discrimination and taking, however difficult, the path of republican equality. In particular we might have imagined a positive response, in tune with the laws of 1905 on the freedom of conscience, to the legitimate, legal request that Islam be treated on the same footing as other religions, beliefs and philosophies. But the whole of the politico-media classes chose differently and responded with negativity and repression].

However, despite the great disappointment experienced by many French Muslim activists and their partner organizations in the wake of the official ban, Delphy represents the views of many other Muslim and non-Muslim activists when she identifies the emergence of pluralist feminisms in France as a 'lueur rose dans un ciel plombé' [a promising glow in a dark sky].[70]

Despite the omnipresence of nativist feminism during the *affaire du foulard* and the exclusion of Muslim women's voices from the mainstream media, it is possible to discern an energetic and vociferous resistance to such discourses on the part of grassroots activists from diverse political, religious and social backgrounds. In particular, there is a developing Muslim women's activism that seeks to rediscover feminism, Islam and republicanism as techniques of trouble. This activism insists above all on the possibility of being French, feminist *and* Muslim, and advocates both a rereading of Islamic sources and a rethinking of French republican principles. This approach is especially threatening to nativist feminist discourses as it breaks down the false dichotomies upon which it depends. Not only do French Muslim feminisms dissolve the *beurette/voilée* dichotomy by which Muslim women are defined as essentially identical or Other to a reified image of 'French womanhood', but they also resist the opposition 'West' versus 'Islam'. By envisaging de-ethnicized understandings of both Islam and French citizenship, Muslim women activists and their supporters imagine a French Muslim femininity that is based, not on a sense of homogenous religious or national communities, but on an active citizenship that draws on shared agendas and partnerships across diverse elements of society. In this way, they avoid both the false universalism of nativist feminism and the isolating relativism of multiculturalism and multi-difference feminism. This practical idealism not only provides a powerful counter-narrative to the 'nativist cultural fundamentalisms' that drive nativist feminist discourses in France but makes an important contribution to an increasingly anxious global debate about national identity and the treatment of minority or marginalized groups.

Notes to Chapter 5

1. The names of these organizations may be translated as follows: The Feminist Collective for Equality, French Muslim Women Politicized, Plural Women, Public Women, The Natives of the Republic, The Science-Pos Bite Back.
2. Edward Said, *Humanism and Democratic Criticism* (Basingstoke: Macmillan, 2004), p. 47.
3. Collectif féministe pour l'égalité, 'Pour les droits des femmes, contre les exclusions, pour un monde plus solidaire' [For women's rights, against the expulsions, for a more united world] <www.lmsi.net/article.php3?id_article+410> [accessed 22 September 2005] (para. 9 of 9).

4. Tariq Ramadan currently resides in Oxford where he is a visiting Professor at St Antony's College. He nonetheless remains the subject of mistrust in France and in the eyes of of the American government, and a number of hate campaigns have been conducted against him. See, Tariq Ramadan, 'My reasons for resigning my position at the university of Notre Dame', <www.tariqramadan.com/articles/my_reasons_for_resigning_my_position_at_the_ university_of_notre_dame> [accessed 3 December 2005].

5. Tariq Ramadan, *Western Muslims and the Future of Islam* (Oxford: Oxford University Press, 2004).

6. Ibid, p. 66.

7. Bencheikh, pp. 148–49.

8. Ramadan, pp. 21–22.

9. Ibid, p. 52.

10. Ibid, p. 115.

11. Laborde, p. 10.

12. Bencheikh, pp. 61–65.

13. Ramadan, p. 5.

14. Ibid, p. 63.

15. Bouzar and Kada, pp. 92–93.

16. Bouzar, *L'Islam des banlieues,* p. 166.

17. *Identités Voilées.* Dir. Sonia Kichah. TV10 Angers & Les Apprentis. 2004.

18. In interview, Dounia Bouzar expressed reservations about the 'anticolonial' approach and transnational affiliations of *Les Indigènes de la République*. In her opinion, such an approach alienates ethnic-majority French and is ultimately counter-productive.

19. See Valentine M. Moghadam, *Globalizing Women: Transnational Feminist Networks* (Baltimore and London: The John Hopkins University Press, 2005), pp. 142–72.

20. The conference was open to all and in total there were over four hundred delegates. See <www. feminismeislamic.org>

21. Aili Mari Tripp highlights some of these dangers in 'Challenges in Transnational Feminist Mobilization', in *Global Feminism: Transnational Women's Activism, Organizing and Human Rights*, ed. by Myra Marx Ferree and Aili Mari Tripp (New York and London: New York University Press, 2006), pp. 296–312.

22. Ismahane Chouder of CFPE raised these concerns with me in interview. Interview conducted on 16 April 2006 in Paris.

23. See Tripp, pp. 296–312.

24. Bouzar, *L'Islam des banlieues*, p. 129.

25. Interview conducted by the author on 16 April 2006 in Paris.

26. Bouzar, *Monsieur Islam n'existe pas: Pour une désislamisation des débats* (Paris: Hachette, 2004), p. 59–60.

27. Amara, p. 48.

28. Kada and Bouzar, p. 51.

29. Ibid, p. 27.

30. Laborde, p. 144.

31. Haideh Moghissi, *Feminism and Islamic Fundamentalism: The Limits of Postmodern Analysis* (London: Zed Books, 1999).

32. In particular, Moghissi complains that Western intellectuals' emphasis on the possibilities for Iranian women within an institutionalized Islamic system often exaggerates the progress that women have made and glosses over the persistence of legally sanctioned gender crimes. Most dangerous of all, she argues, this enthusiasm for Islamic feminist practice legitimizes institutionalized, legalistic Islam and signals defeatism with regard to the pursuit of emancipation outside of an Islamic framework.

33. Tripp, p. 248.

34. Interview conducted by the author on 16 April 2006 in Paris.

35. Interview conducted by the author on 15 April 2006 in Paris.

36. Sonia Kruks, *Retrieving Experience: Subjectivity and Recognition in Feminist Politics* (New York: Cornell University Press, 2001), pp. 107–08.

37. Interview conducted by the author on 14 April 2006 in Paris.
38. Ibid. During the *affaire du foulard*, the feminist critic Elisabeth Badinter adopted a clear nativist feminist position. See Elisabeth Badinter, *Fausse route* (Paris: Odile Jacob, 2003).
39. Paola Bachetta and Nathalie Paulme, 'Co-formations: des spatialités de résistance décoloniales chez les lesbiennes <<of colour>> en France', *Genre, sexualité & société*, 1 (2009) pp. 1–19 <http://gss.revues.org/index810.html> [accessed 10 October 2009]
40. Ibid, pp. 7–9.
41. Winifred Woodhull, 'Postcolonial thought and culture in Francophone North Africa' in *Francophone Postcolonial Studies: A Critical Introduction*, ed. by Charles Forsdick & David Murphy (London: Hodder Arnold, 2003), pp. 211–20 (p. 218).
42. Ibid, p. 217.
43. Interview conducted by the author on 15 April 2006 in Paris.
44. Samuel P. Huntingdon, *The Clash of Civilizations: And the remaking of world order* (Berkshire: Simon and Schuster, 1997).
45. Caroline Fourest, *Frère Tariq: Discours, stratégie et méthode de Tariq Ramadan* (Paris: Grasset, 2005).
46. Kruks, p. 86.
47. Laborde, pp. 230–35.
48. Saïda Kada, 'La femme musulmane doit participer aux grands débats de société' [Muslim women must participate in public debates], <www.oumma.com/imprimer.php3?id_article=950> [accessed 7 November 2005] (para. 21–22)
49. Said, p. 77.
50. Ibid, p. 6.
51. Ibid, pp. 21–22.
52. Ibid, pp. 10–11.
53. Bowen, p. 2.
54. Bencheikh, p. 37.
55. Bouzar, *Monsieur Islam*, p. 34.
56. Bouzar, *L'Islam des banlieues*, p. 172.
57. Bouzar and Kada, p. 59.
58. Ibid, pp. 148–49.
59. Christine Delphy, 'Race, caste et genre en France' [Race, caste and gender in France], <www.lmsi.net/article.php3?id_article=368> [accessed 22, September 2005] (para. 33 of 51)
60. Laborde, pp. 125–48.
61. Bouzar and Kada, p. 59.
62. Christine Delphy, 'Race, caste et genre en France' (para. 48 of 51).
63. Said, p. 27.
64. Ibid, p. 28.
65. Bouzar and Kada, p. 82.
66. Christine Delphy, 'Débat sur le voile au Collectif Droits des femmes' [The Veil Debate at the Women's Rights Collective], <www.lmsi.net/article.php3?id_article=186> [accessed 22/11/05] (para. 8 of 9)
67. Interview conducted by the author on 14 April 2006 in Paris.
68. Bencheikh, p.44.
69. Delphy, 'Race, caste et genre en France' (para. 39 of 51).
70. Christine Delphy, 'Une école pour tous et pour toutes', <multitudes.samizdat.net/une-ecole-pour-tous-et-toutes.html> [accessed 22 November 2005] (para. 1 of 1).

CONCLUSION

When I met her for interview, Houria Bouteldja of *Les Indigenes de la République* commented wryly on the extraordinary consensus generated by the *affaire du foulard*. 'Pendant l'affaire' she remarked '*tout le monde* est devenu féministe' [During the affair, *everybody* was a feminist]. As Bouteldja's irony implies, when *everyone*, including the most chauvinist elements of French society, rallies under the feminist banner, it is enough to set alarm bells ringing. This book has been an attempt to respond to these alarm bells, firstly by exploring the dynamics of feminist representations of Muslim women, and secondly by considering Muslim women's counter-narratives, both as writers and as activists. At a time when humanist and feminist discourses are all too readily harnessed to reactionary political agendas, questioning the nature of certain so-called feminisms seems like an urgent project if feminism is to remain a force for positive change.

As this book has sought to demonstrate, the enthusiastic promotion of women's rights during the headscarf affair signalled not so much a revival as a stagnation of mainstream feminism in France as it saw feminism as an enquiring political agenda displaced by a defence of 'femininity' and in particular a certain idea of 'French femininity' that not only stigmatized those who did not fit the bill, but had little emancipatory potential of its own. As we saw in Part I, the articulation of an idealized, feminized 'Frenchness' is nothing new. Indeed, a genealogy of such discourses may be traced from the nineteenth century onwards. Like colonial-feminism, contemporary nativist feminism equates French, or more broadly Western, culture with an ideal of female emancipation while reducing Muslim-Arab culture to the image of a veiled and oppressed woman. However, the fact that nativist feminism, as Bouteldja remarks, emerged as a site of cultural consensus rather than dissent differentiates it from the feminism of some of its colonial predecessors. While colonial feminists like Suzanne Voilquin and Hubertine Auclert exploited the popular colonial cause to legitimize unpopular feminist demands, nativist feminists have more in common with Marie Bugéja in their tendency to construct conservative models of womanhood as the pinnacle of women's emancipation and to imagine the Republic as guarantor of sexual equality.

Ironically, it was precisely this focus on sexual equality as a defining feature of French society that stifled feminist dissent during the *affaire*. By imagining sexual equality to be a *fait accompli*, nativist feminists neglect feminism's critical imperative in ways that not only erode French Muslim women's freedoms but that inhibit the struggle for women's emancipation as a whole. Indeed, the exclusive focus on sexism within Muslim communities, coupled with an idealization of French womanhood, papers over the sexism that is entrenched in French society and in Western culture more broadly. Although French law sanctions discriminatory practices on the grounds of gender, sexist norms endure in France (as in other Western nations) and these are apparent in the persistence of the traditional division of labour within the family, the underrepresentation of women in public life and the occurrence of domestic violence across all sections of society, to name but a few examples. This state of affairs has only been worsened by the emergence of neo-feminisms that equate women's emancipation with a narrowly defined sexual liberation and promote an ideal of 'femininity' that naturalizes rather than challenges gender norms. Indeed, far from challenging repressive gender norms, nativist feminism facilitates their perpetuation by confusing noble principles with a rather less noble reality. As Laborde points out:

> In this context, the Stasi Commission report's proud statement that 'French society does not accept breaches in gender equality' is historically selective, confuses high-minded principles and practices and, most ironically, takes Muslims to task for not undertaking what the French Republic itself had spectacularly failed to do, beyond the limited confines of its schools: challenging deeply ingrained norms of gender socialization.[1]

By buying into an idea of France as the guardian of women's rights, nativist feminism finds itself complicit with the classic anti-feminist strategy of stifling dissent by persuading women that they already live in the best of all possible worlds.

But it was, of course, the freedoms of Muslim women in particular that were most explicitly and immediately curtailed by the events of 2003–04. Indeed, the irony of the *affaire du foulard* was that nativist feminists disempowered the very women they ostensibly sought to defend. Although nativist feminists supposedly sought to safeguard female autonomy, their caricaturing of religious belief as fundamentally antithetical to the freedom of the individual along with their conviction that the republican school would guarantee liberty through enforcing conformity to French norms left no room for Muslim women to negotiate their freedoms and identities in relation to their existing cultural and affective commitments. Furthermore, this refusal to imagine that Muslim women might rethink their cultural heritage on their own terms aggravated Muslim women's predicament by investing in the conservative Muslim discourses they sought to resist. Kada, remarks: 'En nous disant "Quittez votre religion, enlevez votre foulard, vous voyez bien que l'islam est contre les femmes", ils reprennent à leur compte les interprétations des extrémistes: en s'appuyant sur leur définitions, il font le jeu des intégristes!' [By saying "Abandon your religion, throw off your veil, can't you see that Islam oppresses women" they are accepting the interpretations of the fundamentalists: by using their definitions, they are playing straight into their hands].[2] As Kada's use of the imperative suggests, nativist feminism, despite its professed commitment to women's autonomy, is a coercive strategy seeking to impose 'liberation' from above rather than giving the individual the critical tools with which to carve out her own space of agency and resistance. The contradictions that this desire to emancipate by force entailed were, sadly, made concrete in the act of denying girls an education on 'feminist' grounds.

However, though nativist feminist discourse dominated the media and literary mainstream, it did not, as we have seen, represent the sum total of feminist activism in France, nor did it prevent French Muslim women from developing critical tools of their own. What emerges most clearly from the work of these writers and activists is the desire, not to abandon, but to rehabilitate the republican ideals that were so badly misapplied during the *affaire*. Zouari and Rahmani both reveal how ideals of liberty, equality and solidarity may be betrayed, but they also suggest the devastating consequences of giving up on them altogether. Indeed, Zouari and Rahmani's work insists that minorities have an important interest in notions of identity, belonging and voice and, rather than celebrating a subversive marginality, these writers recognize the urgent necessity for excluded minorities to belong and be seen to belong to the national community so that they may fantasize a sense of identity as a ground from which to speak.

But in order to avoid falling back into the trap of assimilation, notions of identity and belonging must be radically reworked. The activists discussed in the final chapter are, as we have seen, deeply invested in such an enterprise. In order to resist the fossilization of Islamic, feminist and humanist principles into the cultural property of an elite few, these activists seek to breathe new life into them by restoring their potential as interrogative, democratic, critical discourses. In the opinion of the writers and activists considered here, feminism and humanism are not the property of Western societies just as Islam does not exclusively belong to Arab peoples. Instead, they are living and evolving discourses that demand constant interrogation, re-interpretation and renewal in response to developing social and economic contexts. This interrogative work is not the privilege of the academics, politicians, writers and media personalities who monopolized the *affaire du foulard*, but a universal right that French Muslim activists are using to their advantage.

The position of Western Muslim women as both participants in Western democracies, members of the Muslim *umma* and global citizens gives them unique opportunities to engage in this kind of critique. Not only do they have the opportunity to rethink and revalorize Islam from their perspective as Western citizens, but their experience as Muslim women, if acknowledged and integrated by mainstream democratic and feminist discourses, may also reinvigorate Western societies' professed allegiance to gender equality. At a local level, French Muslim women's activism creates a valuable opportunity for France to renew dialogue and rebuild relationships with its religious and ethnic minorities. But the work of these activists also has implications that transcend the French context. In particular, their commitment to a 'practical idealism' that brings the emphasis on difference typical of international influences into dialogue with the universal ideals of the French Republic, suggests ways of avoiding the misuse of humanist, feminist and Islamic ideals without reducing all ideals to oppressive ideologies. This attempt to navigate between the imperialist impulse that so often underpins efforts to 'rescue' subaltern women, and the dangerously complacent relativism that can undermine solidarity and paralyse resistance is a crucial undertaking if feminism is to remain a political force to be reckoned with.

Notes to the Conclusion

1. Laborde, p.131.
2. Bouzar and Kada, p. 42.

BIBLIOGRAPHY

AGAMBEN, GIORGIO, *Homo Sacer: Sovereign Power and Bare Life*, trans. by Daniel Heller-Roazen (Stanford, CA: Stanford University Press, 1998)
——*Remnants of Auschwitz: The Witness and the Archive*, trans. by Daniel Heller-Roazen (New York: Zone Books, 1999)
——*State of Exception*, trans. by Kevin Attell (Chicago, IL: University of Chicago Press, 2005)
AGUSTÍN, LAURA, 'What not to wear — if you want to be French', *Guardian*, 6 August 2008 <www.guardian.co.uk/commentisfree/2008/aug/06/france.islam> [accessed 28 February 2009]
ALLOULA, MALEK, *Le Harem colonial: Images d'un sous-érotisme* (Paris: Garance, 1981)
AMARA, FADELA, and SYLVIA ZAPPI, *Ni putes ni soumises* (Paris: La Découverte, 2003)
ANIDJAR, GIL, *The Jew, The Arab: A History of the Enemy* (Stanford, CA: Stanford University Press, 2003)
AUCLERT, HUBERTINE, *Les Femmes arabes en Algérie* (Paris: Société d'Editions Littéraires, 1900)
——*Les Femmes au gouvernail* (Paris: Marcel Giard, 1923)
BACHETTA, PAOLA, and NATHALIE PAULME, 'Co-formations: Des spatialités de résistance décoloniales chez les lesbiennes «of colour» en France',*Genre, sexualité & société*, 1 (2009) <http://gss.revues.org/index810.html> [accessed 10 October 2009]
BADINTER, ELISABETH, *Fausse route* (Paris: Odile Jacob, 2003)
BADIOU, ALAIN, *Circonstances, 2: Irak, foulard, Allemagne/France* (Paris: Léo Scheer, 2004)
BALIBAR, ETIENNE, and IMMANUEL WALLERSTEIN, *Race, Nation, Class: Ambiguous Identities* (London: Verso, 1991)
BANCEL, NICOLAS, PASCAL BLANCHARD and FRANÇOISE VERGÈS, *La République coloniale: Essai sur une utopie* (Paris: Albin Michel, 2003)
BAUDELAIRE, CHARLES, 'Eloge du maquillage' in *Baudelaire: Œuvres completes*, ed. by Claude Pichois (Paris: Gallimard, 1961), pp. 1182–85
BELLIL, SAMIRA, *Dans l'enfer des tournantes*, 2nd edn (Paris: Editions Denoël, 2003) [first pub. 2002]
BENAÏSSA, AÏCHA, and SOPHIE PONCHELET, *Née en France: Histoire d'une jeune beur* (Paris: Presse Pocket, 1991)
BENCHEIKH, SOHEIB, *Marianne et le Prophète: L'Islam dans la France laïque* (Paris: Grasset, 1998)
BHABHA, HOMI K., *The Location of Culture*, 2nd edn (London: Routledge, 2003) [first pub. 1994]
BLANCHARD, PASCAL, 'La France et sa fracture coloniale', *Nouvel Observateur*, 10 November 2005
BOGUES, ANTHONY, 'John Stuart Mill and "The Negro Question": Race, Colonialism and the Ladder of Civilization', in *Race and Racism in Modern Philosophy*, ed. by Andrew Valls (Ithaca, NY: Cornell University Press, 2005), pp. 217–34
BOUTELDJA, HOURIA, 'De la cérémonie du dévoilement à Alger (1958) à Ni putes ni soumises: L'Instrumentalisation coloniale et néo-coloniale de la cause des femmes' <www.lmsi.net/article.php3?id_article=320> [accessed 5 May 2005]

BOUZAR, DOUNIA, *L'Islam des banlieues: Les Prédicateurs musulmans: Nouveaux travailleurs sociaux?* (Paris: Syros, 2001)

——*Monsieur Islam n'existe pas: Pour une désislamisation des débats* (Paris: Hachette, 2004)

——AND SAÏDA KADA, *L'Une voilée, l'autre pas: Le Témoignage de deux musulmanes françaises* (Paris: Albin Michel, 2003).

BOWEN, JOHN R., *Why the French don't like Headscarves* (Princeton, NJ: Princeton University Press: 2007)

BOWLAN, JEANNE M., 'Civilizing Gender Relations in Algeria: The Paradoxical Case of Marie Bugéja', in CLANCY-SMITH AND GOUDA, eds, DOMESTICATING THE EMPIRE, pp. 175–92

BRAHIMI, DENISE, *Femmes arabes et sœurs musulmanes* (Paris: Editions Tierce, 1984)

BRUBAKER, ROGERS, *Citizenship and Nationhood in France and Germany* (Cambridge, MA: Harvard University Press, 1992)

BUGÉJA, MARIE, *Nos sœurs musulmanes: Nouvelle édition*, 2nd edn (Paris: Editions France Afrique, 1931) [first pub. Algiers, 1921]

——*Visions d'Algérie* (Algiers: Baconnier frères, 1929)

BUISINE, ALAIN, *L'Orient voilé* (Paris: Zulma, 1993)

CLANCY-SMITH, JULIA and FRANCES GOUDA, eds, *Domesticating the Empire: Race, Gender and Family Life in French and Dutch Colonialism* (Charlottesville: University Press of Virginia, 1998)

CLANCY-SMITH, JULIA, 'Islam, Gender and Identities: French Algeria', in DOMESTICATING THE EMPIRE, as previous, pp. 154–74

COHEN, NICK, 'Controversy unveiled', *The Observer*, 24 December 2006 <http://www.guardian.co.uk/theobserver/2006/dec/24/features.magazine167> [accessed January 2007]

COLLECTIF FÉMINISTE POUR L'ÉGALITÉ, 'Pour les droits des femmes, contre les exclusions, pour un monde plus solidaire' <www.lmsi.net/article.php3?id_article+410> [accessed 22 September 2005]

——'Communiqué' <www.saphirnet.info/imprimer.php?id=1663> [accessed 22 September 2005]

COLLECTIF LES MOTS SONT IMPORTANTS, 'Ni putes ni soumises, ou la parole confisquée: Notes sur une réunion publique du mouvement de Mohammed Abdi et Fadela Amara' <www.lmsi.net/php3?id_article=321> [accessed 5 May 2005]

CORNATON, MICHEL, *Les Regroupements de la décolonisation en Algérie* (Paris: Les Editions ouvrières, 1967)

CURTI, LIDIA, *Female Stories, Female Bodies: Narrative, Identity and Representation* (Basingstoke: Macmillan, 1998)

DAUMAS, EUGÈNE, *La Femme arabe*, 2nd edn (Algiers: A. Jourdan, 1912)

DEBRAY, RÉGIS, *Ce que nous voile le voile* (Paris: Gallimard, 2004)

DE GOUGES, OLYMPE, 'Les Droits de la femme', in *Ecrits politiques, 1788–1791*, préface d'Olivier Blanc (Paris: Côté-femmes, 1993), pp. 204–15

DELPHY, CHRISTINE, 'Race, caste et genre en France' <www.lmsi.net/article.php3?id_article=368> [accessed 22 September 2005]

——'Débat sur le voile au Collectif Droits des femmes' <www.lmsi.net/article.php3?id_article=186> [accessed 22 September 2005]

——'Une école pour tous et toutes' <multitudes.samizdat.net/une-ecole-pour-tous-et-toutes.html> [accessed 22 September 2005]

DJAVANN, CHAHDORRT, *Bas les voiles!* (Paris: Gallimard, 2003)

——*Que pense Allah d'Europe* (Paris: Gallimard, 2004)

DONADEY, ANNE, *Recasting Postcolonialism: Women Writing Between Worlds* (Portsmouth, NH: Heinemann, 2001)

DUBET, FRANÇOIS, and DANILO MARTUCELLI, *Dans quelle société vivons nous?* (Paris: Seuil, 1998)

ELHADAD, LYDIA, *Introduction*, in *Souvenirs d'une fille du peuple ou la Saint-simonienne en Egypte, 1834 à 1836*, by Suzanne Voilquin (Paris: François Maspéro, 1978), pp. 5–48

FANON, FRANTZ, *L'An V de la révolution algérienne* (Paris: François Maspéro, 1960)

——*A Dying Colonialism*, trans. by Haakon Chevalier (New York: Grove Press, 1965)

FAVELL, ADRIAN, *Philosophies of Integration: Immigration and the Idea of Citizenship in France and Great Britain* (Basingstoke: Macmillan, 1998)

FEMMES PUBLIQUES, 'Etre féministe, ce n'est pas exclure' <www.lmsi.net/impression. php3?id_article=181> [accessed 16 November 2005]

FERREE, MYRA MARX, and AILI MARI TRIPP, eds, *Global Feminism: Transnational Women's Activism, Organizing and Human Rights* (New York and London: New York University Press, 2006)

FORSDICK, CHARLES, and DAVID MURPHY, eds, *Francophone Postcolonial Studies: A Critical Introduction* (London: Hodder Arnold, 2003)

FOUREST, CAROLINE, *Frère Tariq: Discours, stratégie et méthode de Tariq Ramadan* (Paris: Grasset, 2005)

FREEDMAN, JANE, *Immigration and Insecurity in France* (Aldershot: Ashgate, 2004)

FYSH, PETER, and JIM WOLFREYS, *The Politics of Racism in France* (Basingstoke: Macmillan, 1998)

GAILLARD, JEAN-MICHEL, *Jules Ferry* (Paris: Fayard, 1989)

GEMIE, SHARIF, 'Stasi's Republic: The School and the 'Veil', *Modern and Contemporary France*, 12 (2004), 387–97

GOLDBERG MOSES, CLAIRE, *French Feminism in the Nineteenth Century* (Albany: State University of New York Press, 1984)

——AND LESLIE WAHL RABINE, *Feminism, Socialism and French Romanticism* (Bloomington: Indiana University Press, 1993)

GRESH, ALAIN, *L'Islam, la République et le monde* (Paris: Fayard, 2004)

GROSZ, ELIZABETH, *Volatile Bodies: Toward a Corporeal Feminism* (Bloomington: Indiana University Press, 1994)

GUÉNIF-SOUILAMAS, NACIRA, *Des 'beurettes' aux descendants d'immigrants nord-africains* (Paris: Hachette, 2002)

——and ERIC MACÉ, *Les Féministes et le garçon arabe* (La Tour-d'Aigues: Editions de l'Aube, 2004)

HALL, STUART, and OTHERS, *Policing the Crisis* (London: Macmillan, 1978)

HARGREAVES, ALEC, *Immigration and Identity in Beur Fiction: Voices from the North-African Community in France* (Oxford: Berg, 1997)

——'Testimony, Co-authorship, and Dispossession among Women of Maghrebi Origin in France', *Research in African Literatures*, 37, 1 (2006) 42–54

HENLEY, JON, 'French angry at law to teach glory of colonialism', *The Guardian*, 15 April 2005, section Higher Education <http://www.guardian.co.uk/world/2005/apr/15/ highereducation.artsandhumanities> [accessed 30 November 2005]

HORNE, JANET R., 'In Pursuit of Greater France', in CLANCY-SMITH and GOUDA, eds, *DOMESTICATING THE EMPIRE*, pp. 21–42

HUNTINGDON, SAMUEL P., *The Clash of Civilizations: And the Remaking of World Order* (Berkshire: Simon and Schuster, 1997

KADA, SAÏDA, 'La Femme musulmane doit participer aux grands débats de société' <www. oumma.com/imprimer.php3?id_article=950> [accessed 7 November 2005]

KALTENBACH, JEANNE-HÉLÈNE, and MICHÈLE TRIBALAT, *La République et l'islam: Entre crainte et aveuglement* (Saint-Amand: Gallimard, 2002)

KELLY, DEBRA, *Autobiography and Independence: Self and Identity in North African Writing* (Liverpool: Liverpool University Press, 2005)

KESSAS, FERRUDJA, *Beur's Story* (Paris: L'Harmattan, 1994)

KHOSROKHAVAR, FARHAD, *L'Islam des jeunes* (Paris: Flammarion, 1997)

KICHAH, SONIA, *Identités Voilées*. TV10 Angers & Les Apprentis. 2004

KRISTEVA, JULIA, *Etrangers à nous-mêmes* (Paris: Fayard, 1988)

KRUKS, SONIA, *Retrieving Experience: Subjectivity and Recognition in Feminist Politics* (Ithaca, NY: Cornell University Press, 2001)

LABORDE, CÉCILE, *Critical Republicanism: The Hijab Controversy and Political Philosophy* (Oxford: Oxford University Press: 2008)

LECLERC, ADRIEN, 'De la condition juridique de la femme musulmane en Algérie', *Congrès internationale de sociologie coloniale*, vol.2, *Mémoires soumis au congrès* (Paris: 1901)

LE CORRE, ERWAN, 'La Marche de TOUTES les femmes?' <www.lmsi.net/article.php3?id_article=227> [accessed 28 February 2006]

LEVY, ARIEL, *Female Chauvanist Pigs: Women and the Rise of Raunch Culture* (London: Simon & Schuster, 2006)

LEWIS, REINA, 'On Veiling, Vision and Voyage: Cross-Cultural Dressing and Narratives of Identity', in *Feminist Postcolonial Theory: A Reader*, ed. by Reina Lewis and Sara Mills (Edinburgh: Edinburgh University Press, 2003), pp. 520–41

LOWE, LISA, *Critical Terrains: French and British Orientalisms* (Ithaca, NY: Cornell University Press, 1994)

MACÉ, ERIQUE, 'Entretien avec Erique Macé: Le Féminisme républicaniste est un pseudo féminisme' <www.oumma.com/article.php3?id_article=1297> [accessed 8 December 2005]

McILVANNEY, SIOBHÁN, 'The Articulation of *beur* Female Identity in the Works of Farida Belghoul, Ferrudja Kessas and Soraya Nini', in *Women's Writing in Contemporary France: New Writers, New Literatures in the 1990s*, ed. by Gill Rye and Michael Worton (Manchester: Manchester University Press, 2002), pp. 130–41

MARCIANO-JACOB, CHRISTIANE, *Lettre à un ami musulman: Au délà du voile* (Village-Neuf: Editions du Lys, 2004)

MÉLIANE, LOUBNA, *Vivre libre* (Paris: Oh! Editions, 2003)

MESSAADI, SAKINNA, *'Nos sœurs musulmanes': Ou le mythe féministe, civilisateur, évangélisateur du messianisme colonialiste dans l'Algérie colonisée* (Algiers: Editions Distribution HOUMA, 2001)

MILLIOT, LOUIS, *Etude sur la condition de la femme musulmane au Maghreb* (Paris: J. Rousset 1910)

MOGHADAM, VALENTINE M., *Globalizing Women: Transnational Feminist Networks* (Baltimore, MD, and London: Johns Hopkins University Press, 2005)

MOGHISSI, HAIDEH, *Feminism and Islamic Fundamentalism: The Limits of Postmodern Analysis* (London: Zed Books, 1999)

MUCHIELLI, LAURENT, and VÉRONIQUE LE GOAZIOU, eds, *Quand les banlieues brûlent...: Retour sur les émeutes de novembre 2005* (Paris: La Découverte, 2006)

NINI, SORAYA, *Ils disent que je suis une beurette* (Paris: Fixot, 1993)

'Polémique autour de la définition de "colonisation" et "coloniser" par le Petit Robert', *Le Monde*, 6 September 2006

POMMEROL, MME JEAN, *Une femme chez les Sahariennes: Entre Laghouat et In-Salah* (Paris: Editions Flammarion, 1990) [first pub. 1900]

PONTECORVO, GILLO, *La Bataille d'Alger*. Casbah Film. 1957.

RAHMANI, ZAHIA, *Moze* (Abbeville: Sabine Wespieser Editeur, 2003)

—— *'Musulman' Roman* (Abbeville: Sabine Wespieser Editeur, 2005)

—— (interview) <www.swediteur.com/auteur_3326.html> [accessed 1 September 2005]

RAMADAN, TARIQ, *Western Muslims and the Future of Islam* (Oxford: Oxford University Press, 2004)

—— 'My reasons for resigning my position at the university of Notre Dame', <www.tariqramadan.com/articles/my_reasons_for_resigning_my_position_at_the_university_of_notre_dame> [accessed 3 December 2005]

REID, DONALD, 'The World of Frantz Fanon's *L'Algérie se dévoile*', *French Studies*, 61 (2007), 460–75

ROBINSON, JANE, *Unsuitable for Ladies: An Anthology of Women Travellers* (Oxford: Oxford University Press, 1994)

ROGERS, REBECCA 'Telling Stories about the Colonies: British and French Women in Algeria in the Nineteenth Century', *Gender and History*, 21 (2009), 39–59

ROSELLO, MIREILLE, *France and the Maghreb: Performative Encounters* (Gainesville: University Press of Florida, 2005)

SAID, EDWARD, *Humanism and Democratic Criticism* (Basingstoke: Macmillan, 2004)

SEBBAR, LEÏLA, *Shérazade, 17 ans, brune, frisée, les yeux verts* (Paris: Stock, 1981)

SILVERMAN, MAXIM, *Deconstructing the Nation: Immigration, Racism and Citizenship in Modern France* (London: Routledge, 1992)

SLYOMOVICS, SUSAN, ' "Hassiba Ben Bouali, If You Could See Our Algeria": Women and Public Space in Algeria', in *Political Islam: Essays from Middle East Report*, ed. by Joel Beinin and Joe Sork (Berkeley: University of California Press, 1997), pp. 211–19

STASI, BERNARD, *Laïcité et République. Rapport de la commission de la réflexion sur l'application du principe de laïcité dans la République remis au Président de la République le 11 décembre 2003* (Paris: La Documentation française, 2004)

SUBBARAMAN, SIVIGAMI, 'Catalog-ing Ethnicity: Clothing as Cultural Citizenship', *Interventions*, 1 (1999), 572–89

TALAHITE, ANISSA, 'Constructing Spaces of Transition: "Beur" Women Writers and the Question of Representation', in *Women, Immigration and Identities in France*, ed. by Jane Freedman and Carrie Tarr (Oxford: Berg, 2000), pp. 103–19

TARR, CARRIE, *Reframing Difference: Beur and Banlieue Filmmaking in France* (Manchester: Manchester University Press, 2005)

TÉVANIAN, PIERRE, *Le Voile médiatique* (Paris: Raisons d'agir, 2005)

TITAH, RACHIDA, *La Galerie des absentes: La Femme algérienne dans l'imaginaire masculine* (La Tour-d'Aigues: Editions de l'Aube, 1996)

VIANES, MICHÈLE, *Les Islamistes en manœuvre* (Paris: Hors Commerce, 2004)

——*Un voile sur la République* (Paris: Stock, 2004)

VOILQUIN, SUZANNE, *Souvenirs d'une fille du peuple ou la Saint-simonienne en Egypte, 1834 à 1836*, Introduction de Lydia Elhadad (Paris: François Maspéro, 1978) [first pub. 1866]

WEBER, EUGEN, *Peasants into Frenchmen: The Modernisation of Rural France, 1880–1914* (London: Chatto and Windus, 1977)

WOODHULL, WINIFRED, *Transfigurations of the Maghreb: Feminism, Decolonisation and Literatures* (Minneapolis: University of Minnesota Press, 1993)

YEGENOGLU, MEYDA, *Colonial Fantasies: Towards a Feminist Reading of Orientalism* (Cambridge: Cambridge University Press, 1998)

ZÉGHIDOUR, SLIMANE, *Le Voile et la bannière* (France: Hachette, 1990)

ZOUARI, FAWZIA, *Ce pays dont je meurs*, 2nd edn (Tunisie: L'Or du temps, 2000) [first pub. in France (Paris: Editions Ramsay, 1999)]

——*Ce voile qui déchire la France* (Paris: Ramsay, 2004)

INDEX